高等学校试用教材

建筑类专业英语
给水排水与环境保护
第三册

张文洁　濮宏魁　　　　　主编
岑小平　吴儆武　任　瑞
蒋琴芳　蒋京东　蔡英俊　　编
沈耀良　　　　　　　　　主审

中国建筑工业出版社

《建筑类专业英语》编审委员会

总 主 编　徐铁城
总 主 审　杨匡汉
副总主编　（以姓氏笔画为序）
　　　　　王庆昌　乔梦铎　陆铁镛
　　　　　周保强　蔡英俊
编　　委　（以姓氏笔画为序）
　　　　　王久愉　王学玲　王翰邦　卢世伟
　　　　　孙　玮　李明章　朱满才　向小林
　　　　　向　阳　刘文瑛　余曼筠　孟祥杰
　　　　　张少凡　张文洁　张新建　赵三元
　　　　　阎岫峰　傅兴海　褚羞花　蔡慧俭
　　　　　濮宏魁
责任编辑　刘茂榆　庞大中

前 言

经过几十年的探索,外语教学界许多人认为,工科院校外语教学的主要目的,应该是:"使学生能够利用外语这个工具,通过阅读去获取国外的与本专业有关的科技信息。"这既是我们建设有中国特色的社会主义的客观需要,也是在当前条件下工科院校外语教学可能完成的最高目标。事实上,教学大纲规定要使学生具有"较强"的阅读能力,而对其他方面的能力只有"一般"要求,就是这个意思。

大学本科的一、二年级,为外语教学的基础阶段。就英语来说,这个阶段要求掌握的词汇量为2400个(去掉遗忘,平均每个课时10个单词)。加上中学阶段已经学会的1600个单词,基础阶段结束时应掌握的词汇量为4000个。仅仅掌握4000个单词,能否看懂专业英文书刊呢?还不能。据统计,掌握4000个单词,阅读一般的英文科技文献,生词量仍将有6%左右,即平均每百词有六个生词,还不能自由阅读。国外的外语教学专家认为,生词量在3%以下,才能不借助词典,自由阅读。此时可以通过上下文的联系,把不认识的生词猜出来。那么,怎么样才能把6%的生词量降低到3%以下呢?自然,需要让学生增加一部分词汇积累。问题是,要增加多少单词?要增加哪一些单词?统计资料表明,在每一个专业的科技文献中,本专业最常用的科技术语大约只有几百个,而且它们在文献中重复出现的频率很高。因此,在已经掌握4000单词的基础上,在专业阅读阶段中,有针对性地通过大量阅读,扩充大约1000个与本专业密切有关的科技词汇,便可以逐步达到自由阅读本专业科技文献的目的。

早在八十年代中期,建设部系统院校外语教学研究会就组织编写了一套《土木建筑系列英语》,分八个专业,共12册。每个专业可选读其中的3、4册。那套教材在有关院校相应的专业使用多年,学生和任课教师反映良好。但是,根据当时的情况,那套教材定的起点较低(1000词起点),已不适合今天学生的情况。为此,在得到建设部人事教育劳动司的大力支持,并征得五个相关专业教学指导委员会同意之后,由建设部系统十几所院校一百余名外语教师和专业课教师按照统一的编写规划和要求,编写了这一套《建筑类专业英语》教材。

《建筑类专业英语》是根据国家教委颁发的《大学英语专业阅读阶段教学基本要求》编写的专业阅读教材,按照建筑类院校共同设置的五个较大的专业类别对口编写。五个专业类别为:建筑学与城市规划;建筑工程(即工业与民用建筑);给水排水与环境保护;暖通、空调与燃气;建筑管理与财务会计。每个专业类别分别编写三册专业英语阅读教材,供该专业类别的学生在修完基础阶段英语后,在第五至第七学期专业阅读阶段使用,每学期一册。

上述五种专业英语教材语言规范,题材广泛,覆盖相关专业各自的主要内容:包括专业基础课,专业主干课及主要专业选修课,语言材料的难易度切合学生的实际水平;词汇以大学英语"通用词汇表"的4000个单词为起点，每个专业类别的三册书将增加1000—1200个阅读本专业必需掌握的词汇。本教材重视语言技能训练，突出对阅读、翻译和写作能力的培养，以求达到《大学英语专业阅读阶段教学基本要求》所提出的教学目标："通过指导学生阅读有关专业的英语书刊和文献，使他们进一步提高阅读和翻译科技资料的能力，并能以英语为工具获取专业所需的信息。"

《建筑类专业英语》每册16个单元，每个单元一篇正课文（TEXT），两篇副课文（Reading Material A & B），每个单元平均2000个词，三册48个单元，总共约有十万个词，相当于原版书三百多页。要培养较强的阅读能力，读十万个词的文献，是起码的要求。如果专业课教师在第六和第七学期，在学生通过学习本教材已经掌握了数百个专业科技词汇的基础上，配合专业课程的学习，再指定学生看一部分相应的专业英语科技文献，那将会既促进专业课的学习，又提高英语阅读能力，实为两得之举。

本教材不仅适用于在校学生，对于有志提高专业英语阅读能力的建筑行业广大在职工程技术人员，也是一套适用的自学教材。

建设部人事教育劳动司高教处和中国建设教育协会对这套教材的编写自始至终给予关注和支持；中国建筑工业出版社第五编辑室密切配合，参与从制定编写方案到审稿各个阶段的重要会议，给了我们很多帮助；在编写过程中，各参编学校相关专业的许多专家、教授对材料的选取、译文的审定都提出了许多宝贵意见；本书在编写过程中，借鉴并采用了重庆建筑大学任慧清、吴瑞玲、张慰声、郭定寰、张显模、刘焕粤等同志所编写的《给水排水专业英语教材》第一册、第三册中的部分内容，同时还承王国民、周晓蕾、乐毅全等同志大力协助，谨此致谢。

《建筑类专业英语》是我们编写对口专业阅读教材的又一次尝试，由于编写者水平及经验有限，教材中不妥之处在所难免，敬请广大读者批评指正。

《建筑类专业英语》
编审委员会

Contents

UNIT ONE
- Text   An Introduction to Water Supply and Sanitation Provisions 1
- Reading Material A   Water Demand 6
- B   Water Treatment in Developing Countries 9

UNIT TWO
- Text   Water Quality Criteria 12
- Reading Material A   Drinking Water Standards in the U.S. 17
- B   Setting Standards for the Mediterranean Sea 18

UNIT THREE
- Text   Microbiological Examination 21
- Reading Material A   Ecological Principles 27
- B   Sampling and Analysis 29

UNIT FOUR
- Text   Role of Monitoring in Water Quality Management 31
- Reading Material A   Sources of Water Pollution 35
- B   Water-related Disease 38

UNIT FIVE
- Text   Mechanism of Coagulation 41
- Reading Material A   Drainlaying 46
- B   Ion Exchange 49

UNIT SIX
- Text   Overall Effects of Pollution by Wastewaters 52
- Reading Material A   Wastewater Chemical Analyses 56
- B   Sorption on Wastewater Solids: Elimination of Biological Activity 59

UNIT SEVEN
- Text   Tertiary Treatment of Wastewater 65
- Reading Material A   Activated Sludge Treatment of Wastewater 71
- B   Land Treatment of Wastewater 74

UNIT EIGHT
- Text   The Role of the Engineer in Water Pollution Abatement 76
- Reading Material A   Disinfection 80
- B   Nitrogen and Phosphorus Removal 83

UNIT NINE
- Text   The Concept of Sustainable Development 86

Reading Material A Environmental Stress as a Source of Conflict ······ 91
              B Equity and the Common Interest ······ 93
UNIT TEN
  Text   Assessment of Environmental Impacts ······ 96
  Reading Material A Environmental Impact ······ 100
              B Environmental Assessment ······ 102
UNIT ELEVEN
  Text   Man and His Environment ······ 106
  Reading Material A A Preface to Air Pollution and Acid Rain ······ 111
              B Effects of Air Pollution on Health ······ 113
UNIT TWELVE
  Text   Biological Design of Activated Sludge ······ 115
  Reading Material A Landfills ······ 120
              B Disposal of Sludge Containing Heavy Metals ······ 122
UNIT THIRTEEN
  Text   Energy, Economy and Environment ······ 124
  Reading Material A The Growth of Cities ······ 129
              B The Situation in Industrial World Cities ······ 132
UNIT FOURTEEN
  Text   Ecology—Its Relation to Other Sciences and
            Its Relevance to Civilization ······ 135
  Reading Material A Elements of Ecology ······ 139
              B Role of Consumers in Food Web Dynamics ······ 141
UNIT FIFTEEN
  Text   The Environmental Ethic ······ 144
  Reading Material A Resolution of Environmental Conflicts (Part I) ······ 149
              B Resolution of Environmental Conflicts (Part II) ······ 150
UNIT SIXTEEN
  Text   EPA Must Look to the Future ······ 153
  Reading Material A EMAP Shifts Focus to Research ······ 157
              B States Try Out "Pollution Prevention Permits" ······ 159
Appendix I   Vocabulary ······ 162
Appendix II   Translation for Reference ······ 169
Appendix III Key to Exercises ······ 192

UNIT ONE

Text   An Introduction to Water Supply
           and Sanitation Provisions

[1]   Water is probably the most important natural resource in the world since without it life cannot exist and industry cannot operate. Unlike many other raw materials there is no substitute for water in many of its uses. Water plays a vital role in the development of communities since a reliable supply of water is an essential prerequisite for the establishment of a permanent community. Unfortunately, the liquid and solid wastes from such a community have a considerable potential for environmental pollution. In primitive civilizations the remedy for this pollution problem was simply to move the community to another suitable site. In more advanced civilizations such upheavals become impracticable and measures must be taken to protect and augment water supplies and for the satisfactory disposal of waste materials. The concept of water as a natural resource which must be carefully managed is very necessary as growing populations and industrial developments demand ever-increasing supplies of water.

[2]   The importance of water supply and sanitation provisions was recognized centuries ago in ancient civilizations. Archaeological evidence shows the existence of latrines and drains in Neolithic dwellings and the Minoan civilization in Crete 2000 years B.C. had clay water and sewage pipes with flushing toilets in the houses.[①] The Romans had highly developed water supply and drainage systems and their cities used large amounts of water with continuously operating fountains being a major source of supply for the majority of the population although wealthy families had their own piped supplies.[②] Large aqueducts, some of which still remain, were constructed over distances up to 80 km to bring adequate supplies of good-quality water into the cities. Stone sewers in the streets removed surfacewater and collected the discharges from latrines for conveyance beyond the city limits. With the demise of the Roman Empire most of their public works installations fell into disuse and for centuries water supply and sanitation provisions were virtually non-existent.[③] In the Middle Ages, towns started to develop at important crossing points on rivers and these rivers usually provided a convenient source of water and an apparently convenient means of waste disposal. Although sewers were built in the larger towns they were intended solely for the removal of surfacewater and in the UK the discharge of foul sewage to the sewers was forbidden by law until 1815. Sanitary provisions were usually minimal: in 1579 one street in London with sixty houses had three communal latrines. Discharges of liquid and solid wastes from windows into the street were common and it is not surprising that life expectancy was less than half the current figure in the developed world. In an attempt to improve matters a law was passed in 1847 which made it obligatory in London for cesspit and latrine waste to be discharged to the sewers.[④] London's sewers drained to the Thames, from which much of the city's water was obtained, and in addition the poor state of

repair of many of the sewers allowed the contents to leak into the aquifer which was the other main source of water. The inevitable consequences of this state of affairs were that water sources became increasingly contaminated by sewage, the Thames became objectionable to both sight and smell, and most seriously, waterborne diseases became rampant in the city. The Broad Street Pump outbreak of cholera in 1854 which caused 10,000 deaths provided the evidence for Dr. John Snow to demonstrate the connection between sewage pollution of water and enteric diseases like cholera and typhoid. Public outcry resulted in the commissioning of the first major public health engineering works of modern times; Bazalgette's intercepting sewers which collected sewage discharges and conveyed them downstream of London for discharge to the estuary, and water abstraction from Teddington on the non-tidal part of the river. Thus by 1870 waterborne outbreaks had been largely brought under control in the UK and similar developments were taking place in Western Europe and the cities of the USA. The Industrial Revolution greatly increased the urban water demand and the late nineteenth century saw the construction of major water-supply schemes involving large upland impoundments of which the Elan Valley scheme for Birmingham and the Croton and Catskill reservoirs serving New York are examples.

[3]　　Only by continual and costly attention to water quality control has it been possible to virtually eradicate waterborne diseases from developed countries. Such achievements must not, however, be allowed to mask the appalling situation regarding water supply and sanitation in much of the developing world.⑤ A survey in 1975 found that 80% of the world's rural population and 23% of the urban population had no reasonable access to a safe water supply. The sanitation situation was even worse with 85% of the rural population and 25% of the urban population having no sanitary provision at all. The growth of population in developing countries, due to the high birth rate, is such that unless strenuous efforts to increase water supply and sanitation facilities are made, the percentage of the world's population with satisfactory facilities would actually decrease in the future. The United Nations Organization has therefore designated the period 1981-90 as the International Drinking Water Supply and Sanitation Decade with the aim of providing safe water and adequate sanitation for all. Such a target will be difficult to achieve, involving as it must large investments in finance and manpower, although it has been estimated that the cost of meeting the Decade target would be about 5% of global spending on armaments during the same period.⑥

[4]　　In developed countries, demands for water are now fairly static and basic water quality-control measures are well established. However, many of the existing water-supply and sewage schemes are now relatively old so that their reconstruction will pose problems in the future. In addition, as knowledge of the effects of all forms of environmental pollution increases so new potential hazards appear, for example there is current concern about the possible carcinogenic hazards arising from the presence of minute concentrations of some organic compounds in water. Thus, throughout the world, various aspects of water quality control will continue to be vital in safeguarding public health.

New Words and Expressions

provision [prəu'viʒən]	n.	设备，装置
prerequisite * [ˌpriː'rekwizit]	n.	先决条件，前提
upheaval [ʌp'hiːvəl]	n.	动乱，剧变
augment * [ɔːg'ment]	vt.	扩大，增加，加强
latrine [lə'triːn]	n.	（沟形、坑形的）厕所
dwelling ['dweliŋ]	n.	住宅，住所
conveyance [kən'veiəns]	n.	运送，输送
demise [di'maiz]	n.	死亡，灭亡，终止
fall into		陷入，陷于
foul * [faul]	a.	污浊的，腐烂的
minimal * ['miniməl]	a.	最低限度的，最小的
communal ['kɔmjunəl]	a.	公有的，公用的
life expectancy		估计寿命，平均寿命
cesspit ['sespit]	n.	粪坑，污水坑
contaminate * [kən'tæmineit]	vt.	污染，弄脏
objectionable * [əb'dʒekʃənəbl]	a.	令人讨厌、作呕的
rampant ['ræmpənt]	a.	蔓延的，猖獗的
enteric [en'terik]	a.	肠的
outcry ['autkrai]	n.	强烈抗议或反对
intercept * [ˌintə'sept]	vt.	截流
abstraction [æb'strækʃən]	n.	引水
impoundment [im'paundmənt]	n.	贮水（池）
eradicate [i'rædikeit]	vt.	根除，消灭，杜绝
appalling [ə'pɔːliŋ]	a.	令人震惊的，骇人的
regarding [ri'gɑːdiŋ]	prep.	关于，就…而论
strenuous ['strenjuəs]	a.	奋发的，努力的
designate... as... *		指定，指派
armament ['ɑːməmənt]	n.	武器，器械
pose * [pəuz]	vt.	提出，形成

Notes

①Neolithic [ˌniː(ː)liː'liθik]（公元前 10 000 年左右中东地区和以后发展至其他地区的）新石器时代的；the Minoan [mi'nəuən] civilization（公元前 3000～1100 年古希腊克里特为中心的青铜器时代的）米诺斯（Minos）文化（亦称克里特文化）；Crete（希腊南部的）克里

特岛。

②with continuously operating fountains being a major source of supply for the majority of the population…为独立结构，补充说明。

③Roman Empire 罗马帝国（指公元前27年到公元476年的罗马奴隶制国家）。

④…for cesspit and latrine waste to be discharged to the sewers. 带逻辑主语的不定式短语为 which 定语从句中 made 的宾语。

⑤…regarding water supply and sanitation in much of the developing world. 为 situation 的定语。

⑥…as it must…省略形式的方式状语从句，意为 as it inevitably happens，此处"must"为"必然要"，"必定要"。

Exercises

Reading Comprehension

I. Are these statements true (T) or false (F) according to the text?

1. Since the demand for supplies of water is always on the increase with growing populations and industrial developments, it is necessary to form the idea that water as a natural resource must be carefully protected and managed. (　)

2. It was the Romans that recognized the importance of water supply and sanitation provisions and highly developed them, but with the collapse of the Roman Empire, all the public works installations were abandoned and water supply and sanitation provisions were no longer existent for several hundred years. (　)

3. Before 1815, it was forbidden to discharge foul sewage to the sewers by law in the UK, nor was it to discharge liquid and solid wastes from windows into the street. (　)

4. In some developed countries, achievements have been made in getting rid of waterborne diseases by continual and costly attention to water quality control, but the situation is still terrible in much of the developing world. (　)

5. It seems quite disappointing that the demands for water quality control will never be met in developed countries, for new potential hazards appear with the increasing knowledge of the effects of all forms of environmental pollution. (　)

II. Match Column A with Column B to form meaningful sentences according to the text.

A	B
1. Many raw materials have their substitutes in many of their uses	a. the percentage of the world's population with satisfactory facilities would actually decrease in the future

2. In the Middle Ages, sanitary situation was poor and sanitation provisions were usually minimal

3. The Broad Street pump outbreak of cholera in 1854 caused 10,000 deaths,

4. The major water-supply schemes involving large upland impoundments were constructed in the late 19th century

5. If strenuous efforts to increase water supply and sanitation facilities were not to be made

b. but as for water, there is none

c. in order to meet the urban water demand increased by the Industrial Revolution

d. which provided the evidence to prove forcibly the link between sewage pollution of water and enteric diseases

e. so the fact won't surprise you that life expectancy was less than half the current figure in the developed world

Vocabulary

I. Fill in the blanks with the expressions given below. Change the forms if necessary.

| communal | fall | into disuse | prerequisite | strenuous |
| provisions | rampant | solely | | |

1. I am afraid nobody can understand the meaning of the word, for it _____ for quite a long time.
2. Is it stated in the marriage law that everything owned by a husband and wife is considered _____ property?
3. He was thinking of resigning his position on the school paper _____ on account of his age.
4. The paper deals with the nation's problems, ranging from _____ inflation to a lowering of literacy levels.
5. A minimum _____ for this job is three years' experience and a good command of English.

II. Complete each of the following statements with one of the four choices given below.
1. The principal told the boys and girls that Mr. Wang was ill and Miss Li would be his _____ to give the English lecture to them.
   A. supply   B. substitute   C. place   D. post
2. Her knowledge of English is _____ for the job, although she is not fluent in the language.
   A. perfect   B. efficient   C. available   C. adequate

5

3. The European people had been carrying out a hard struggle against Fascists during the Second World War, and they won a complete victory with the _____ of the Third Reich in 1945.
   A. demise B. break C. ruin D. split
4. Because of the essential role played by water in supporting human life it also has, if _____, great potential for transmitting a wide variety of diseases and illnesses.
   A. augmented B. conveyed C. contaminated D. discharged
5. With the water supply and sanitation situation improved, cholera has been _____ in the region.
   A. escaped B. erased C. eradicated D. erected

Writing   Selecting the Key Words (1)

Key words are informative words that can give the information about what a piece of writing is mainly talking about. They are often nouns and verbs, etc.
For Example:
Read the following text and find out the key words

With the rapid industrialization of the States, air pollution is posing a problem. Fertilizer and steel plants, cement industries, thermal power plants and paper mills are among the units which cause air pollution.

Automobiles also cause air pollution as they emit smoke which contains hydrocarbon, nitrous oxide and carbon monoxide.

The Air Act was passed in Congress in 1982 and came into effect in 1983.

Key words:
Air pollution, Pollutant, Air Act
Directions: Read the text of this Unit and find out three to five key words.

Reading Material A

Water Demand

In addition to the water required for survival, other domestic uses of water are highly desirable, e.g. for personal hygiene, washing of utensils and clothes, etc. The amount of water used for these other domestic purposes will be governed by the availability of water in the community judged on both amount and cost bases. In very primitive communities water demands of around 2.5 l/person day have been recorded but as life styles develop, a water demand of about 10 l/person day is normal in the absence of a piped supply and where water has to be carried some distance to the house. The provision of a central stand-pipe supply in a village will probably increase the water demand to about 25 l/person day and the demand with an individual house tap in a low-income community is likely to be about 50 l/person day. In developed countries and the high-value urban housing areas of developing countries the provision of multiple taps, flush toilets, washing machines and dishwashers will greatly increase water demand for domestic purposes so that demands of several hundred litres per person day are common.

Industrial processes consume considerable amounts of water and in manufacturing areas industrial water demand may equal or even exceed the domestic demand. Some typical industrial water demands are, however, very much dependent upon such factors as the age of the plant, the cost of water and the incentive for in-plant recycling. Many industrial uses of water do not require a potable supply and there is increasing use of lower-grade sources, such as a sewage effluent, to satisfy at least part of the industrial demand. ① Industrial water demand is closely related to industrial productivity and is therefore likely to be subject to change in differing economic circumstances. Increasing costs of water and charges for wastewater collection and treatment exert considerable pressures for reductions in the water used by industry.

In many developed countries all water consumers are metered so that, at least in theory, demand could be regulated by pricing policy. ② However, the UK does not have a general policy of metering individual domestic supplies although the 1973 Water Act makes provision for the installation of meters and some authorities now offer metering as an option. ③ Most domestic consumers in the UK pay for their water on the basis of a charge related essentially to the size of the property and its value so that they have no incentive to economize in their use of water. ④ It has always been argued that the cost of installing and reading meters would far outweigh the potential savings which might accrue. Indeed, evidence from other countries where domestic metering is practised is somewhat conflicting and it is by no means clear that the introduction of metering would produce a sustained reduction in water consumption. ⑤ Some form of sliding-scale tariff for metered water to discourage excessive consumption is a possibility but it must be remembered that an ample supply of safe water is a primary requirement in the maintenance of public health. ⑥ Poorer members of a community should not therefore be forced into undesirable restrictions on water usage by economic pressures. ⑦ The justification for installing domestic water meters in the UK is thus essentially related to the provision of an equitable means of payment for the service in which the consumer has some degree of control over the size of the bill.

In a complex distribution system it is inevitable that there will be a certain amount of leakage and waste. In supply systems which are fully metered it is not unusual for about 25% of the water entering the system to be unaccounted for and there is no reason to suppose that the losses would be any less in unmetered systems. ⑧ This loss is made up of leakages, fire-fighting usage, unauthorized connections, ect. ⑨

In temperate zones almost all of the domestic water supply and much of the industrial supply find their way back into the sewers so that the dry weather flow (d. w. f.) of sewage could be expected to be of the same order as the flow of water supplied to the area.⑩ In warm climates a proportion of the water will be used for garden watering or otherwise lost by evaporation so that only 70~80% may enter the sewers.

Treatment plants and their associated collection and distribution systems are expensive items of capital expenditure which are often designed to have a useful life of 30 years or more. For this reason and to enable efficient development and utilization of water resources it is necessary to be able to predict future water demands. Domestic water demand is the product of the *per capita* demand and the population. The *per capita* demand will tend towards a ceiling value related to the standard of living of the community and its environmental conditions. Although in many developed countries populations are more or less static in numbers the developing world is experiencing large increases in population. The economic prosperity of an area will have a considerable influence on industrial activity and hence industrial water consumption. As productivity increases, so will water consumption until the point where the cost of water becomes a significant item in overall costs and means of reducing consumption then become financially attractive. The prediction of future industrial demands for water is thus fraught with difficulties.

Notes

① Sewage effluent 污水厂出水。
② 在许多发达国家中，用户用水表计量（付费）。因此，至少从理论上说，用水量是可以用价格政策来调控的。to meter (*v*.) 用仪器计量。
③ make provision for 为……作好准备，采取措施。
④ Most domestic consumers in the UK pay for their water on the basis of a charge related essentially to the size of the property and its value … 英国国内许多用户支付水费是根据他们财产的多少和价值来确定的，……
⑤ a sustained reduction 不断的减少。
⑥ Some form of sliding-scale tariff for metered water to discourage excessive consumption is a possibility …
  为了阻止浪费用水，计量用水可以采用某种浮动价目表的形式……
⑦ 因而不应迫使一社区的穷人因为经济原因而接受令人不快的用水限制。
⑧ to be unaccounted for … 未被计入。
⑨ unauthorized connections 未经批准（私自）安装的自来水管接头。
⑩ to be of the same order 同一情况。

8

Reading Material B

Water Treatment in Developing Countries

Water is our most abundant raw material and, in its natural state, one of our purest. All the same, for many uses the available water is still not pure enough, and therefore some impurity or other often has to be treated or removed in order to make the available water fit to use. When we talk about the different properties of various waters, we are actually talking about the impurities which they contain. As a result, water treatment is a technology which is concerned with the impurities in waters, rather than with the water itself. In developing countries, every effort must be made to keep the treatment as simple as possible to try to ensure low cost, ease of construction, reliability in operation and to enable operation and maintenance to be satisfactorily undertaken by local labour. Failure to satisfy these basic aims will almost certainly produce many problems and will often lead to the abandonment of the scheme with reversion to the traditional unimproved sources.

Storage

Storage can provide a useful measure of purification for most surface waters although it cannot be relied upon to produce much removal of turbidity. The disinfecting action of sunlight normally gives fairly rapid reductions in the numbers of faecal bacteria. To obtain the maximum benefit from storage it is important to ensure that short-circuiting in the basin is prevented by suitable baffles.① A disadvantage of storage in hot climates is the considerable evaporation losses which can occur. The design of storage facilities should be such as to prevent the formation of shallow areas at the edges which could provide mosquito-breeding sites.② If the settlement provided by storage does not give sufficient removal of suspended matter the choice for further treatment involves consideration of chemical coagulation and/or filtration techniques.

Coagulation

The use of chemicals for coagulation brings a further level of complexity to the treatment process and should only be adopted if the necessary skills are available locally. Chemical coagulation will only be successful if the appropriate dose can be determined and then applied to the water in such a manner as to ensure adequate mixing and flocculation. The most useful form of chemical feeder is one based on hydraulic control of a solution such as the Marriotte vessel which provides a constant rate of discharge regardless of the level in the storage container.③

The coagulant must be added at a point of turbulence such as a weir or in a baffled channel and flocculation is best achieved in a baffled basin connected to a settling basin. In practice it is difficult to prevent floc carry- over from the settling basin so that the output water quality may at times have fairly high turbidity levels. ④ A more satisfactory water may therefore arise by omitting the coagulation stage and proceeding directly with filtration.

Filtration

Although some simplified types of rapid sand filter are available the slow sand filter is likely to be the most satisfactory form of treatment process for many developing-country installations. Slow filtration is able to provide high removals of many physical, chemical and bacteriological contaminants from water with the advantages of simplicity in construction and use. No chemicals are required and no sludge is produced. Cleaning by removal of the top surface at intervals of a month or more is labour intensive but this is not normally a problem in developing countries. ⑤ The relatively large area requirements for a slow filter are unlikely to cause problems for small supplies and the cost of construction can be reduced by using locally available sand or substitute materials such as rice husks. It is usually possible to operate slow filters at rates of about $5m^3/m^2d$ with raw water turbidities of up to 50 NTU whilst producing a filtrate of <1 NTU.

Disinfection

If disinfection is required the previously stated problems related to chemical dosing must again be faced. Chlorine is the only practicable disinfectant but the availability of the gaseous form is likely to be restricted and in any event the hazards of handling chlorine gas make it unsuitable for rural supplies. A more suitable source of chlorine for such installations is bleaching powder which is about 30% available chlorine and is easy to handle although it loses its strength when exposed to the atmosphere and to light. High-test hypochlorite (HTH) in granular or tablet form has a higher available chlorine content (70%) and is stable in storage but more costly. ⑥ Sodium hypochlorite solution is another possible source of chlorine. Dosage should be by means of the same type of simple hydraulic feeder as discussed for coagulants. For very small supplies simple pot chlorinators using a pot or jar with a few tiny holes and filled with a mixture of bleaching powder and sand can give a chlorine residual for about 2 weeks before recharging is necessary. The attainment of the correct dose of chlorine is important since too low a dose will give a false sense of security and too high a dose will give a chlorine taste to the water which will probably result in rejection of the supply by the consumers in favour of traditional sources.

Notes

①baffles 隔板。

②设计储水设备时务必注意在储水池的边缘不致形成供蚊子滋生的浅洼。

③…the Marriotte vessel which provides a constant rate of discharge…保持恒定流量的马里奥特容器……

④事实上沉淀池里很难避免没有絮凝体的留存物，这样，输出的水质常会出现颇高的混浊度。

⑤labour intensive 费劲的细活。

⑥High-test hypochlorite (HTH) in granular or tablet form…颗粒状或片状的优质次氯酸盐。

UNIT TWO

Text   Water Quality Criteria

[1]   Municipal water will be used for several purposes—washing, drinking, waste disposal and as industrial water. The quality requirements will be set by the most critical of these uses, that is, human consumption. The criteria will reflect the need to produce water which is

   (a) hygienic with a minimum of pathogens and toxins;
   (b) aesthetically acceptable and potable;
   (c) non-corrosive to the distribution system;
   (d) can be produced for the least cost.

[2]   To meet these conditions, several sets of standards have been proposed and are continually being revised. The specific concentrations proposed are suggested as those which will not adversely affect water quality. The general types of criteria for drinking water supplies are described for the following parameters: microbiological, health and toxicity, and aesthetic properties of the water.

[3]   **Microbiological Criteria for Drinking Water**
Microbiological standards for drinking waters are considered to be the most important and most widely quoted standards. Direct tests for pathogens are difficult because of the low number of pathogens present and the large number of different types of pathogen which can be present. The routine microbiological testing of waters relies upon the enumeration of the non-pathogenic coliform bacteria. A common standard is that the average number of coliforms is less than one per 100ml of sample with specification of statistical variation and sampling frequency.

[4]   **Health and Toxicity Criteria for Drinking Water**
Several different types of compound are considered harmful, including both organic and inorganic species. Metals such as lead, chromium and cadmium are toxic and the maximum allowable concentrations are usually less than 0.1 and often less than 0.01 mg litre^{-1}; similar criteria apply to cyanide. Standards for toxic organic compounds have been recommended only relatively recently; the large number of substances and the difficulties of analysis are major problems, but an increasing number of substances are included in drinking water criteria. General parameters like carbon chloroform extract (often <1mg litre^{-1}) provide some assessment of organic content. Some groups of materials, for example organophosphates and carbonates, can be grouped together (<0.1mg litre^{-1}) while other chemicals are covered by specific criteria, for example endrin (<0.001mg litre^{-1}), lindane (<0.056mg litre^{-1}) and DDT (<0.042mg litre^{-1}). As many of the organic compounds are likely to be carcinogenic (causing cancer), mutagenic (causing mutation) or teratogenic (causing malformation), the effects may take many years to appear. The standards are likely to be subject to revision, but their inclusion in water quality criteria has resulted in an increased use of processes like activated carbon adsorp-

tion for the removal of organic molecules.

[5]   Several other chemicals are specified because they influence human health, nitrate and fluoride ions being the most significant. ① Nitrate ions (NO_3^-) may cause methaemoglobinaemia in infants (children less than 6 months old). The concentration of nitrate in drinking water is often limited to <10 or <50 mg litre^{-1}; if this condition is not met, alternative water supplies must be used for feeding infants. Excessive amounts of fluoride ions (F^-) in drinking water (>1.5 mg litre^{-1}) result in a mottling of tooth enamel and in extreme cases a blackening of teeth and eventually failure of the structure of the teeth. ② Some other chemicals have specific effects; for example sulphate ions, particularly if present together with magnesium ions, have a laxative effect on new users. ③

[6]   **Aesthetic Criteria for Drinking Water**

The production of a drinking water which is aesthetically acceptable is generally regarded as necessary to assure users of the hygienic quality of the water. The physical tests for turbidity, colour, taste, and odour are designed to ensure that the water will be potable and aesthetically pleasing. The general standards require the production of water which has properties within certain limits, for example less than 5 colour units and unobjectionable taste and odour. Specific chemicals are subject to additional restriction; chlorine ions impart a salty taste to water if present in concentrations greater than 200 mg litre^{-1} while phenolic compounds are restricted partly because of their tendency to form chlorophenols which are highly odorous.

[7]   **Drinking Water Quality Standards and Raw Water Quality**

Any classification of water quality criteria tends to be arbitrary because of the overlap of the classifications. The criteria for toxins are the most easily classified as the concentration in water which is considered to have no adverse effect on consumers. However, long-term effects of toxins are difficult to determine and the interaction of different toxins usually results in increased total toxicity. Also, because of the large volume of water consumed, even 'non-toxic' species like chloride ions can have adverse effects.

[8]   In general, raw water supplies are chosen to provide the highest water quality and/or the least expensive treatment. As many materials are little affected by conventional water treatment processes, this often means that the concentrations of the materials in the raw water supply must be similar to those recommended for drinking water. As the presence of pollution in water will tend to be associated with pathogens, toxins and a high concentration of soluble materials, raw waters should contain low concentrations of materials which indicate pollution. Raw water criteria for oxygen demand (chemical oxygen demand $<$ 10 mg litre^{-1}, five-day biochemical oxygen demand $<$ 6 mg litre^{-1}), grease ($<$1 mg litre^{-1}), ammonia ($<$0.5 mg litre^{-1}), carbon chloroform extract ($<$0.5 mg litre^{-1}) and total nitrogen are intended to minimize these effects.

New Words and Expressions

critical ['krɪtɪkəl]	a.	挑剔的
hygienic [haɪ'dʒiːnɪk]	a.	卫生的
aesthetically [iːs'θetɪkəli]	ad.	美（学）地
corrosive * [kə'rəusɪv]	a.	腐蚀的
enumeration [ɪˌnjuːmə'reɪʃən]	n.	计数
coliform ['kɔlifɔːm]	n.	大肠杆菌
specification * [ˌspesɪfɪ'keɪʃən]	n.	说明，规格
cyanide ['saɪənaɪd]	n.	氰化物
chloroform ['klɔrəfɔːm]	n.	氯仿，三氯甲烷
extract * [ɪk'strækt]	n.	提取物
organophosphate [ˌɔːgənəu'fɔsfeɪt]	n.	有机磷酸盐
carbonate ['kɑːbəneɪt]	n.	碳酸盐
endrin ['endrɪn]	n.	异狄氏剂（一种杀虫剂）
lindane ['lɪndeɪn]	n.	高丙体六六六，林丹
mutagenic [ˌmjuːtə'dʒenɪk]	a.	致突变的
mutation [mjuː'teɪʃən]	n.	突变
teratogenic [ˌterətəu'dʒenɪk]	a.	致畸形形成的
malformation [ˌmælfɔː'meɪʃən]	n.	畸形（体）
inclusion * [ɪn'kluːʒən]	n.	包括，内含
adsorption * [æd'sɔːpʃən]	n.	吸附（作用）
fluoride ['fluəraɪd]	n./a.	氟化物（的）
methaemoglobinaemia [met'hiːməuˌgləubɪ'niːmɪə]	n.	高铁血红蛋白血（症）
mottling ['mɔtlɪŋ]	n.	斑驳状，杂色
enamel [ɪ'næməl]	n.	珐琅质
sulphate ['sʌlfeɪt]	n.	硫酸（盐）
magnesium * [mæg'niːzɪəm]	n.	镁
laxative ['læksətɪv]	a.	致轻泻的
impart * [ɪm'pɑːt]	vt.	给予，传递
phenolic [fɪ'nɔlɪk]	a.	苯酚的
chlorophenol [ˌklɔːrə'fiːnəl]	n.	氯（苯）酚
overlap * [ˌəuvə'læp]	n.	覆叠，部分相同
chloride * ['klɔːraɪd]	n.	氯化物
soluble ['sɔljubl]	a.	可溶的
nitrogen ['naɪtrədʒən]	n.	氮

14

Notes

① …, nitrate and fluoride ions being the most significant. 独立结构，补充说明。
② 谓语动词短语 result in 后面有三个宾语：a mottling of tooth enamel, a blackening of teeth 及 failure of the structure of the teeth。
③ 句中 if 从句中形容词 present 前省略了 it is。

Exercises

Reading Comprehension

Ⅰ. Are these statements true (T) or false (F) according to the text?
1. The water quality requirements will be decided by its uses—washing, drinking, waste disposal and as industrial water. (　　)
2. Since conventional water treatment processes are unable to remove many materials effectively, the raw water supplies must be chosen by the standards for drinking waters. (　　)
3. The most widely used standards for drinking waters are microbiological standards, but the direct microbiological tests for pathogens are not an easy job because there exist a small number of pathogens and a large number of different types of pathogen. (　　)
4. The large number of substances in drinking waters and the difficulties of analysis enable standards for toxic organic compounds to be recommended recently. (　　)
5. Aesthetically acceptable drinking water will assure users of the hygienic quality of water, which can be obtained by the physical tests for turbidity, colour, taste and odour. (　　)

Ⅱ. Match Column A with Column B to form meaningful sentences according to the text.

A

1. There are several uses of municipal water, of which the most demanding is drinking water
2. The normal microbiological tests of water are conducted
3. Health and toxicity standards tend to be revised,

B

a. one is of the highest water quality and the other is of the least cost treatment
b. for the unfavourable effects of many organic compounds may not be deter-mined until many years later
c. for the purpose of making the portable and aesthetically pleasing water available

4. The physical tests for turbidity, colour, taste and odour are designed
5. There are two requirements for the choice of raw water supplies:

d. by which the water quality criteria will be determined
e. on the basis of the amount of the non-pathogenic coliform bacteria existing in waters

Vocabulary

I. Fill in the blanks with the expressions given below. Change the forms if necessary.

| adsorption | critical | impart | malformation |
| overlap | routine | soluble | |

1. It is very difficult to determine which individual should be blamed for the mistake because of the _____ of responsibility.
2. Unlike common saccharin, this one is only _____ in hot liquid.
3. Soil type as well as climate are _____ factors in controlling the feasibility and design of a land treatment process.
4. He had sufficient _____ work to carry him through the whole day.
5. A pregnant woman must be very cautious in taking medicines, for some of them will lead to _____ of the baby.

II. Complete each of the following statements with one of the four choices given below.
1. The similar standards for drinking water _____ the raw water supplies since conventional water treatment processes are not very effective.
   A. apply for   B. apply in   C. apply with   D. apply to
2. While the chloride ion concentration is limited to 200 mg litre^{-1} because of the salty taste, chloride ion concentrations in excess of 600mg litre^{-1} _____ to lead to kidney damage.
   A. are easily   B. are likely   C. are possible   D. are probably
3. I used to _____ very severe colds but my persistence in physical exercise for a few years has changed the situation.
   A. subject to   B. be subject to   C. be subjected to   D. be subjective to
4. Many people think that television _____ both children and adults though it occupies most of their leisure time.
   A. has bad effects on   B. has bad effects to
   C. has bad affect on   D. has bad affect to
5. He _____ me _____ his full support for my plan and his readiness to help.
   A. ensured…by   B. ensured…as
   C. assured…of   D. assured…with

Writing   Selecting the Key Words (2)

Directions: Read the text of Unit two and find out 3 to 5 key words.

Reading Material A

Drinking Water Standards in the U. S.

Drinking water standards are equally if not more important to public health than stream standards.① These standards have a long history. In 1914, faced with the questionable quality of potable water in the towns along their routes, the railroad industry asked the U. S. Public Health Service (USPHS) to suggest standards which would describe a good drinking water.② As a result of this problem, the first USPHS Drinking Water Standards were born. There was no law passed to require that all towns abide by these standards, but it was established that interstate transportation would not be allowed to stop at towns which could not provide water of adequate quality. Over the years most water supplies in the United States have not been closely regulated, and the high-quality water provided by municipal systems has been as much the result of the professional pride of the water industry personnel as any governmental restrictions.

Because of a growing concern with the quality of some of the urban water supplies and reports that not all waters are as pure and safe as people have always assumed, the federal government passed the Safe Drinking Water Act in late 1974. This law authorizes the EPA to set minimum national drinking water standards. The EPA has published some of these standards, which are quite similar to the USPHS Water Standards. Potable water standards used to describe the contaminants can be divided into three categories: physical, bacteriological and chemical.

Physical standards include color, turbidity and odor, all of which are not dangerous in themselves but could, if present in excessive amounts, drive people to drink other, perhaps less safe, water.

Bacteriological standards are in terms of coliforms, the indicators of pollution by wastes from warm-blooded animals.③ Tests for pathogens are almost never attempted. The present EPA standard calls for a concentration of coliforms of less than 1 per 100 ml water. This standard is a classical example of how the principle of expediency is used to set standards.④ Before modern water treatment plants were commonplace, the bacteriological standard stood at 10 coliforms/100ml. In 1946, this was changed to the present level of 1/100ml. In reality, with modern methods we can attain about 0. 01 coliforms/100ml. It is, however, not expedient to do this because the extra measure of public health attained by lowering the permissible coliform level would not be worth the price we would have to pay.

Chemical standards include a long list of chemical contaminants beginning with arsenic and ending with zinc. Two classifications exist, the first being a suggested limit, the latter a maximum allowable limit. Arsenic, for example, has a suggested limit of 0.01 mg/l. This concentration has, from experience, been shown to be a safe level even when ingested over an extended period. The maximum allowable arsenic level is 0.05 mg/l, which is still under the toxic threshold but close enough to create public health concern.⑤ On the other hand, some chemicals such as chlorides have no maximum allowable limits since at concentrations above the suggested limits the water becomes unfit to drink on the basis of taste or odor.

Over the years, the battles for clean water have moved from the courtroom through the congressional chambers to the administrative offices of EPA and state departments of natural resources. Permitting systems have replaced inconsistent, one-case-at-a-time judicial proceedings as ambient water quality standards and effluent standards are sought. Tough decisions lie ahead as current water programs are administered, particularly the NPDES permits for polluters discharging to waterways and the pretreatment guidelines for polluters discharging to municipal sewer systems. Even tougher decisions must be faced in the future as regulations are developed for the control of toxic substances.

Notes

①就公共卫生而言，如果说饮用水水质标准不比河水水质标准更重要的话，它们也是同等重要的。
②U. S. Public Health Service (USPHS)　美国公共卫生署
③warm-blooded animals　温血动物（指体温从 98 至 118 华氏度的哺乳动物或鸟类）。
④环保局制定的现有标准要求每 100ml 水中大肠杆菌的密度小于 1。这一典型例证说明我们在制定水质标准中采取了一种权宜之计。
⑤the toxic threshold　中毒界限。

Reading Material B

Setting Standards for the Mediterranean Sea

Developing water quality criteria for the Mediterranean is a key part of the Mediterranean Action Plan. All countries party to the Barcelona Convention, which acts as a legal framework for pollution control measures, support its aims, but the emergence of new standards can pose legal and economic difficulties.①

Most of the quality standards for the Mediterranean are related to the health of people rather than the environment. AS such they are the responsibility of the World Health Organization (WHO) and take the form of guidelines and recommendations on the basis of expert opinion. Unlike other WHO recommendations, under the terms of the Barcelona Convention contracting states have to include criteria and standards as part of their statutory programmes, and so become legally binding.

Currently recreational water quality and seafood quality are the main focus for WHO. Mediterranean countries attract large numbers of tourists to their coastlines. Rapid and uncontrolled development together with discharge of municipal and industrial waste has caused deterioration of coastal water quality. Rightly or wrongly, increases in some health problems among local and holiday populations are attributed to bathing in polluted waters. Expansion in the range of recreational activities to include diving, wind-surfing and underwater fishing also adds to the quality coverage necessary in terms of area, depth and risk assessment.[2]

Development of standards for recreational water use is therefore a complicated issue. To ensure adequate health protection, an upper tolerance limit to the degree of pollution by sewage needs to be defined. Unfortunately, establishing a satisfactory quality-effect correlation has not yet been achieved.

With seafood, sewage pollution poses an immediate or acute health hazard. Contamination by bacterial and microbial pathogens is most common, though algal biotoxins in shellfish are affecting some areas, particularly the Adriatic.

Chemical pollutants in seafood create long-term rather than acute health hazards. Diagnosis can be difficult because symptoms are less specific and chemicals can be ingested from other sources. At present quality standards are set in terms of upper acceptable limits for concentrations of selected chemicals in seafood, but this affords only partial protection. Standards tend to be designed on the basis of national consumption patterns, which can leave high seafood consumers at risks. Analysing seafood for chemicals also requires sophisticated techniques that some Mediterranean countries find difficult to carry out on a routine basis.

So far, interim quality criteria have been adopted by member states for bathing waters, mercury, used lubricating oils, cadmium compounds, organotins, organohalogens, organophosphorus compounds, persistent synthetic materials, radioactive substances, pathogenic microorganisms, shellfish waters, and carcinogenic, teratogenic and mutagenic substances. These represent minimum standards: some countries have stricter controls.

Introducing new standards would require change in the majority of countries to maintain heterogeneity.[3] Differences in where standards are enshrined in the national legislative frameworks can make such changes difficult to implement legally and economically. This is often the case where not only the standard but frequency of sampling methods of analysis and interpretation of results are prescribed by the law.

Complying with standards assumes the existence of an institutional infrastructure to monitor and make decisions based on results obtained. Remediation measures may involve capital costs to build treatment plants or remove sources of contamination. Introducing new standards can impact developed and developing countries in different ways. Developed countries may already have the institutional infrastructure and necessary control measures in place. If standards are revised to tighter limits, this may require upgrading and redesign of control structures at significant cost.

With developing countries, the problem is of creating new quality standards, rather than amending old ones. Economically, this has greater implications than legal problems. Rapid development along coastlines has often taken place without pollution control infrastructure being incorporated. Costs involved in effecting preventive and/or remedial measures are proving to be a major stumbling block and implementation of necessity, has to be in stages.

Enforcement is a further problem for both developed and developing countries. Monitoring of seawater, effluents and seafood is often carried out as part of the duties of public health, food or water laboratories, or sometimes marine research laboratories. As the more sophisticated laboratories are often in towns and cities far from the coast, samples are frequently transported long distances for analysis. More coastal laboratories are springing up, but these require funds for equipment and materials, which in developing countries usually have to be paid for in hard currency.

Notes

① "All countries party to the Barcelona…support its aims, but…"
所有国家都参加了巴塞罗那大会，并支持大会制定的目标。巴塞罗那大会是一个为控制污染采取一系列措施的立法机构，但是…

② 由于扩大了包括潜泳、风帆冲浪和水下捕鱼在内的各项娱乐活动范围，鉴于对面积、深度和风险估价诸方面的考虑，也有必要增加合格水质的面积。

③ 采用新标准将要求大多数国家改变各自认可沿用的做法。

UNIT THREE

Text   Microbiological Examination

[1]   Because of their small size, observation of micro-organisms with the naked eye is impossible and in the case of the simpler micro-organisms their physical features do not provide positive identification.① With bacteria it is necessary to utilize their biochemical or metabolic properties to aid identification of individual species. Living specimens are often difficult to observe because they usually have little colour and thus do not stand out against the liquid background. Staining of dead specimens is useful in some cases but the staining and mounting technique may itself alter some of the cell characteristics.

[2]   An optical microscope has a maximum magnification of about $1000\times$ with a limit of resolution of about $0.2\mu m$. Hence most viruses will be invisible with an optical microscope and only limited detail of the structure of a bacterial cell can be observed. For more detailed examination it is necessary to use an electron microscope which can provide magnifications of around $50,000\times$ with a limit of resolution of about $0.01nm$.

[3]   Study of living specimens, which is only possible under an optical microscope, is necessary to determine whether or not an organism is motile. A hanging drop slide must be used in this case and it is important to differentiate between Brownian movement, a random vibrational motion common to all colloids, and true motility which is a rapid shooting or wriggling movement.

[4]   In many situations it is necessary to assess the number of micro-organisms present in a water sample. With the larger micro-organisms like algae, estimation of numbers and actual identification of species can be achieved using a special microscope slide containing a depression of known volume. Numbers are obtained by counting the appropriate micro-organisms in the chamber, aided by a grid etched onto the slide.②

[5]   An estimate of the number of living bacteria (viable cell count) in a water sample may be obtained with a plate count using nutrient agar medium. A 1-ml sample of the water, diluted if necessary, is mixed with liquefied agar at 40℃ in a petri dish. The agar sets to a jelly thus fixing the bacterial cells in position. The plate is then incubated under appropriate conditions (72 h at 22℃ for natural water bacteria, 24 h at 37℃ for bacteria originating from animals or man). At the end of incubation the individual bacteria will have produced colonies visible to the naked eye and the number of colonies is assumed to be a function of the viable cells in the original sample. In practice such plate counts do not give the total population of a sample, since no single medium and temperature combination will permit all bacteria to reproduce. However, viable counts at the two temperatures using a wide-spectrum medium do give an overall picture of the bacterial quality and pollution history of a sample.

[6]   To determine the presence of a particular genus or species of bacteria it is necessary to

utilize its characteristic behaviour by supplying special selective media and/or incubation conditions which are suitable only for the bacteria under investigation. Many serious diseases are related to microbiological contamination of water, most of them due to pathogenic bacteria excreted by people suffering from or carrying the disease.③ Whilst it is possible to examine a water for the presence of a specific pathogen a more sensitive test employs an indicator organism *Escherichia coli* which is a normal inhabitant of the human intestine and is excreted in large numbers. Its presence in water thus indicates human excretal contamination and the sample is therefore potentially dangerous in that pathogenic faecal bacteria *might* also be present. Coliform bacteria in general have the ability to ferment lactose to produce acid and gas. Detection of coliforms can be achieved using a lactose medium inoculated with serial dilutions of the sample. The appearance of acid and gas after 24 h at 37℃ is taken as positive indication of the presence of coliform bacteria, results being expressed with the aid of statistical tables as most probable number (MPN) /100 ml. As a confirmatory test for *Escherichia coli*, positive tubes are subcultured in fresh medium for 24 h at 44℃ under which conditions only E. *coli* will grow to give acid and gas.

[7]　An alternative technique for bacteriological analysis, which is now popular, uses special membrane filter papers with a pore size such that bacteria can be separated from suspension. The bacteria retained on the paper are then placed in contact with an absorbent pad containing the appropriate nutrient medium in a small plastic petri dish and incubated. Identification of a particular species of bacteria is made on the basis of the type of nutrient provided and often on the appearance (colour, sheen) of the colonies formed. Counting the colonies provides the necessary quantitative information. The membrane filter technique is very convenient for field testing although the cost of the materials is likely to be higher than for the conventional methods of analysis.

New Words and Expressions

organism ['ɔːgənizəm]　　　　　　　　　n.　生物体，有机物
identification * [aiˌdentifiˈkeiʃən]　　　n.　识别，鉴别
metabolic [ˌmetəˈbɔlik]　　　　　　　　a.　新陈代谢的
stand out　　　　　　　　　　　　　　　　引人注目，醒目
stain [stein]　　　　　　　　　　　　　vt./n.　着色，染色
mount [maunt]　　　　　　　　　　　　n.　载片
magnification * [ˌmægnifiˈkeiʃən]　　　n.　放大（率）
resolution [ˌrezəluːʃən]　　　　　　　　n.　晰象，分辨
motile [ˈməutail]　　　　　　　　　　　a.　运动的
differentiate * [ˌdifəˈrenʃieit]　　　　　vt.　区分，分别
random * [ˈrændəm]　　　　　　　　　　a.　随机的，不规则的
vibrational * [vaiˈbreiʃənl]　　　　　　　a.　振动的

colloid ['kɔlɔid]	n. /a.	胶体（的），胶质（的）
motility [məu'tiləti]	n.	运动
shooting ['ʃu:tiŋ]	n.	直射
wriggle ['rigl]	vt.	蠕动，扭动
depression * [di'preʃən]	n.	低压
chamber ['tʃeimbə]	n.	小室
grid * [grid]	n.	格子，格栅
etch * [etʃ]	vt.	刻蚀
plate [pleit]	n.	平皿
a plate count		平皿读数
agar ['eigə:]	n.	琼脂
liquefy ['likwifai]	vt.	液化，稀释
petri ['pi:tri]	n.	皮氏培养皿
set to		转化
jelly ['dʒeli]	n.	胶冻，胶状物
incubate ['inkjubeit]	vt.	（细菌）培养
originate from		来源于
colony ['kɔləni]	n.	菌落，群体
population [ˌpɔpju'leiʃən]	n.	总数，全体
genus ['dʒi:nəs]	n.	类，种类
excrete [ek'skri:t]	vt.	排泄，分泌
whilst = while	conj.	尽管，虽然
intestine [in'testin]	n.	肠
faecal ['fi:kəl]	a.	粪便的，排泄物的
ferment ['fə:ment]	vt. /n.	发酵
lactose ['læktəus]	n.	乳糖
inoculate [i'nɔkjuleit]	vt.	移植，培养
serial ['siəriəl]	a.	系列的
confirmatory [kən'fə:mətəri]	a.	起确定作用的
subculture [ˌsʌb'kʌltʃə]	vt.	再次培养
suspension * [sə'spenʃən]	n.	悬浮液（体）
retain [ri'tein]	vt.	残留
in contact with		与…有联系的
absorbent [əb'sɔ:bənt]	a.	有吸收作用的
sheen [ʃi:n]	n.	光泽，光彩

Notes

① in the case of 就……而论。
② aided by a grid etched onto the slide 过去分词短语做状语；其中 etched onto the slide 是 grid 的定语。
③ … most of them due to pathogenic bacteria excreted by people suffering from or carrying the disease. 独立结构，excreted … 过去分词短语作定语，修饰 bacteria。

Exercises

Reading Comprehension

Ⅰ. Are these statements true (T) or false (F) according to the text?
   1. Micro-organisms are too small to be observed with the naked eye and as for the simpler ones their physical features are plain to be identified. ( )
   2. The electron microscope, having a maximum magnification of about 50,000× with a limit of resolution of about 0.01 nm, is much more helpful than the optical microscope, for the former can provide more details of the structure of a bacterial cell than the latter. ( )
   3. An overall picture of the bacterial quality and pollution history of a sample cannot be obtained with plate counts which do not provide the total population of a sample. It can only be gained with viable counts at the two temperatures using a wide-spectrum medium. ( )
   4. It has been found out that many serious diseases result from microbiological pollution of water which is totally caused by pathogenic bacteria excreted by people who suffer from or carry the disease. ( )
   5. An alternative technique for bacteriological analysis is the membrane filter technique, which is very original and convenient although the cost is much higher. ( )

Ⅱ. Match Column A with Column B to form meaningful sentences according to the text.

A	B
1. With little colour, living specimens are difficult to observe	a. you can utilize a plate count employing nutrient agar medium
2. Brownian movement is a random vibrational motion common to all colloids	b. according to the type of nutrient used

3. If you want to estimate the number of living bacteria in a water sample
4. Coliforms can be detected by means of lactose medium
5. A particular species of bacteria is identified

c. which is inoculated with serial dilutions of the sample
d. while true motility is a rapid shooting or wriggling movement
e. so staining of dead specimens is often used in some cases

Vocabulary

I. Fill in the blanks with the expressions given below. Change the forms if necessary.

| contamination | depression | inhabitant |
| nutrient | positive | resolution | viable |

1. The process of the _____ of a chemical mixture into simple substances was shown to the students in the lab.
2. You can notice the _____ of the mercury in the thermometer with the air-conditioner beginning to work.
3. The human fetus usually becomes _____ by the end of the seventh month.
4. It is a normal _____ of the intestines of both man and animals.
5. The factory is charged with the _____ of the river by industrial waste.

II. Complete each of the following statements with one of the four choices given below.
1. _____ a highly intelligent animal like the seal, elementary training is not difficult.
   A. In case   B. In case of   C. In the case of   D. In no case
2. A number of diseases depend upon the _____ organism spending part of its life-cycle in water or in an intermediate host which lives in water.
   A. pathogenic   B. metabolic   C. confirmatory   D. pathological
3. The grading of milk is usually made _____ bacterial content.
   A. at the base of   B. at the basis of
   C. on the base of   D. on the basis of
4. White is the _____ colour for a wedding gown in the western world but in China Red is.
   A. common   B. conventional   C. convenient   D. contemporary
5. The jade is so pure that no imperfections are visible at a hundred times _____.
   A. simplification B. amplification C. enlargement   D. magnification

Writing   Outline Writing (1)

To write an outline of an article, you must first of all identify the main ideas in the paragraphs and then express them by using noun phrases (topic outline) or simple sentences (sentence outline).

Topic outline is one that uses incomplete sentences, e.g. nouns, noun phrases etc. while sentence outline uses complete sentences.

For example:

The Topic Outline
a) Three Main Groups of Oil
b) Uses and Importance of Mineral Oil
c) History and Origin of Mineral Oil

The Sentence Outline
a) Oil falls into three categories: animal, vegetable and mineral.
b) Of them mineral oil is the most useful and has changed our life.
c) The oil originated in the distant past and has formed from living things in the sea.

Directions: Now read the text of Unit Three again and then complete the outline by matching the paragraph numbers in Column A with their proper topic outline in Column B.

A	B
1. Para. 1	a. the way of estimating the number of living bacteria in a water sample
2. Para. 2	b. an alternative technique for bacteriological analysis
3. para. 3	c. using biochemical or metabolic properties of bacteria to aid identification of individualspecies
4. para. 4	d. the way of assessing the number of micro-organisms present in a water sample
5. para. 5	e. the way of determining the presence of living bacteria
6. para. 6	f. the way of studying living specimens
7. para. 7	g. the reason for the use of the electron microscope instead of the optical microscope

Reading Material A

Ecological Principles

In all communities of living organisms the various forms of life are interdependent to a greater or lesser extent. This interdependence is essentially nutritional, described as a trophic relationship, and is exemplified by the cycle of organic productivity and the carbon and nitrogen cycles. A biological community and the environment in which it is found form an ecosystem and the science of such systems is known as ecology.

The autotrophes in an ecosystem, i. e. green plants and some bacteria, are termed *producers* since they synthesize organic matter from inorganic constituents.① Heterotrophic animals are known as consumers since they require ready-made organic food and may be subdivided into herbivores (plant eaters) and carnivores (meat eaters).② Heterotrophic plants are termed *decomposers* since they break down the organic matter in dead plants and animals and in animal excreta. Some of the products of decomposition are utilized for their own growth and energy requirements, but others are released as simple inorganic compounds suitable for plant uptake. Solar radiation provides the only external energy source and permits the synthesis of carbohydrates and other organic products which are then transferred to the heterotrophic phase of the cycle along with oxygen resulting from photosynthesis.③ In exchange, carbon dioxide, water and inorganic salts resulting from the activities of animals and bacteria are returned to the autotrophes. It should be noted that whilst carbon follows a cyclical path in such a system, energy flow is one-way only. It is important to remember that a continual energy input is thus necessary to allow the system to function. The loss of some part of the energy input to heat and entropy which inevitably occurs in biological systems can be considered as analogous to friction losses in a mechanical system.④ In fact the efficiency in terms of energy conversion of biological systems is very low and the further away an organism is from the original energy input the lower will be the proportion of that energy available to the particular organism.

In an aquatic environment the interdependence of organisms takes the form of a complex food web within which are many food chains with successive links being composed of different species in a predator-prey relationship with adjacent links.⑤ Thus a typical food chain for a river would be

algae → rotifer → mayfly → minnow → pike

The successive links in the food chain contain fewer but larger individual organisms and the community can be pictured in the form of an Eltonian pyramid of numbers (Fig. 3-1). Each level in the pyramid is known as trophic level. Organisms occupying the same level compete for a common food, but those on a higher level are predatory on the lower level. Under natural conditions such an ecosystem can remain dynamically balanced over long periods, but changes in water quality or other environmental factors can completely upset the balance. Toxic materials tend to give a particular percentage kill of the population regardless of the population density, whereas the effect of such factors as shortage of food is more likely to be significant with dense populations. A clean surface water will normally contain many different forms of life, but none will be dominant and the community will be well balanced. Serious organic pollution of the water would produce conditions unsuitable for most of the higher forms of life so that the community would become one of one or two simple life forms which would be present in very large numbers because of the absence of predators.

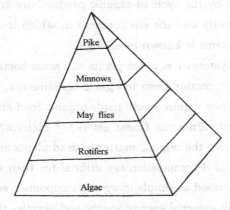

Fig 3-1 An Eltontian pyramid of numbers

Because of the low efficiency of ecological processes the number of organisms at the first trophic level required to support an organism at the top of the pyramid becomes very large.⑥ As a result, food chains in nature do not contain more than five or possibly six trophic levels.

Notes

①生态系中的自养菌，即绿色植物及某些细菌，称为生产者，因为它们把无机组分合成为有机物质。

②consumers 消费者（指生态系食物链上摄食其它有机体或部分有机物的一个营养组）。

③herbivore 食草动物；carnivore 食肉动物；carbohydrate 碳水化合物；photosynthesis 光合作用。

④entropy 熵。

⑤在水生环境中，有机体的相互依赖形成了一种有许多连续不断链节的食物链组成复杂的食物网，这些链节中包括了不同种类的生物，它们相邻间是一种捕食者同被捕食者的关系。

⑥由于生态过程的低效率，要维持金字塔顶层有机体所需要的第一层（即底层）的营养有机体的数目就变得非常庞大。

Reading Material B

Sampling and Analysis

To obtain a true indication of the nature of a water or wastewater it is first necessary to ensure that the sample is actually representative of the source.

The collection of a representative sample from a source of uniform quality poses few problems and a single grab sample will be satisfactory. [1] A grab sample will also be sufficient if the purpose of sampling is simply to provide a spot check to see whether particular limits have been complied with. [2] However, most raw waters and wastewaters are highly variable in both quality and quantity so that a grab sample is unlikely to provide a meaningful picture of the nature of the source. This point is illustrated in Fig. 3-2 which shows typical flow and strength variations in a sewer. To obtain an accurate assessment in this situation it is necessary to produce a composite sample by collecting individual samples at known time intervals throughout the period and measuring the flow at the same time. By bulking the individual samples in proportion to the appropriate flows an integrated composite sample is obtained. [3] Similar procedures are often necessary when sampling streams and rivers and with large channel sections it may be desirable to sample at several points across the section and at several depths. Various automatic devices are available to collect composite samples and these may operate on either a time basis or on a flow-proportional basis. Sampling of industrial wastewater discharges may be even more difficult since they are often intermittent in nature. In these circumstances it is important that the nature of the operations producing the discharge is fully understood so that an appropriate sampling programme can be drawn up to obtain a true picture of the discharge.

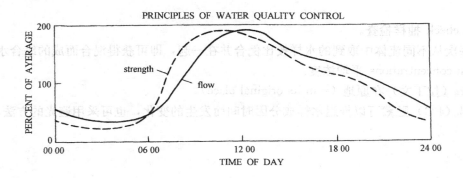

Fig. 3-2 Typical flow and strength variations in a sewer during dry weather.

When designing a sampling programme it is vital that the objective of the exercise be clearly specified, e.g. to estimate maximum or mean concentrations, to detect changes or trends, to estimate percentiles or to provide a basis for industrial effluent charges. [4] The degree of uncertainty which can be tolerated in the answer must also be specified and it is also necessary to bear in mind the resources available for sampling and analysis. For example, it may be found that to reduce the uncertainty of the results by a few percent might require twice the number of samples thus making the whole exercise uneconomic. It is therefore important to set a realistic level for the uncertainty of the results, based on the intended use. Ideally, all analyses should be carried out on the sample immediately after collection and certainly the quicker the analysis can be done the more likely it is that the results will be a true assessment of the actual nature of the liquid *in situ*.⑤ With characteristics which are likely to be unstable such as dissolved gases, oxidizable or reducible constituents, etc., the analyses must be carried out in the field or the sample must be suitably treated to fix the concentrations of unstable materials. Changes in the composition of a sample with time can be retarded by storage at low temperature (4℃) and the exclusion of light is also advisable.⑥ The more polluted a sample is, the shorter the time which can be allowed between sampling and analysis if significant errors are to be avoided.

Common analyses in the field of water quality control are usually based on relatively straightforward analytical principles. Quantitative analysis may be carried out by gravimetric, volumetric or colorimetric methods. Certain constituents may be determined by various types of electrode and there is increasing interest in the development of automated techniques for continuous monitoring of important parameters. It must be appreciated that, because of the low concentrations of impurities in water, laboratory work is often of a microanalytical nature requiring the use of careful procedures.

Notes

①从水质均匀的水源中收集有代表性的水样并不困难，而且，只要随意地取样一次就足够了。
②spot check 抽样检查。
③把每次从不同流体中取到的水样按比例合并在一起，即可获得混合而成的综合水样。
④mean concentrations 平均浓度。
⑤*in situ*（拉丁文）在原地（＝in its original place）。
⑥低温（4℃）贮藏可以推迟水样成分因时间而发生的变化，也可采用避光的方法。

UNIT FOUR

Text Role of Monitoring in Water Quality Management

[1]   From the law arise various water quality management strategies-each with its own way of using the results of water quality monitoring. ① The spectrum ranges from a "crisis management" approach to the "no-pollutant-discharge" approach. Crisis management generally uses monitoring on a special study basis and is often utilized when there are limited resources available. It also represents some of the earlier forms of water quality management from which more sophisticated approaches have subsequently evolved. The no-pollutant-discharge approach, on the other hand, tends to focus its monitoring efforts on discharges, not on the receiving water.

[2]   In practice, most water quality management agencies operate somewhere between the above two extremes. The exact nature of information needed on water quality is a function of administrative interpretation of the law. As there may be numerous implications in a given law regarding the need to understand the behavior of water quality, it is up to the staff of each agency to decide on what they want to emphasize in monitoring. ② Needs for understanding water quality behavior may be implied in *legal goals*, *functions and powers of management* provided to reach the goals, or they may be *directly stated* as monitoring requirements. To more fully appreciate these implications, first consider the legal goal of fishable and swimmable. How does an agency, particularly a state-wide or nation-wide agency, obtain information on water quality that permits it to state whether the goal is met? Is there a clear relationship between the goal and the data obtained to measure success in its accomplishment?

[3]   Next consider that most water quality management laws provide a number of management functions and powers (management "tools") to be utilized in managing the quality of water. Each of these tools requires information on the quality of the water if it is to be implemented fairly and effectively. The exact information needs of each tool are not usually spelled out in the law but rather are defined by the staff charged with implementation. These water quality management professionals must often answer difficult questions, such as the following. How does an agency identify exactly what information it needs to properly implement its management tools? What information is needed to state quantitatively that stream standards are met? What water quality information is needed to write a discharge permit? What water quality information is needed to issue a loan for construction of a wastewater treatment plant?

[4]   Workable answers to these questions can be derived from the management strategy chosen to implement the law. To design water quality monitoring systems that support water quality management, this strategy must be identified and its information needs defined. ③ The connection between the *data collected* by monitoring and *its use* within a management agency is an important element in the success of any water quality monitoring system design.

[5]   Finally, beyond the above implications for monitoring within a water quality management agency, there are directly stated monitoring requirements in many water quality management laws. For example, section 305 (b) of the Federal Clean Water Act requires that states prepare a report which describes the water quality of all navigable waters in the state. This rather straightforward requirement for ambient water quality monitoring is often the justification for fixed-station monitoring operated by states. In this role, assessment monitoring is used to determine whether legal goals are being met. There is, however, not a clear design connection between most ambient monitoring systems and goal assessment. For this reason, assessing goal achievement with ambient monitoring data is difficult. The need for current research and development in this area is evidenced by the continuing evolution of 305 (b) report guidance by U.S. EPA and the current redesign of the NASQAN (National Stream Quality Accounting Network) program by the U.S. Geological Survey.④

[6]   Thus, the role of monitoring in management, while being weakly guided by the law setting up the management agency, is very much open to interpretation by the personnel implementing the law. Defining the role the staff has chosen to employ is the first step in designing an effective water quality monitoring (information) system that supports management decision making in a quantitative manner.

New Words and Expressions

strategy ['strætidʒi]	n.	战略，策略
spectrum* ['spektrəm]	n.	范围
range from…to…		从…到…不等
sophisticated* [sə'fistikeitid]	a.	采用先进技术的
subsequently ['sʌbsikwəntli]	ad.	后来，接着
evolve [i'vɔlv]	vi.	发展，演变
tend to		往往，趋向于
focus ['fəukəs]	vt./n.	集中
in practice		实际上
agency ['eidʒənsi]	n.	部门，机构
extreme [ik'stri:m]	n.	极端
function ['fʌŋkʃən]	n.	依据，随…变化
administrative [əd'ministrətiv]	a.	管理的，行政的
decide on		决定，选定
fishable ['fiʃəbl]	a.	有鱼可捕的
implement ['implimənt]	vt.	实施，执行
spell out		详细说明
not…but rather		不是…而是
charge [tʃɑ:dʒ]	vt.	使承担责任

32

professional [prəʊˈfeɪʃənəl]	n.	专业人员，行家
quantitatively [ˈkwɒntɪteɪtɪvli]	adv.	定量地
discharge permit		排污许可证
issue [ˈɪsjuː]	vt.	配给，发行
workable* [ˈwɜːkəbl]	a.	切实可行的
derive from		由…得出
navigable [ˈnævɪgəbl]	a.	可通航的
straightforward* [ˌstreɪtˈfɔːwəd]	a.	明确的，肯定的
justification [ˌdʒʌstɪfɪˈkeɪʃən]	n.	以…为理由，证明为正当
in this role		在这项工作中
evidence [ˈevɪdəns]	vt.	证明，作为…的依据
evolution [ˌiːvəˈluːʃən]	n.	进化，发展
be open to		可利用的，容易受到

Notes

① From the law arise various water quality management strategies … 全部倒装句，主语是 strategies。

② …regarding the need to understand the behavior of water quality, … 定语，修饰 implications。

③ … and its information needs defined 中 defined 之前省略了 to be。

④ U.S. EPA 是 "the United States Environmental Protection Agency" 的缩写。

Exercises

Reading Comprehension

Ⅰ. Are these statements true (T) or false (F) according to the text?

1. There are various water quality management strategies resulting from the law, which vary from a "crisis management" way to the "no-pollutant-discharge" way, and some more sophisticated ways have developed from them. ( )

2. It is the staff of water quality management agencies that decide on what they are in favour of emphasizing in monitoring according to their interpretation of the law. ( )

3. The success of a water quality monitoring system design depends entirely on the connection between the data collected by monitoring and its use within a management agency. ( )

4. Assessing goal achievement with ambient monitoring data is difficult since most ambient monitoring systems are not clearly related in design to goal assessment. ( )

5. The role of monitoring in management is not spelled out in the law but rather is interpreted by the personnel applying the law.   (   )

II. Match Column A with Column B to form meaningful sentences according to the text.

A	B
1. In legal goals, functions and powers of management you may find	a. according to their interpretation
2. The answers to those difficult questions that water quality management professionals are required to answer come from	b. the suggested requirements for understanding water quality behavior
3. The strategy should be determined and its information be defined	c. the management strategy used to implement the law
4. In order to fully understand the law, the first consideration should be given to	d. the legal goal of fishable and swimmable
5. It is the personnel applying the law who determine the role of monitoring in management	e. before water quality monitoring systems are designed

Vocabulary

I. Fill in the blanks with the expressions given below. Change the forms if necessary.

> ambient   assessment   derive ··· from   implication
> range from ··· to   spectrum   strategy

1. He needs to improve his _____ before he can call himself a good tennis player.
2. This exhibition covers the entire _____ of Japanese aggression history.
3. The _____ air about the earth is called atmosphere.
4. Reactions to the news that a new oil terminal is to be built _____ bitterness and hostility _____ cautious optimism.
5. Reading skills require that when you come across a new word while reading, you should not look it up in the dictionary if you can _____ its meaning _____ the context.

II. Complete each of the following statements with one of the four choices given below.

1. The new equipment is too _____ for the unskilled worker to operate.
   A. delicate   B. sophisticated   C. superior   D. elegant
2. Donations from all walks of life are needed to _____ our child-careprogrammes.
   A. provide   B. confirm   C. compliment   D. implement
3. The possible economic benefit of the participation in the General Agreement on Tariffs

and Trade _____ in his newly-published book.

　　A. is spelled down　B. is spelled off　　　C. is spelled out　　D. is spelled up

4. He found it hard to _____ his thought _____ one thing for longer than five minutes. So he decided to consult a psychiatrist.

　　A. put ··· on　　　B. put ··· at　　　C. focus ··· on　　D. focus ··· at

5. Second-generation measurements of air quality _____ when more accurate and rapid data were required.

　　A. evolved　　　B. revolved　　　C. resolved of　　D. revoluted

Writing　　Outline Writing (2)

Directions: Read the text of Unit Four again and write a topic outline of each paragraph of the text.

Reading Material A

Sources of Water Pollution

The United States has more than 40,000 factories that use water, and their industrial wastes are probably the greatest single water pollution problem.

Organic wastes from industrial plants, at present-day treatment levels, are equal in polluting potential to the *untreated* raw sewage of the entire population of the United States.① In most cases the organic wastes, as potent as they might be, are at least treatable, in or out of the plant. Inorganic industrial wastes are much trickier to control, and potentially more hazardous. Chromium from metal-plating plants is an old source of trouble, but mercury discharges have only recently received their due attention.

As important as these and other well-known "heavy metals" might be, many scientists are much more concerned with the unknown chemicals. Industry is creating a fantastic array of new chemicals each year, all of which eventually find their way to the water. For most of these, not even the chemical formulas are known, much less their acute, chronic or genetic toxicity.②

Another industrial waste is heat. Heated discharges can drastically alter the ecology of a stream of lake. This alteration is sometimes called beneficial, perhaps because of better fishing or an ice-free docking area. The deleterious effects of heat, in addition to promoting modifications of ecological systems, include a lessening of dissolved oxygen solubility and increases in metabolic activity.③ Dissolved oxygen is vital to healthy aquatic communities, and the warmer the water the more difficult it is to get oxygen into solution. Simultaneously, the metabolic activity of aerobic (oxygen-using) aquatic species increases, thus demanding more oxygen. It is a small wonder, therefore, that the vast majority of fish kills due to oxygen depletion occur in the summer. ④

Municipal waste is a source of water pollution second in importance only to industrial wastes. Around the turn of the century, most discharges from municipalities received no treatment whatsoever. In the United States, sewage from 24 million people was flowing directly into our watercourses. Since that time, the population has increased, and so has the contribution from municipal discharges. It is estimated that presently the population equivalent of municipal discharges to watercourses is about 100 million. Even with the billions of dollars spent on building wastewater treatment plants, the contribution from municipal pollution sources has not been significantly reduced. We seem to be holding our own, however, and at least are not falling further behind.

One problem, especially in the older cities on the east coast of the United States, is the sewerage systems. When the cities were first built, the engineers realized that sewers were necessary for both strormwater and sanitary wastes, and they saw no reason why both stormwater and sanitary wastes should not flow in the same pipelines. After all, they both ended up in the same river or lake. Such sewers are now known as *combined sewers*. ⑤

As years passed and populations increased, the need for the treatment of sanitary wastes became obvious, and two-sewer systems were built, one to carry stormwater and the other, sanitary waste. Such systems are known as *separate sewers*. ⑥

Almost all of the cities with combined sewers have built treatment plants which can treat the *dry weather flow*, or in other words, sanitary wastes. As long as it doesn't rain, they can provide sufficient treatment. When the rains come, however, the flows swell to many times the dry weather flow and most of it must be bypassed directly into a river or lake. This overflow contains sewage as well as stormwater, and has a high polluting capacity. All attempts to capture this excess flow for subsequent treatment, such as storage in underground caverns and rubber balloons, are expensive. ⑦ However, the alternative solution, separating the sewers, is estimated at a staggering $ 60 billion for the major cities in the United States.

In addition to industrial and municipal wastes, water pollution emanates from many other sources.

Agricultural wastes, should they all flow into a stream, would have a population equivalent of about 2 billion. Fortunately, very little of it does reach streams. The problems are intensifying, however, with the increase in the size and number of feed lots. ⑧ Feed lots are cattle pens constructed for the purpose of fattening up the cattle before slaughter. These are usually close to slaughterhouses (hence cities) and a large number of animals are packed into a small space. Drainage from these lots has an extremely high pollutional strength.

Sediment from land erosion can also be classified as a pollutant. Sediment consists of mostly inorganic material washed into a stream as a result of farming, construction or mining operations. The detrimental effects of sediment include interference with the spawning of fish by covering gravel beds; interference with light penetration, thus making food more difficult to find; and direct damage to gill structures. In the long run, sediment could well be one of our most harmful pollutants.

The concern with pollution from petroleum compounds is relatively new, starting to a large extent with the Torrey Canyon disaster in 1967. Ignoring maps showing submerged rocks, the huge tanker loaded with crude oil plowed into a reef in the English Channel.⑨ Almost immediately, oil began seeping out, and both the French and British became concerned. Rescue efforts failed and the Royal Air Force attempted to set it on fire, with little success. Almost all of the oil eventually leaked out and splashed on the beaches of France and England. The French started the back-breaking chore of spreading straw on the beaches, allowing the straw to adsorb the oil, and then collecting and burning the oil-soaked straw. The English, being more sophisticated, used detergents to disperse the oil and then flushed the emulsion off the beaches. Time has shown the French way to be best, since the English detergents have now been shown to be potentially more harmful to coastal ecology than the oil would have been.

Although the Torrey Canyon disaster was the first big spill, many have followed it. It is estimated that there are no fewer than 10,000 serious oil spills in the United States every year. In addition, the contribution from routine operations such as flushing oil tankers may well exceed all the oil spills.

The acute effect of oil on birds, fish and microorganisms is reasonably well cataloged. What is not so well understood, and potentially more harmful, is the subtle effect on aquatic life. Salmon, for example, have been known to find their home stream by the specific smell (or taste) of the water, caused in large part by the hydrocarbons present. If man continues to pour (even unintentionally) hydrocarbons into salmon rivers, it is possible that the salmon will become so confused that they will refuse to enter their spawning stream.

Another form of industrial pollution, much of it willed to us by our ancestors, is acid mine drainage. The problem is caused by the leaching of sulfur-laden water from old abandoned mines (as well as some active mines). On contact with air, these compounds are soon oxidized to sulfuric acid, a deadly poison to all living matter.

It should be amply clear, therefore, that water can be polluted by many types of waste products.

Notes

①就当今废水的处理水平而言，工厂排出的有机废物其污染程度同全美人口所排出的未经处理的原污水相同。
②对其中大多数的化学物质来说，连它们的化学式也鲜为人知，更不用说其剧烈、长期或遗传的毒性了。
③dissolved oxygen solubility 溶解氧的可溶性。
④fish kills（水污染引起的）鱼殇，鱼难。

⑤combined sewers 合流排水管。
⑥separate sewers 分流排水管。
⑦为了随后进行的污水处理，控制这种过度的流量而进行的所有尝试，如 用地下洞穴和橡胶囊来贮存，均颇费财力。
⑧ "feed lots" 饲养圈；圈栏肥育地。
⑨由于没注意地图上标明的暗礁，装满原油的大油船急速地冲向英吉利海峡的礁石。

Reading Material B

Water-related Disease

There are about two dozen infectious diseases, the incidence of which can be influenced by water. These diseases may be due to viruses, bacteria, protozoa or worms and although their control and detection is based in part on the nature of the causative agent it is often more helpful to consider the water-related aspects of the spread of infection.① In the context of diseases associated with water there has in the past been some confusion about the terminology applied. Bradley has developed a more specific classification system for water-related diseases which differentiates between the various forms of infections and their transmission routes.

Waterborne Disease

The commonest form of water-related disease and certainly that which causes most harm on a global scale includes those diseases spread by the contamination of water by human faeces or urine. With this type of disease infection occurs when the pathogenic organism gains access to water which is then consumed by a person who does not have immunity to the disease.② The majority of diseases in this category, cholera, typhoid, bacillary dysentery, etc., follow a classical faecal-oral transmission route and outbreaks are characterized by simultaneous illness amongst a number of people using the same source of water.③ It should be appreciated that although these diseases can be waterborne they can also be spread by any other route which permits direct ingestion of faecal matter from a person suffering from that disease. Poor personal hygiene of workers in food handling and preparation activities would provide an obvious infection route. The situation is further complicated in that some people may be carriers of diseases like typhoid so that although they exhibit no outward signs of the disease their excreta contain the pathogens.④ Screening for such a carrier state is often practised with potential employees in the water-supply industry.⑤

There are other waterborne diseases in which the infection pattern is not so simple. Well's disease (leptospirosis) is transmitted in the urine of infected rats and the causative organism is able to penetrate the skin so that external contact with contaminated sewage or flood water can spread the disease.

Water-washed disease

As described above, infections which are transmitted by the ingestion of faecally contaminated water can also be spread by more direct contact between faeces and mouth. In the case of poor hygiene, due to inadequate water supply for washing, the spread of infection may be reduced by providing additional water, the quality of which becomes a secondary consideration. Water in this context is a cleansing agent and since it is not ingested the normal quality requirements need not be paramount. Clearly waterborne faecal-oral diseases may also be classified as water-washed diseases and many of the diarrhoeal infections in tropical climates behave as water-washed rather than waterborne diseases.

A second group of diseases can also be classified as water-washed. These include a number of skin and eye infections which whilst not normally fatal have a serious debilitating effect on sufferers. The diseases of this type include bacterial ulcers and scabies and trachoma. They tend to be associated with hot dry climates and their incidence can be significantly reduced if ample water is available for personal washing.

Water-based Disease

A number of diseases depend upon the pathogenic organism spending part of its life-cycle in water or in an intermediate host which lives in water.⑥ Thus infection of man cannot occur by immediate ingestion of or contact with the organism excreted by a sufferer. Most of the diseases in this class are caused by worms which infest the sufferer and produce eggs which are discharged in faeces or urine. Infection often occurs by penetration of the skin rather than by consumption of the water.

Schistosomiasis (also called bilharzia) is probably the most important example of this class of disease. The transmission pattern of schistosomiasis is relatively complex in comparison with waterborne diseases. If a sufferer excretes into water, eggs from the worms hatch into larvae which can live for only 24 h unless they find a particular species of snail which acts as an intermediate host. The larvae then develop in a cyst in the snail's liver which after about 6 weeks bursts and releases minute free-swimming cercariae which can live in water for about 48 h. The cercariae have the property of being able to puncture the skin of man and other animals and they can then migrate through the body via skin, veins, lungs, arteries and liver in a period of around 8 weeks. The parasite then develops in the veins of the wall of the bladder, or of the intestine, into a worm which may live several years and which will discharge enormous number of eggs. It is unfortunate that schistosomiasis is often spread by irrigation schemes which unless carefully designed and operated, tend to provide suitable habitats for the snail host as well as increasing the likelihood of contact with the water by agricultural workers.⑦

Control measures for schistosomiasis include, as well as the obvious prevention of excretal contamination of water, creation of conditions unfavourable to the presence of the snails, prevention of human contact with potentially contaminated water and the insertion of a 48-h delay period after removal of snails, before access to the water is permitted. Unfortunately such measures are not easy to enforce and there may often be a conflict between the needs of schistosomiasis control and the desire to obtain agricultural and economic benefits from irrigation schemes in which some degree of water contact is inevitable.

Guinea worm is another water-based disease which is widespread in the tropics. In this case the intermediate host is cyclops, a small crustacean, and human infection occurs following the ingestion of water containing infected cyclops. Control of guinea worm, which can bring marked improvements in the health of the population, is essentially based on protection of water sources, particularly springs and wells. The provision of sloping hardstandings and parapets round water sources will effectively prevent the access of eggs to the water.

Notes

①causative agent 致病因素；病因。
②此类疾病的病菌进入水源，而用水的人对这种疾病又无免疫能力的话，就会被感染上。
③simultaneous illness 同时患病。
④The situation is further complicated in that some people may be carriers of diseases like typhoid ……"
　由于有些人本身是霍乱等疾病的带菌者，情况就变得更加复杂了……
⑤在自来水供水行业中，对那些可能聘用的雇员都要进行是否带菌的检查。
⑥intermediate host 中介基质；中间寄生（指寄生物在其体内或体上进行无性繁殖的寄生）。
⑦不幸的是吸血虫病常常通过灌溉工程传播；除非精心设计和施工，不然这些工程除了增加农业工人接触这种水源的可能性外，还往往成为蜗牛寄生的栖息地。

UNIT FIVE

Text   Mechanism of Coagulation

[1] Naturally occurring silt particles suspended in water are difficult to remove because they are very small, often colloidal in size, and they possess negative charges and thus are prevented from coming together to form larger particles which could more readily be settled out.[①] The removal of these particles by settling requires first that their charges be neutralized, and second that the particles be encouraged to collide with each other. The charge neutralization is commonly termed coagulation, and the building at larger flocs from the small particles is called flocculation. Now we are going to study the mechanism in a more detailed way.

[2] Although chemical coagulation is a widely used process the mechanisms by which it operates are not fully understood in spite of considerable research effort. Basic colloid stability considerations have been applied to coagulation in attempts to offer explanations for the observed results. The stability of hydrophobic colloid suspensions can be explained by consideration of forces acting on the particles as shown in Fig. 5-1. Mutual repulsion arises from the electrostatic surface charges but destabilization can be achieved by the addition of ions of opposite charge to reduce the repulsive forces and permit the molecular attraction forces to become dominant. In this context the value of the zeta potential, the electrical potential at the edge of the particle agglomerate, is of some significance. In theory a zero zeta potential should provide the best conditions for coagulation. However, when dealing with the heterogeneous suspensions found in water it seems that there are many complicating factors and zeta potential measurements are not always of much value in operational circumstances.

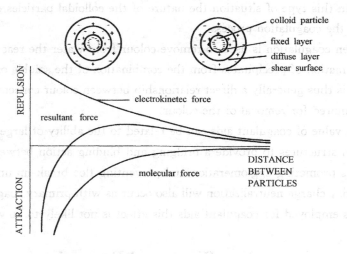

Fig. 5-1 Forces acting on a floc particle.

[3] In the case of relatively low suspended solids concentrations, coagulation usually occurs

41

by enmeshment in insoluble hydrolysis products formed as the result of a reaction between the coagulant and the water.② In this "sweep coagulation" the nature of the original suspended matter is of little significance and it is the properties of the hydrolysis product which control the reaction. Unfortunately, the behaviour of coagulants when added to water can be highly complex. The most popular coagulant for water treatment is aluminium sulphate (alum) $Al_2(SO_4)_3$ and the complex reactions which take place following its addition to water are often simplified as:

$$Al_2(SO_4)_3 + 6H_2O \rightarrow \underline{2Al(OH)_3} + 3H_2SO_4$$
$$3H_2SO_4 + 3Ca(HCO_3)_2 \rightarrow 3CaSO_4 + 6H_2CO_3$$
$$6H_2CO_3 \rightarrow 6CO_2 + 6H_2O$$

i.e. overall

$$Al_2(SO_4)_3 + 3Ca(HCO_3)_2 \rightarrow \underline{2Al(OH)_3} + 3CaSO_4 + 6CO_2$$

The simplified reactions are now known to be far removed from the actual situation. The hydrolysis products of aluminium are very complex, their nature being affected by such factors as the age and strength of the coagulant solution.③ Hydrolysis products of aluminium include compounds of the form

$$[Al(H_2O)_5OH]^{2+} \quad \text{and} \quad [Al_6(OH)_{15}]^{3+}$$

and sulphate complexes may also appear. As a result the actual reactions taking place are difficult to specify.

[4]　With higher suspended solids concentrations the colloidal theory can provide a basis for explaining the observed reactions. Thus destabilization of a colloidal suspension occurs due to the adsorption of strongly charged partially hydrolysed metallic ions. Continued adsorption results in charge reversal and restabilization of the suspension which does occur with high coagulant doses. In this type of situation the nature of the colloidal particles does therefore have an influence on the coagulation process.

[5]　When coagulation is used to remove colour from water the reaction appears to depend upon the formation of precipitates from the combination of the soluble organics and the coagulant. There is thus generally a direct relationship between colour concentration and the dose of coagulant required for removal of the colour.

[6]　The value of coagulant aids can be related to the ability of large molecules in the form of long-chain structures to provide a bridging and binding action between adjacent suspended particles thus promoting agglomeration and preventing floc break-up under shear. With ionic coagulant aids, charge neutralization will also occur as with primary coagulants although at the normal doses employed for coagulant aids this effect is not likely to be very important.④

New Words and Expressions

neutralization [ˌnjuːtrəlaiˈzeiʃən]　　　　n.　　　中和

flocculation	[ˌflɔkju'leiʃən]	n.	絮凝
mechanism *	['mekənizəm]	n.	机理
apply to			运用，应用
in attempt to			试图
hydrophobic	[ˌhaidrəu'fəubik]	a.	恐水的，疏水的
repulsion *	[ri'pʌlʃən]	n.	排斥
electrostatic *	[iˌlektrəu'stætik]	a.	静电的
charge	[tʃɑːdʒ]	n.	电荷，负荷
destabilization	[diːˌsteibilai'zeiʃən]	n.	脱稳（作用）
repulsive	[ri'pʌlsiv]	a.	排斥的，令人生厌的
molecular *	[məu'lekjulə]	a.	分子的
dominant *	['dɔminənt]	a.	显性的，显著的
potential	[pəu'tenʃəl]	n.	电位，电势
zeta potential			ζ 电位
agglomerate	[ə'glɔməreit]	n.	烧结块
heterogeneous *	[ˌhetərəu'dʒiːnjəs]	a.	非均匀的，异类的
complicate	['kɔmplikeit]	vt.	使复杂
in the case of			就…而论，那…来说
enmeshment	[in'meʃmənt]	n.	吸附，包入作用
insoluble *	[in'sɔljubl]	a.	不溶解的
hydrolysis	[hai'drɔlisis]	n.	水解（作用）
sulphate	['sʌlfeit]	n.	硫酸
aluminium sulphate			硫酸铝
specify	['spesifai]	vt.	详细说明
partially	['pɑːʃəli]	ad.	部分地
hydrolyse	['haidrəlaiz]	v.	水解
reversal *	[ri'vəːsəl]	n.	改变，反向
restabilization	[risteibilai'zeiʃən]	n.	再稳定
removal	[ri'muːvəl]	n.	清除
long-chain			一系列，一连串
bridging	['bridʒiŋ]	n. /a.	桥接（的）
binding	['baindiŋ]	n. /a.	粘合（的），束缚（的）
break-up			分离，分解

Notes

① 句首中，现在分词短语 Naturally occurring 及名词 silt 修饰 particles；过去分词短语 suspended in water 后置修饰。

②"..., coagulation usually occurs by enmeshment in insoluble hydrolysis products formed as the result of a reaction between the coagulant and the water" 中 by enmeshment 做方式状语；in insoluble ... and the water 做地点状语；formed as ... and the water 过去分词短语做定语。

③..., their nature being affected by such factors as the age and strength of the coagulant solution 独立结构，状语，补充说明。

④as with primary coagulants，省略形式的方式状语从句。

Exercises

Reading Comprehension

Ⅰ. Are these statements true (T) or false (F) according to the text?

1. The removal of naturally occuring silt particles suspended in water needs to neutralize their charges and thereby encourage them to collide with each other. ( )

2. Since a zero zeta potential should theoretically provide the best conditions for coagulation, the value of the zeta potential is considered of great importance in dealing with the heterogeneous suspensions found in water. ( )

3. It is not the nature of the original suspended matter but the properties of the hydrolysis product that control the reaction between the coagulant and the water. ( )

4. Charge reversal and restabilization of the suspension resulting from the absorption of strongly charged partially hydrolysed metallic ions do happen with high coagulant doses. ( )

5. The use of both primary coagulants and ionic coagulant aids will make the charge neutralized. ( )

Ⅱ. Match Column A with Column B to form meaningful sentences according to according to the text.

A	B
1. The process of taking away electricity contained in the particles suspended in water	a. is called flocculation
2. The process of encourage particles to collide with each other	b. thus providing the promotion of agglomeration and the prevention of floc break-up under shear
3. Theoretically speaking, the conditions for coagulation are the most favourable	c. the dose of coagulant used to remove the colour

4. Generally speaking, colour concentration is related to
5. Large molecules in the form of long-chain structures have the ability to hold suspended particles together,

d. is termed coagulation
e. when zeta potential is at zero

Vocabulary

I. Fill in the blanks with the expressions given below. Change the forms if necessary.

```
dominant      heterogeneous    in attempt to    mutual
repulsive     significance     shear
```

1. By our _____ love, we mean the love that each of us has for the other.
2. You can never overestimate the _____ of the discovery of penicillin.
3. The father had a very _____ nature, so all the rest of the members in the family did what he wanted.
4. The young actress refused to play the role of a _____ character in the play.
5. Her father sent her to the warm south _____ restore her health.

II. Complete each of the following statements with one of the four choices given below.
1. Scientific discoveries are often _____ industrial production methods.
   A. applied for   B. applying for   C. applied to   D. applying to
2. The removal of many impurities in water and wastewater present as colloidal solids can be achieved by promoting agglomeration of such particles by _____ with or without the use of a coagulant followed by sedimentation or flotation.
   A. neutralization   B. destabilization   C. restabilization   D. flocculation
3. The contract _____ red tiles, not slates, for the roof and teak flooring throughout.
   A. specializes   B. specifies   C. requires   D. demands
4. Our house is _____ a busy road so it can be very noisy during the day.
   A. adjacent to   B. adjacent by   C. near at   D. nearby
5. The moon was _____ hidden behind the clouds so we could not see all of it.
   A. completely   B. fully   C. nearly   D. partially

Writing   Outline Writing (3)

Directions: Read the text of Unit Five and match the paragraph numbers in Column A with proper sentences in Column B to form a sentence outline.

A	B
1. Para. One	a. Chemical coagulation is widely used but its mechanisms are not completely understood.
2. Para. Two	b. Coagulation is used to remove colour from water.
3. Para. Three	c. The charge neutralization is coagulation and the building at large flocs from the small particles is flocculation.
4. Para. Four	d. How coagulation usually happens in lower suspended solids contentrations.
5. Para. Five	e. The ability of large molecules in the form of long-chain structure makes coagulant aids valuable.
6. Para. Six	f. Coagulation is used in higher suspended solid concentrations.

Reading Material A

Drainlaying

Pipes under roads should be laid with from 900mm to 1.2m of cover and pipes under fields and gardens with at least 600 mm of cover. For lesser depths, particularly where there is likelihood of heavy traffic, special protection of the pipes may be neccessary.① The drain trench should be as narrow as possible, so as to reduce the backfill load on the pipe to the minimum. Local soft spots in the trench bottom should be stabilised by tamping in granular material and large boulders and tree roots should be removed and replaced, by tamped granular material.

The drainage pipeline should be laid so as to provide flexibility and flexible joints are normally preferable to rigid joints, for the following reasons:

1. A minimum of skill is required in laying and is quicker, more reliable and cheaper.
2. Because of increased speed of laying, the time the trench is kept open is reduced to the minimum, with a possible reduction in pumping and less risk of the trench bottom becoming muddy.
3. The flexible joints reduce the risk of fracture of the pipeline, due to the ground movement, backfill of superimposed loads.
4. The pipeline may be tested immediately after laying.
5. Rectifying faults is quick and easy.
6. There is less delay in laying, due to wet or freezing site conditions.

Types of bedding

Class A: this type of bedding is used for rigid pipes such as vitrified clay and asbestos-ce-

46

ment. ② It is used where additional supporting strength of the pipe is required under roads, or where there is a risk of disturbing the pipeline after laying, such as when excavations have to be made alongside it at a later date. ③ Fig. 5-2 shows class A bedding, which is carried out as follows:

1. A layer of concrete at least 50 mm thick should be spread along the prepared trench bottom.
2. The pipes should be supported clear of this concrete by means of blocks or cradles placed under the pipes and a piece of resilient material about 14 mm thick placed between the pipes and the supporting blocks. The total clearance under the pipes should not be less than 100mm.
3. The pipes should be tested and a piece of compressed board cut to the profile of the pipe, placed at the face of each pipe joint, as shown in Fig. 5-2.
4. A 1 : 2 : 4 concrete, using 14 mm maximum size aggregate; giving a minimum 28 days cube strength of 20 MN/m^2 should be carefully placed under the pipes between the profiles and extended up to the barrel of the pipes to the required height.
5. The trench should be backfilled by first placing three layers of selected soil, free from hard objects, to a depth of 100 mm each and carefully compacting each layer by hand tamping separately. The trench can now be backfilled, but a mechanical rammer should not be used until there is a minimum cover over the pipe of 600mm.

Class B: this is the usual method of bedding, of both rigid and flexible pipes. Fig. 5-3 shows class B bedding, which is carried out as follows:

1. The trench bottom should be prepared and granular material consisting of broken stone or gravel 5 to 10 mm in size should be spread along the prepared trench bottom, to a depth of at least 100 mm; after compacting, the top should be levelled off.
2. Socket holes should be formed where neccessary to allow the pipeline to rest uniformly on top of the granular material.
3. The pipeline should be laid and tested and granular material placed at either side of rigid pipes, to a depth of half the diameter of the pipe. For pitch fibre pipes the granular material should be brought up to the top of the pipe, and for unplasticised polyvinyl chloride pipe the granular material should be carried up to a minimum height of 100 mm above the crown of the pipe. ④ For all types of pipes the granular material should be carefully compacted by hand tamping and the main backfill should be placed as described for class A bedding.

Class D: where the soil is reasonably dry, soft and fine grained, the pipes may be laid directly on the trench bottom. Fig. 5-4 shows class D bedding, which is carried out as follows:

1. The trench bottom should be prepared by accurately trimming by hand and socket holes cut out, so that the soil will be in contact with the pipe barrel over the whole length of the pipeline. If too much soil is removed, it must be replaced to the correct level and thoroughly

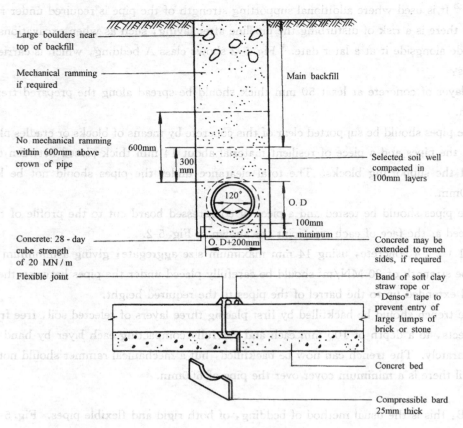

Fig. 5-2 Class A bedding

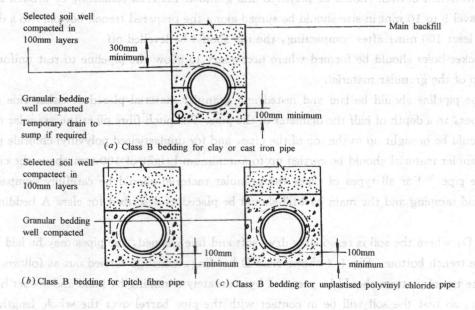

(a) Class B bedding for clay or cast iron pipe

(b) Class B bedding for pitch fibre pipe   (c) Class B bedding for unplastised polyvinyl chloride pipe

Fig. 5-3 Class B bedding

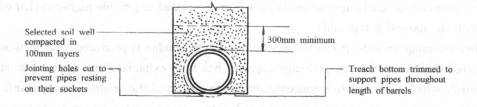

Fig. 5-4 Class D bedding

rammed.

2. The pipes should be laid and tested and the trench backfilled in 100 mm layers up to a level of 300 mm above the pipes. The main backfill should then be placed as described for class A bedding.

Pipes laid under buildings

The placing of drains under buildings should wherever possible be avoided, but if there is no other alternative the following points should be observed:
1. The drain should be laid in a straight line and at one gradient.
2. Access for cleansing should be provided to all parts of the drain.⑤
3. Manholes placed inside the building should have double-sealed covers.
4. Flexible joints should be used and the pipe surrounded by 150 mm of granular material, or concrete, with a piece of compressed board 25 mm thick at the face of each pipe joint to maintain flexibility.

Notes

①如果小于该深度，特别是在交通繁忙的地段，那里的下水道需特别加以保护。
②vitrified clay 陶土（管）。
③这类管道垫层用于道路下面的下水道需增加支撑强度的地方，或用于管道埋设后有可能遭受损坏的地方，如今后得沿着管道进行挖掘工程等。
④unplasticised polyvinyl chlorid 未增塑的聚氯乙烯（即硬质聚氯乙烯）。
⑤应该为下水道的所有各部分设置进行清洁工作的入口。

Reading Material B

Ion Exchange

Certain natural materials, notably zeolites which are complex sodium alumino-silicates and greensands, have the property of exchanging one ion in their structure for another ion in solution.① Synthetic ion-exchange materials have been developed to provide higher exchange capacities than the natural compounds.

Ion-exchange treatment has the advantage that no sludge is produced, but it must be remembered that when the ion-exchange capacity has been exhausted the material must be regenerated, which gives rise to a concentrated waste stream of the original contaminant. Industrial waste-waters, such as metal finishing effluents, can be treated by ion exchange as an alternative to precipitation methods, but again the commonest use of ion exchange is for water softening or deminreralization in the case of high pressure boiler feed waters where high-purity water is essential.②

When used for water softening, natural zeolites will exchange their sodiumions for the calcium and magnesium ions in the water, thus giving complete removal of hardness, i.e. representing a zeolite by Na_2X

$$\left.\begin{array}{l}Ca^{++}\\Mg^{++}\end{array}\right\} + Na_2X \rightarrow \left.\begin{array}{l}Ca\\Mg\end{array}\right\} X + 2Na^+$$

The finished water is thus high in sodium, which is not likely to be troublesome unless the water was originally very hard. When all sodium ions in the structure have been exchanged, no further removal of hardness occurs. Regeneration can be achieved using a salt solution to provide a high concentration of sodium ions to reverse the exchange reaction,

$$\left.\begin{array}{l}Ca\\Mg\end{array}\right\} X + 2NaCl \rightarrow Na_2X + \left.\begin{array}{l}Ca\\Mg\end{array}\right\} Cl_2$$

the hardness being released as a concentrated chloride stream. A natural sodium cycle zeolite will have an exchange capacity of about 200 gram equivalents/m³ with a regenerant requirement of about 5 equivalents /equivalent exchanged.③ Synthetic sodium cycle resins may have doubled the exchange capacity with about half the regenerant requirement, but have a higher capital cost.

Hydrogen cycle cation exchangers produced from natural or synthetic carbonaceous compounds are also available and will also give a water of zero hardness.④ They exchange all cations for hydrogen ions so that the product stream is acidic and their main use is as the first stage in demineralization operations.

$$\left.\begin{array}{l}Ca^{++}\\Mg^{++}\\2Na^+\end{array}\right\} + H_2Z \rightarrow \left.\begin{array}{l}Ca\\Mg\\2Na\end{array}\right\} Z + 2H^+$$

Regeneration is by acid treatment:

$$\left.\begin{array}{l}Ca\\Mg\\2Na\end{array}\right\} Z + 2H^+ \rightarrow H_2Z + \left\{\begin{array}{l}Ca^{++}\\Mg^{++}\\2Na^{++}\end{array}\right.$$

Typical performance characteristics for a hydrogen cycle exchanger are 1000 gram equivalents/m³ exchange capacity and a regenerant requirement of about 3 equivalents/ equivalent exchanged. Anion exchangers which are usually synthetic ammonia derivatives will accept the product water from a hydrogen cycle exchanger and produce demineralized water for laboratory and other specialized uses as well as for boiler feed water.⑤

A strong anion exchanger R OH, where R represents the organic structure will remove all anions:

$$\left.\begin{array}{l} HNO_3 \\ H_2SO_4 \\ HCl \\ H_2SiO_3 \\ H_2CO_3 \end{array}\right\} + R\ OH \rightarrow R \left\{\begin{array}{l} NO_3 \\ SO_4 \\ Cl \\ SiO_3 \\ CO_3 \end{array}\right. + H_2O$$

A strong base is necessary for regeneration

$$R\left\{\begin{array}{l} NO_3 \\ SO_4 \\ Cl \\ SiO_3 \\ CO_3 \end{array}\right. + NaOH \rightarrow R\ OH + Na\left\{\begin{array}{l} NO_3 \\ SO_4 \\ Cl \\ SiO_3 \\ CO_3 \end{array}\right.$$

Weak anion-exchangers remove strong anions but not carbonates and silicates.

Typical anion-exchanger performance would be 800 gram equivalents/m³ exchange capacity and 6 equivalents/equivalent exchanged regenerant capacity.

Ion-exchange materials are normally used in units similar to pressure filters and it is possible to combine cation and anion resins in a single mixed-bed unit. The feedwater to an ion-exchange plant should be free of suspended matter, since this would tend to coat the surfaces of the exchange medium and reduce its efficiency. Organic matter in the feed can also cause fouling of the exchanger, although the development of macroporous materials with their internal surface area inaccessible to large organic molecules reduces the problems of organic fouling.⑥

Notes

① 某些天然材料,特别是像络合钠、铝硅酸盐络合物和绿砂之类的沸石,它们的特性是能把自己结构中的离子和溶液中的另一个离子交换。
② Industrial waste-waters, … to precipitation methods, …。
   可用离子交换代替沉淀法来处理工业废水,如处理金属表面处理产生的废水,……。
   feed waters 给(供)水。
③ gram equivalents/m³ 克当量/立方米。
④ 从天然或合成含碳化合物中产生的氢循环阳离子交换剂也是可以用的,它也能使水达到零硬度。
⑤ anion exchanger 阴离子交换剂。
⑥ 尽管研制的大孔材料,因为它们里层的表面能使有机大分子无法进入离子交换器,所以减少了有机污垢的形成,但是进料中的有机物质也能造成离子交换器的污染。

UNIT SIX

Text   Overall Effects of Pollution by Wastewaters

[1]   Any body of water is capable of assimilating a certain amount of pollution without serious effects because of the dilution and self-purification factors which are present. If additional pollution occurs the nature of the receiving water will be altered and its suitability for various uses may be impaired. An understanding of the effects of pullution and the control measures which are available is thus of considerable importance to the efficient management of water resources.

[2]   When considering pollution by wastewaters there are of course other effects than the creation of DO deficits. ① Depending on the dilution available there will be significant increases in dissolved solids, organic content, nutrients such as N and P, colour and turbidity. All of these constituents may give rise to undesirable changes in water quality particularly as regards downstream abstraction. ② Nutrient build-up is a serious problem in lakes and very slow-moving waters but is not likely to be so troublesome with rivers. It should be remembered, however, that in many river abstraction schemes for water supply, raw water is stored in large shallow reservoirs prior to treatment. Even quite low nutrient contents in the water can result in prolific algal growths giving a water much more difficult to treat than the original river water. ③

[3]   All lakes undergo a natural change in their characteristics which in the absence of man may take thousands of years. A lake in a 'wilderness' catchment receives inflow from largely barren surroundings and thus collects little in the way of organic food and inorganic nutrients. Such nutrient-deficient waters are termed oligotrophic and are characterized by low TDS levels, very low turbidities and small biological populations. ④ As the catchment becomes older (in almost geological time scale) there is a gradual increase in nutrient levels and hence in biological productivity, with a consequent deterioration in water quality. Eventually, as nutrient levels and biological production increase, the water becomes nutrient-rich or eutrophic. Nutrients are recycled and in extreme cases the water may become heavily polluted by vegetation, low DO levels will occur due to rotting plants and during darkness anaerobic conditions may well exist. The eventual fate of all lakes is to become eutrophic, but the rate at which this end point is reached can be greatly accelerated by artificial enrichment due to human activities. Nitrogen and phosphorus are the most important nutrients in the context of eutrophication and since some algae can fix atmospheric nitrogen it is generally accepted that phosphorus is the limiting nutrient in water. The level of phosphorus above which algal growth becomes excessive depends upon many factors. Phosphates occur in sewage effluents due partly to human excretion and partly to their use in synthetic detergents.

[4]   Serious pollution which often occurs in industrialized areas can have very profound ef-

fects on a river system and reduction of river pollution in such system is inevitably an expensive operation usually taking many years to achieve. Ideally it would be desirable for every river to be unpolluted, full of fish and aesthetically pleasing. In an industrialized country it became economically impossible to prevent all river pollution and it is necessary to take an overall view of water resources and to classify rivers as suitable for particular purposes.

[5]   River pollution is clearly undesirable for many reasons:
1. Contamination of water supplies—additional load on treatment plants.
2. Restriction of recreational use.
3. Effect on fish life.
4. Creation of nuisances—appearance and odour.
5. Hindrance to navigation by banks of deposited solids.

A typical water use classification might thus be (in decreasing order of quality requirements):
1. Domestic water supply.
2. Industrial water supply.
3. Commercial fishing.
4. Irrigation.
5. Recreation and amenity.
6. Transportation.
7. Waste disposal.

[6]   Each use has specific requirements for quality and quantity of water and some uses may be incompatible. Irrigation is a consumptive use in that water used in this way does not find its way back into the river system. Considerable volumes of cooling water are lost by evaporation. The others are not in general consumptive although they usually have a detrimental effect on quality. Thus water abstracted for domestic supply is returned as sewage effluent. The conservation of water resources depends on multipurpose use of water wherever possible.

New Words and Expressions

assimilate [ə'simileit]	vt.	同化，吸收
deficit ['defisit]	n.	缺乏，不足
give rise to		引起，导致
build-up ['bildʌp]	n.	产生，形成
prolific [prəulifik]	a.	多产的，有生殖力的
wilderness ['wildənis]	n.	荒野
catchment ['kætʃmənt]	n.	流域，集水处
barren ['bærən]	a.	荒芜的，贫瘠的
in the way of		关于
term [təːm]	vt.	把……叫做
inorganic * [ˌinɔːgænik]	a.	无机的，人造的

deficient [dɪˈfɪʃənt]		a.	缺乏的，不足的
oligotrophic [ˌɒlɪɡəʊˈtrɒfɪk]		a.	贫营养的
productivity * [ˌprɒdʌkˈtɪvɪti]		n.	生产率
eutrophic [juːˈtrɒfɪk]		a.	富营养的
vegetation [ˌvedʒɪˈteɪʃən]		n.	植被，草木
rot [rɒt]		vi.	腐朽
enrichment [ɪnˈrɪtʃmənt]		n.	富集
in the context			在……方面
eutrophication [juːˌtrɒfɪˈkeɪʃən]		n.	富有养分
phosphate [ˈfɒsfeɪt]		n.	磷酸盐（脂）
excretion [ekˈskriːʃən]		n.	排泄（物），分泌（物）
synthetic detergent			合成洗涤剂
profound [prəʊˈfaʊnd]		a.	深远的，深刻的
inevitably [ɪnˈevɪtəbli]		ad.	不可避免地
take a view of			抱……观点
restriction [rɪˈstrɪkʃən]		n.	限制
hindrance [ˈhɪndrəns]		n.	障碍，妨碍
bank [bæŋk]		n.	堆
fishing [ˈfɪʃɪŋ]		n.	鱼场
recreation [ˌrekrɪˈeɪʃən]		n.	消遣娱乐
amenity [əˈmiːnəti]		n.	愉快
incompatible [ˌɪnkəmˈpætəbl]		a.	不相容的，不一致的
consumptive [kənˈsʌmptɪv]		a.	消耗性的，消费的

Notes

①DO = dissolved oxygen。

②"… particularly as regards downstream abstraction." 在句中做状语，其中 as regards 为词组介词，在作用和意义上等于 in regard to 或 with regard to，意为"至于"，"关于"。

③句中"prolific algal growths giving a water much more difficult to treat than the original river water" 是带逻辑主语的动名词短语，做介词 in 的宾语。

④TDS = total dissolved solid。

Exercises

Reading Comprehension

1. Are these statements true (T) or false (F) according to the text?

1. Water has the capacity to solve the pollution in it with the presence of its two properties—dilution and self-purification. （　）
2. What makes the water treatment more difficult is prolific algal growths resulting from low nutrient contents in the water. （　）
3. Naturally all lakes on the earth will undergo the change from oligotrophic to eutrophic, but human activities have sped up the process. （　）
4. The reduction of water pollution is a high cost and time-consuming operation. That's why it is only a dream now for every river to be free from pollution and full of fish. （　）
5. Irrigation consumes large quantities of water, during which the water usually returns to the river system with some loss, but hygienic and unpolluted. （　）

II. Match Column A with Column B to form meaningful sentences according to the text.

A

1. To manage water resources efficiently
2. The increases in dissolved solids, organic content, nutrients, colour and turbidity may lead to
3. It may take thousands of years for all lakes to undergo a natural change in their characteristics
4. Because of its great spending, the prevention of rivers from all pollution seems impossible
5. The quality requirement of domestic water supply is the highest

B

a. without the consideration of the presence of man.
b. it is necessary to understand the effects of pollution and the control measures.
c. while that of waste disposal the lowest.
d. so it's necessary to classify rivers as suitable for particular purposes in order to make full use of water resources.
e. unfavourable changes in water quality.

Vocabulary

I. Fill in the blanks with the expressions given below. Change the forms if necessary.

| aesthetically | as regards | deterioration | excessive |
| give rise to | impair | prolific | |

1. I was afraid that my father's health _____ through overwork and I hoped that he would slow down.
2. Haydn was a _____ composer who wrote as many as 104 symphonies.
3. A sudden _____ in the weather spoiled our holidays.
4. The hotel is situated in a natural scenery area with _____ pleasing environment and

modern amenities as well.

5. The depression _____ widespread unemployment, which led to a lot of crimes.

II. Complete each of the following statements with one of the four choices given below.

1. The achievement of self-cleansing velocity in sewers is particularly important in tropical areas since in those conditions, organic deposits will rapidly become _____ and the resultant production of hydrogen sulphide can cause serious damage to the sewer.
   A. entrophic   B. anaerobic   C. inorganic   D. prolific

2. Travellers choose to stay in the hotels which can provide them with more _____ facilities.
   A. amazement   B. entertained   C. relaxation   D. recreational

3. He was able to complete his studies without _____, although he was somewhat slow.
   A. hindrance   B. nuisance   C. barrier   D. dilemma

4. What causes the friction between the husband and wife may be their _____ temper.
   A. incomparable   B. incompatible   C. incompetent   D. incomprehensible

5. Inequality of property, _____ the exploitation of the masses of the poor by a rich minority, breeds class conflict.
   A. resulting from   B. preventing   C. resulting in   D. putting forward

Writing   Outline Writing (4)

Directions: Read the text of Unit Six and write a sentence outline of each paragraph.

Reading Material A

Wastewater Chemical Analyses

Suspended solids determination and BOD are the most common and most important analyses for evaluation of the performance of a sewage treatment works or in assessing the waste assimilative capacity of a receiving water.[①] It should be noted that these two parameters are commonly mandated and regulated by the discharge permit. The values on suspended solids concentration also give a measure of the sludge production in the clarifiers.

Suspended Solids are characterized as filterable, settleable, and nonsettleable. To find the concentration of suspended solids in a wastewater sample, a measured volume of the sample is filtered through a preweighed standard glass-fiber filter and the residue retained on the filter then constitutes the suspended (or filterable) solids. Total suspended solids are obtained by weighing the filter with the retained solids and then subtracting the weight of the filter.

The Settleable Solids are measured in a conical cylinder 40cm (15 in.) high that has a graduated tip in ml and holds 1 liter of sample (Imhoff cone).[②] The volume of solids settling into the tip of the inverted cone is normally read after 1hr. The sides of the cone should be gently stirred with a rod after a lapse of 45 min in order to effect the deposition of the solids that would otherwise stick to the sides. A Zone Settling Test is similar except it can be performed in a standard 1-liter graduated cylinder and the settling of the top of the solids layer is recorded periodically in shorter time intervals. This test provides information on the design and performance of settling units. Between 2 and 5 ml of sludge is ordinarily deposited by 1 liter of raw domestic sewage. The performance of settling tanks is generally considered to be satisfactory when the effluent contains no more than 0.5 ml of settleable solids. The percentage removal of the settleable solids in the treatment plant is computed as $100 \times (a-b)/a$, where a is the volume of settleable solids of the raw influent, and b is that of the effluent.

Turbidity caused by suspended solids and other components (some soluble organic compounds) can be related to transparency. For this purpose, a Secchi disc is used.[3] This white rounded plate is submerged during the test in the water or wastewater and the depth at which visibility of the disc is lost is then the measure of turbidity. These depths are relatively small for wastewater (a fraction of 1 m). For surface waters, they range from about 1 m for typical slightly polluted waters to over 10m for clean stream and lakes. The Secchi disc procedure is primarily a field method for turbidity estimation. In the laboratory, turbidity is measured visually by a Jackson candle turbidimeter or by special turbidimeters or nepthelometers measuring optical light-scattering properties of turbidity causing particles in water.[4]

Volatile Suspended Solids are determined by igniting the filter residue at 550℃. The remaining residue (ash) is then weighed and represents the fixed (mineral) solids. The difference between the total suspended solids and mineral solids concentrations is the volatile solids. This value is often related to the organic content of the suspended solids although this may not be correct since the loss by ignition also contains some volatile mineral components. The organic suspended solids are of importance as they have a lower specific gravity and do not settle readily. When all the suspended particles are removed from the sewage, the remaining solids are either colloids or dissolved ions and salts.

The Dissolved Oxygen content of water and wastewater determines whether the water or treatment process is aerobic [dissolved oxygen (DO) concentration $\gg 0$] or anaerobic (DO = 0). The DO analysis is one of the key tests in water pollution and wastewater treatment control. The wet DO content determination is by the Winkler (iodometric) titration method.[5] Today, the DO test is performed mostly by membrane electrode probes.

Oxygen Saturation

Table 6-1

Temperature	0℃	5℃	10℃	15℃	20℃	25℃	30℃
Freshwater	14.6	12.8	11.3	10.1	9.1	8.3	7.6mg/l
Seawater	11.3	10.0	9.0	8.1	7.4	6.7	6.2mg/l

The dissolved oxygen content in waters cannot usually exceed its saturation value, which depends on temperature, salinity, and, to a lesser degree, barometric pressure. The DO saturation values are given in Table 6-1.

The Oxygen Deficit, *D*, is the difference in mg/liter between the measured oxygen concentration and the saturation concentration at the sample temperature. The reaeration rate, that is, the rate at which new oxygen is supplied to the water from the atmosphere, is proportional to the oxygen deficit.⑥

The degree of organic pollution of water or wastewater is best expressed as the amount of oxygen needed to oxidize the organics. Several analytical measurements are available from which the chemical oxygen demand (COD) and biochemical oxygen demand (BOD) are the most common.

Total oxygen demand (TOD) and total organic carbon (TOC) are analyses that rely on laboratory instruments and are becoming popular as a result of their ease of measurement and short time requirements.

The Chemical Oxygen Demand (COD) is a measure of the oxygen equivalent in mg of O_2/liter of the organic matter of the sample that can be oxidized by a strong chemical oxidant. As an oxidant, Standard Methods (APHA, AWWA, WPCF) recommend potassium dichromate ($K_2Cr_2O_7$), whereas German and British methods recommend potassium permanganate ($KMnO_4$). The COD analysis is a "wet" laboratory procedure.⑦ Oxidation of most organic compounds is 95-100% of the theoretical value. Some organic components are not completely oxidized by this method but few are not oxidized at all. These organics include benzene, pyridine, and toluene. On the other hand, the chemical oxidant employed in the analysis will oxidize some inorganic compounds such as ferrous iron, sulfides, and secondary manganese.⑧ Because of these problems, the COD values of wastewaters with different compositions cannot be compared; however, the COD values do represent the relative strength of organic pollution of samples of similar composition.

Notes

①评价污水处理工厂的工作状况或评估受纳水体对废水的同化能力，最常用和最重要分析法有悬浮固体的测定及生化需氧量的分析。
②可沉淀固体可以用一只标有毫升刻度的、可盛一升水样的40厘米（15英寸）高的圆锥形管（即英霍夫锥形管）测定。
③Secchi disc 透明度板，赛克板。
④Jackson candle turbidimeter 杰克逊烛光浊度计。
⑤Winkler titration method 温克勒滴定法（即测定溶解氧的碘量滴定法）。
⑥reaeration rate 复氧速率。
⑦ "wet" laboratory procedure "湿法"实验室过程。
⑧ferrous iron 亚铁。

Reading Material B

Sorption on Wastewater Solids: Elimination of Biological Activity
(A Thesis Model for Your Reference)

Abstract: Sorption was found to be greatly affected by the biological activity in wastewater solids. Two experimental techniques, cyanide treatment and pasteurization, were developed for eliminating the biological activity during isotherm measurements. Both methods are effective, however, pasteurization is recommended over cyanide treatment because of toxicity of the latter

Key words: biological activity, cyanide, isotherm, pasteurization, solids, sorption.

Sorption on wastewater solids is an important mechanism for removal of organic compounds in biological wastewater treatment systems. During isotherm measurements, biological activity in wastewater solids, especially in activated sludge that contains a substantial amount of active biomass, must be controlled to obtain accurate sorption isotherms. Otherwise, measurements of changing aqueous phase compound concentrations could include the effect of biodegradation, resulting in apparent sorption capacities greater than actually achieved.[1] Several methods, such as lyophilization, autoclaving, and dry heating have been reported for controlling of biological activity in sludge.[2] These methods, however, involved drying the sludge, which changes the surface properties and alters the original structure of the biomass. The objective of this communication is to present other methods that avoid the changes in biomass properties and sorption capacity for elimination of the biological activity in wastewater solids.

Materials and Methods

Wastewater solids were collected from the Fairfield, Ohio, Wastewater Treatment Plant. Activated sludge was used as the test adsorbent because it has the highest level of biological activity. Carbon tetrachloride and methylene blue dye were used as adsorbates. Carbon tetrachloride was analyzed using EPA Method 601 (1982), and methylene blue dye was determined with a Beckman Model 25 spectrophotometer equipped with a clinical sipper system. Detailed experimental method for measuring sorption isotherms can be found in our previous work.

Results and Discussion

Cyanide treatment. Elimination of the biological activity of sludge with cyanide treatment was attempted based on the reported potent inhibition of methanogenesis and carbon metabolism by cyanide (Yang et al., 1980; Smith et al., 1985; Fedorak et al., 1986).[3] The minimum contact time and minimum cyanide dosage required for controlling the biodegradation were determined using activated sludge in isotherm measurements. During the experiments, the sludge was contacted with cyanide at different concentrations for 2, 6, and 24 hours, respectively. The treated sludge was separated from the solution for subsequent use in sorption isotherms using carbon tetrachloride. The sludge was separated from the cyanide solution after treatment to minimize any possible interference with the isotherm measurement or analytical determination of test compound.

Carbon tetrachloride was added at a concentration of 0.5 mg/L to a series of bottles containing the sludge treated at different cyanide dosages. A range of contact times were used to optimize the sludge treatment conditions. All sample bottles were mixed for 6 hours. After equilibration, a 5-mL whole sample (both liquid and solids) was analyzed for the concentration of carbon tetrachloride remaining in each sample bottle. Figure 6-1 presents the results of the above experiments, where the ratio of the equilibrium concentration (C_e) to the initial concentration (C_0) is plotted as a function of cyanide dosage for three contact times. The cyanide dosage was based on the dry weight of sludge. The solid curves are the best fit curves to show the trend of experimental data. Theoretically, a complete control of biodegradation is achieved when C_e/C_0 is unity. As can be seen from the data in Fig. 6-1, the control of biodegradation was very effective at contact times of 6 hours and 24 hours over a range of cyanide to sludge ratios. The biodegradation was almost completely eliminated when a 24-hour contact time was used for cyanide dosages between 0.1 to 0.2 g/g. Higher cyanide dosage does not appear to enhance the control of biodegradation.

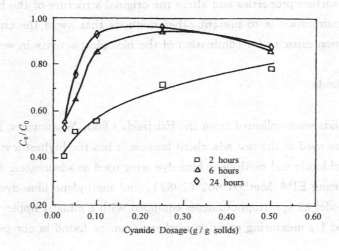

Fig. 6-1 Effect of cyanide: biomass ratio and contact time on biodegradation of carbon tatrachloride on activated sludge.

It can be concluded from the above discussion that effective control of biological activity can be achieved with cyanide dosage between 0.1 to 0.2 g/g of sludge and a pretreatment contact time of 24 hours. Therefore, a recommended procedure for cyanide pretreatment is as follows:

1. Add 0.1 to 0.2 g/g cyanide to dry weight solid to centrifuge bottles containing sludge solution.
2. Stir the solution on a multiple magnetic stirrer at approximately 80 to 100 rpm for about 24 hours. ④
3. Separate the solids from the liquid phase by centrifugation before sorption isotherm measurement. ⑤
4. Use the moist solids for sorption isotherm measurements.

Pasteurization. Although cyanide treatment was demonstrated to be effective in eliminating biodegradation, the extreme toxicity of cyanide makes this method less attractive. An attempt was made to find a safer method that could also control the biological activity effectively. Pasteurization has long been successfully used in the food industry for destroying bacteria. Moretti and Neufeld (1989) also applied this method to inactivate the microorganisms in sludge. The objective of this study was to determine the proper temperature and the heating time of this technique. In this study, 85 ℃ was chosen as the optimum temperature. ⑥ Results of different heating times were evaluated. As shown in Fig. 6-2, heating at 85 ℃ for 30 minutes essentially eliminated biological activity. Therefore, the recommended procedure for pasteurization is as follows:

1. Gradually heat the sludge to 85 ℃.
2. Maintain the temperature for 30 to 40 minutes.
3. Cool the sludge down to room temperature before use in the isotherm measurement.

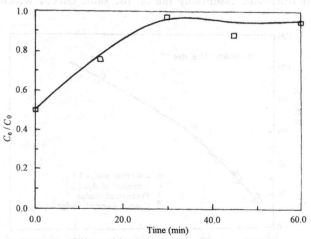

Fig. 6-2 Effect of biomass heating time at 85 ℃ on biodegradation of carbon tetrachloride on activated sludge

Using the above conditions, whole samples containing carbon tetrachloride with both untreated and pasteurized sludges were analyzed after 6-hour equilibrium contact time. Results shown in Table 6-2 clearly indicate that pasteurization is a very effective method for eliminating the biological activity of biomass. Although the whole sample concentration of carbon tetrachloride with untreated sludge decreased from 0.1 to an average of 0.04 mg/l, the concentration in the whole sample with pasteurized sludge remained basically unchanged.

Whole sample analysis of carbon tetrachloride on control and pastourized activated sludge.

Table 6-2

Sample No.	Type of sludge	C_0, mg/l	C_e, mg/l	(C_e) ave, mg/l
1	Control*	0.1	0.042	
2	Control*	0.1	0.036	0.039
3	pasteurized	0.1	0.101	
4	pasteurized	0.1	0.097	
5	pasteurized	0.1	0.103	0.100
6	pasteurized	0.1	0.101	
7	pasteurized	0.1	0.098	

* Control indicates untreated sludge.

Effect of pretreatment of wastewater solids on sorption isotherms. To demonstrate that pretreatment by cyanide or pasteurization did not alter the sorption characteristics, isotherms on untreated, cyanide-treated, and pasteurized activated sludge were measured using methylene blue dye.[7] The dye was chosen as the test compound because it is nonbiodegradable, nonvolatile, and easily measured colorimetrically. The isotherms are plotted in Fig. 6-3. Results document that all the isotherms essentially fall on the same curve, which indicates that pre-

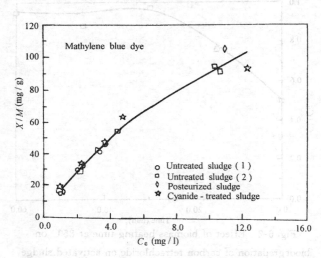

Fig. 6-3 Isotherms of methyiene blue dye on untreated, cyanide-treated, pasteurized activated sludge.

treatment by either cyanide or pasteurization has no significant effect on the sorption characteristics of wastewater solids and that both cyanide treatment and pasteurization are effective for elimination of biological activity during isotherm measurements. From a practical point of view, however, pasteurization is safer and easier to use than cyanide treatment.

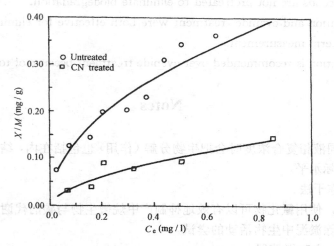

Fig. 6-4 Isotherms of carbon tetrachloride on untreated and cyanlde-treated activated sludge.

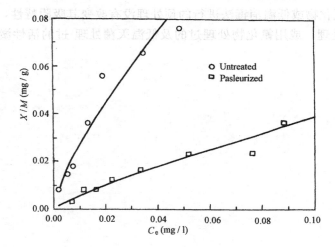

Fig. 6-5 Isotherms of carbon tetrachloride on untreated and pasteurized activated sludge.

Isotherms for carbon tetrachloride on untreated and cyanide-treated activated sludge are shown in Fig. 6-4, and the isotherms on untreated and pasteurized activated sludge are shown in Fig. 6-5. Both Figures 6-4 and 6-5 show that biodegradation must be eliminated to obtain accurate sorption isotherm capacities for biodegradable toxic organic compounds. The difference between the two isotherms was due to biodegradation of carbon tetrachloride by live biomass in activated sludge.

Conclusions

The following conclusions can be made based on the present study:

* Apparent sorption capacities for organics on biomass can be greatly affected by biological activity if the solids are not pretreated to eliminate biodegradation.

* Pasteurization and cyanide treatment were both effective for eliminating biological activity during isotherm measurements.

* Pasteurization is recommended over cyanide treatment because of toxicity of the latter.

Notes

①此外，测定不同液相复合浓度时会把生物分解（作用）也包括在内，结果造成其吸附能力明显超过了实际水平。
②lyophilization 冻干法。
③根据报导所述，使用氰化物可以有效地抑制产甲烷微生物与碳的代谢作用，从而进行了氰化处理法消除淤泥中生物活动的尝试。
④magnetic stirrer 电磁搅拌器。
⑤在测定等温吸附线前，用离心分离法将固体从液相中分离出来。
⑥optimum temperature 最佳温度。
⑦为了证明采用氰化物或低温消毒法进行的预处理没有改变其吸附特性，通过使用亚甲蓝染料法对未经处理、或用氰化物处理过的及低温灭菌处理过的活性淤泥进行等温线测定。

UNIT SEVEN

Text　　　Tertiary Treatment of Wastewater

[1]　　Primary and biological treatments make up the conventional wastewater treatment plant. However, secondary treatment plant effluents still contain a significant amount of various types of pollutants. Suspended solids, in addition to contributing to BOD, can settle out in streams and form unsightly mud banks.① The BOD, if discharged into a stream with low flow, can still cause damage to aquatic life by depressing the DO.② Neither primary nor secondary treatment is effective in removing phosphorus and other nutrients or toxic substances.

[2]　　Suspended solids can be effectively removed by a simple device called a pebble filter which consists of a box full of pebbles hung over the edge of the secondary clarifier so that all water must travel through the filter bed. The actual mechanism of how the pebbles catch the floc is unknown. What is known is that the effluent through a pebble filter is clear.

[3]　　A sophisticated, and hence marketable gadget is the *microstrainer*. The microstrainer is a large drum covered with a stainless steel sheet with small holes in it. The dirty water is pumped into the drum and the clearwater filters through. As the drum rotates, the holes are cleaned with spray.

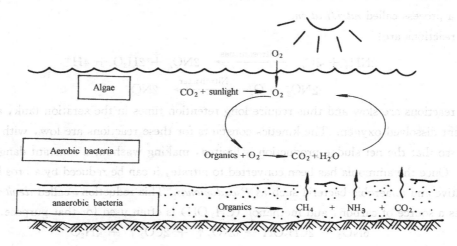

Fig 7-1　Simplified reactions within an oxidation pond

[4]　　For BOD removal, by far the most popular advanced treatment method is the polishing pond, often called the *oxidation pond*. This is essentially a hole in the ground, a large pond used to confine the plant effluent before it is discharged. Such ponds are designed to be aerobic, since light penetration for algal growth is important, hence a large surface area is needed. The reactions occurring within an oxidation pond are depicted in Fig. 7-1. Oxidation ponds are sometimes used as the only treatment step if the water flow is small and the pond area is large.

[5]   *Activated carbon adsorption* is another method of BOD removal, and this process has the added advantage that inorganics as well as organics are removed. The mechanism of adsorption on activated carbon is both chemical and physical, with tiny crevices catching and holding colloidal and smaller particles.③ An activated carbon column is a completely enclosed tube with dirty water pumped up from the bottom and the clear water exiting at the top.④ As the carbon becomes saturated with various materials, it must be removed from the column and regenerated, or cleaned. Removal is often continuous, with clean carbon being added at the top of the column. The cleaning or regeneration is usually done by heating the carbon in the absence of oxygen. A slight loss in efficiency is noted with regeneration, and some virgin carbon must always be added to ensure effective performance.

[6]   Nitrogen removal can be accomplished in two ways. The first method makes use of the fact that even after secondary treatment, most of the nitrogen exists as ammonia. Increasing the pH produces the following reaction:⑤

$$NH_4^+ + OH^- \rightarrow NH_3 \uparrow + H_2O$$

Much of the dissolved ammonia gas can then be expelled from the water into the atmosphere. The resulting air pollution problem has not been resolved.

[7]   A second method of getting rid of nitrogen is to first treat the waste thoroughly enough to produce nitrate ions. This usually involves longer detention times in secondary treatment, during which bacteria such as *Nitrobacter* and *Nitrosomonas* convert ammonia nitrogen to NO_3^-, a process called *nitrification*.

These reactions are:

$$2NH_4^+ + 3O_2 \xrightarrow{\text{Nitrosomonas}} 2NO_2^- + 2H_2O + 4H^+$$

$$2NO_2^- + O_2 \xrightarrow{\text{Nitrobacter}} 2NO_3^-$$

These reactions are slow and thus require long retention times in the aeration tank, as well as sufficient dissolved oxygen. The kinetics constants for these reactions are low, with very low yields, so that the net sludge production is limited, making washout a constant danger.

[8]   Once the ammonia has been converted to nitrate, it can be reduced by a broad range of facultative and anaerobic bacteria such as *Pseudomonas*. This reduction, called *denitrification*, requires a source of carbon, and methanol (CH_3OH) is often used for that purpose.

$$6NO_3^- + 2CH_3OH \rightarrow 6NO_2^- \uparrow + 2CO_2 \uparrow + 4H_2O$$

$$6NO_2^- + 3CH_3OH \rightarrow 3N_2 \uparrow + 3CO_2 \uparrow + 3H_2O + 6OH^-$$

[9]   Phosphate removal is almost always done chemically. The most popular chemicals used for phosphorus removal are lime $Ca(OH)_2$, and alum, $Al_2(SO_4)_3$. The calcium ion, in the presence of high pH, will combine with phosphate to form a white, insoluble precipitate called calcium hydroxyapatite which is settled out and removed. Insoluble calcium carbonate is also formed and removed and can be recycled by burning in a furnace.

$$CaCO_3 \xrightarrow{\Delta} CO_2 + CaO$$

Quick lime, CaO, is slaked by adding water,

$$CaO + H_2O \rightarrow Ca(OH)_2$$

thus forming lime which can be reused.

[10]   The aluminum ion from alum precipitates out as poorly soluble aluminum phosphate,

$$Al^{+++} + PO_4^{---} \rightarrow AlPO_4 \downarrow$$

and also forms aluminum hydroxides,

$$Al^{+++} + 3OH^- \rightarrow Al(OH)_3 \downarrow$$

which are sticky flocs and help to settle out the phosphates. The most common point of alum dosing is in the final clarifier.

[11]   The amount of alum required to achieve a given level of phosphorus removal depends on the amount of phosphorus in the water, as well as other constituents. The sludge produced can be calculated using stoichiometric relationships.

[12]   Using such a technique as alum precipitation of phosphorus, (and a bonus of more efficient SS and BOD removal due to the formation of $Al(OH_3)$, we now have attained our effluent goal:⑥

	Raw Wastewater	Following Primary Treatment	Following Secondary Treatment	Following Tertiary Treatment
BOD. mg/l	250	175	15	10
SS mg/l	220	60	15	10
P mg/l	8	7	6	0.5

[13]   An alternative to high-technology advanced wastewater treatment systems is to spray secondary effluent on land and allow the soil micro-organisms to degrade the remaining organics. Such systems, known as *land treatment*, have been employed for many years in Europe, but only recently have been used in North America. They appear to represent a reasonable alternative to complex and expensive systems, especially for smaller communities.⑦

[14]   Probably the most promising land treatment method is irrigation. Commonly, from 1000 to 2000 hectares of land are required for every 1 m^3/sec of wastewater flow, depending on the crop and soil.⑧ Nutrients such as N and P remaining in the secondary effluent are of course beneficial to the crops.

New Words and Expressions

significant [sig'nifikənt]	a.	相当数量的
contribute to		对……产生影响
unsightly [ʌn'saitli]	a.	不雅观的，难看的
flow [fləu]	n.	流量（速）

depress [di'pres]		vi.	降低，减少
moving ['mu:viŋ]		a.	移动的，活动的
marketable ['mɑ:kitəbl]		a.	有销路的
gadget ['gædʒit]		n.	小装置
microstrainer [ˌmaikrəu'streinə]		n.	微应变器
oxidation * [ˌɔksi'deiʃən]		n.	氧化（作用）
aerobic [ɛə'rəubik]		a.	有氧的
penetration * [ˌpeni'treiʃən]		n.	穿透
depict * [di'pikt]		vt.	描绘
crevice ['krevis]		n.	缝隙
enclosed [in'kləuzd]		a.	封闭式的
regenerate [ri'dʒenəreit]		vt.	还原，再生
expel [ik'spel]		vt.	排出
thoroughly ['θʌrəli]		ad.	彻底地
nitrobacter ['naitrəu'bæktə]		n.	硝化杆菌
convert ··· to			转变成
nitrification [ˌnaitrifi'keiʃən]		n.	氮的硝化（作用）
retention * [ri'tenʃən]		n.	保持，停留
constant ['kɔnstənt]		n.	恒量
washout ['wɔʃaut]		n.	冲洗
yield [ji:ld]		n.	效率，产量
facultative ['fækəltətiv]		a.	兼性的
pseudomonas [ˌpsju:'dɔmənəs]		n.	假单胞菌属
denitrification [di:ˌnaitrifi'keiʃən]		n.	脱硝（作用）
lime [laim]		n.	石灰
alum ['æləm]		n.	明矾
calcium ['kælsiəm]		n.	钙
hydroxyapatite [haiˌdrɔksi'æpətait]		n.	碱式磷酸钙
slake [sleik]		vt.	熟化
carbonate [ˌkɑ:bənit]		n.	碳酸钙
stoichiometric [stɔikiəu'metrik]		a.	化学计量的
degrade * [di'greid]		vt.	降低，减少

Notes

①BOD = biochemical oxygen demand 生化需氧量。

②DO = dissolved oxygen 溶解氧。

③句中 with tiny crevices catching and holding colloidal and smaller particles 为独立结构，补

充说明主句。

④句中 with dirty water pumped up from the bottom and the clear water existing at the top 为独立结构，逻辑主语分别为 dirty water 和 the clear water。

⑤increasing the pH 为动名词短语作主语，pH=hydrogen-ion concentration，氢离子浓度。

⑥SS = suspended solids 悬浮固体。

⑦句中 They 代表上句提到的 such systems。

⑧sec = second 秒。

Exercises

Reading Comprehension

I. Are these statements true (T) or false (F) according to the text?

1. Tertiary treatment is necessary in wastewater treatment for neither primary nor secondary treatment can effectively remove phosphorus and other nutrients or toxic substances. ( )

2. The most advanced treatment for BOD removal is activated carbon adsorption, by which both in organics and inorganics can be removed. ( )

3. It seems that neither of the two ways of nitrogen removal is preferable. ( )

4. Lime and alum are the most popular chemicals used for phosphorus removal, but the latter is even more popular than the former with a bonus of more efficient SS and BOD removal. ( )

5. The best wastewater treatment known as land treatment is nowadays widely used in the world with the advantage of being simple and inexpensive. ( )

II. Match Column A with Column B to form meaningful sentences according to the text.

A	B
1. It's known that a simple device called a pebble filter can be used to remove suspended solids effectively,	a. the amount of phosphorus existing in water and other constituents.
2. The most popular advanced treatment method of BOD removal is the oxidation pond	b. one of which will result in air pollution problem
3. There are two methods of getting rid of nitrogen,	c. while the other method is activated carbon adsorption which has the advantage of removing both organics and inorganics.

4. The amount of alum required to remove phosphorus to a given level is determined by
5. The process of spraying effluent on land and allowing the soil micro-organisms to degrade the remaining organics is known as

d. land treatment is considered a reasonable alternative to high-technology advanced wastewater treatment systems
e. but how the device works is unknown

Vocabulary

I. Fill in the blanks with the expressions given below. Change the form if necessary.

| beneficial | conventional | expel | marketable |
| promising | saturate | virgin | |

1. In such a small house it is necessary to have some method of _____ the smell of cooking from the kitchen.
2. The tourists showed their great interests in the town _____ with charm.
3. A system of strict discipline has a _____ effect on conduct.
4. The mind of a child is _____ soil, it is not full of firmly held ideas and opinions that prevent it receiving new ones.
5. I believe they are the most _____ young people in this field.

II. Complete each of the following statements with one of the four choices given below.

1. The old people _____ nearly 40 per cent of the total population of the city.
    A. consist of   B. are composed of
    C. make up   D. are made up of
2. The dregs _____ and the coffee was clear.
    A. settled for   B. settled in
    C. settled up   D. settled out
3. The new policy _____ immensely _____ the economic development of the country.
    A. contributes … to   B. contributes … with
    C. contributes … for   D. contributes … about
4. Removal of certain soluble inorganic materials can be achieved by the addition of suitable reagents to _____ the soluble impurities _____ insoluble precipitates which can then be flocculated and removed by sedimentation.
    A. exchange … into   B. alter … into
    C. convert … into   D. transform … into
5. He felt embarrassed, being questioned _____ a large number of people.
    A. at the present of   B. in the presence of

C. at the presence of D. in the present of

Writing   Summary Writing (1)

Summarizing means writing a short version of an article. To write a summary, you must skim the article so as to have a general idea of the material, underline the main points, make a list of all the points to be used and then with this list write the summary in an Introduction-Body-Conclusions structure with transition words like "but", "and", "however", "also", etc.

Directions: The following is a summary of the text of Unit Seven and there are several words missing. Now fill in the blanks with some of the words given below. irrigation, tertiary treatment, chemically, calcium hydroxyapatite, primary, suspended solids, land treatment, activated carbon adsorption, effluent goal, secondary

Tertiary treatment is necessary for neither __1__ nor __2__ treatment is effective in removing phosphorus and other nutrients or toxic substances.

There are various ways and devices used in __3__. Both a pebble and a microstrainer are used for the removal of __4__; an oxidation pond and __5__ for BOD removal. Nitrogen removal is accomplished in two ways while phosphate removal is done __6__. Lime and alum are the most popular chemicals used for this purpose. An alternative to the high-technology advanced wastewater treatment systems is known as __7__, of which the most promising method is __8__.

Reading Material A

Activated Sludge Treatment of Wastewater

The basic components of an activated sludge sewage treatment system include an aeration tank and a secondary settling basin or clarifier. Primary effluent is mixed with settled solids that are recycled from the secondary clarifier and then introduced into the aeration tank. Compressed air is injected continuously into the mixture, through porous diffusers located at the bottom of the tank, along one side.

In the aeration tank, microorganisms consume the dissolved organic pollutants as food. The microbes absorb and aerobically decompose the organics, using oxygen provided in the compressed air; water, carbon dioxide, and other stable compounds are formed.[①] In addition to providing oxygen, the compressed air thoroughly mixes the microbes and wastewater together, as it rapidly bubbles up to the surface from the diffusers. Sometimes mechanical propellerlike mixers, located at the liquid surface, are used instead of compressed air and diffusers. The churning action of the propeller blades mixes air with the wastewater and keeps the contents of the tank in a uniform suspension.

The aerobic microoganisms in the tank grow and multiply, forming an active suspension of biological solids called *activated sludge*. The combination of the activated sludge and the wastewater in the aeration tank is called *the mixed liquor*. In the basic or conventional activated sludge treatment system, a tank detention time of about six hours is required for thorough stabilization of most of the organics in the mixed liquor.

After about six hours of aeration, the mixed liquor flows to the secondary or final clarifier, in which the activated sludge solids settle out by gravity. The clarified water near the surface called the *supernatant*, is discharged over an effluent weir; the settled sludge is pumped out from a sludge hopper at the bottom of the tank.② Recycling a portion of the sludge back to the inlet of the aeration tank is an essential characteristic of this treatment process. The settled sludge is in an "active" state. In other words, the microbes are well acclimated to the wastewater and, given the opportunity, will readily absorb and decompose more organics by their metabolism.③

By pumping about 30 percent of the wastewater flow from the bottom of the clarifier back to the head of the aeration tank, the activated sludge process can be maintained continuously. When mixed with the primary efflluent, the "hungry" microbes quickly begin to absorb and metabolize the fresh "food" in the form of BOD causing organics. Since the microbes multiply and increase greatly in numbers, it is not possible to recycle or return all the sludge to the aeration tank. The excess sludge, called *waste activated sludge*, must eventually be treated and disposed of (along with sludge from the primary tanks.) Sludge management is a major aspect of wastewater treatment.

Several modifications of the conventional activated sludge process have been developed; these serve to increase treatment plant capacity or to reduce the tank volume requirements.

A process called *step aeration* provides multiple feed points of the primary effluent into the aeration tank. By introducing the organics into the tank in increments or "steps", rather than only once at the head of the tank, the oxygen demand is spread more uniformly over the length of the tank.④ In this manner, greater treatment plant capacities can be obtained in a given volume of aeration tank than can be obtained using the conventional process.

For treating small sewage flow rates from surburban residential developments, hotels, schools and other relatively isolated wastewater sources, a process called *extended aeration* is often used. These small systems are generally in the form of prefabricated steel tanks and are called "package plants". (Conventional tanks, on the other hand, are usually made with cast-in-place reinforced concrete). In the extended aeration system, the aeration tank and secondary clarifier are built in a single unit.

There are two important distinctions between an extended aeration system and a conventional system. First, screened or comminuted sewage is directed into the extended aeration tank without any primary settling. Second, the detention time or aeration period is about 30 h, whereas the conventional system's detention time is about 6h.

Another difference is that the extended aeration process operates with F/M ratios as low as 0.05. This means that there is a large population of microorganisms compared to the amount of food (organics). The low F/M ratio and the "extended" period of aeration allow for the stabilization of most of the organics in the wastewater. But eventually some sludge has to be removed from the aeration tank for disposal.

In yet another modification of the activated sludge process, the influent sewage is mixed and aerated with return activated sludge for only about 30 min. This process is called *contact stabilization*.⑤ The short contact period of 30 min is sufficient for the microorganisms to absorb the organic pollutants, but not to stabilize them.

After the short contact time, the mixed liquor enters a clarifier and the activated sludge settles out, the clarified sewage flows over effluent weirs. The settled sludge is pumped into another aerated tank, called *a reaeration or stabilization tank*. The contents of the stabilization tank are aerated for about three hours, allowing the microbes to decompose the absorbed organic material. The total size of a contact stabilization tank is generally less than that of a conventional plant. This is because the volume of activated sludge being stabilized in the reaeration tank is considerably less than the total wastewater flow.⑥

A typical installation consists of a field-erected circular steel tnak, with an inner tank providing a zone for clarification. The annular volume between the inner tank and the outer tank wall provides the room or zones for contact, reaeration, and sludge storage.⑦ An "air-lift" type of pump is usually used to transfer sludge between zones of the tank. With some minor modification of piping and baffling arrangements, a contact stabilization system can also be operated in the step aeration or in the extended aeration mode.

Notes

①微生物利用压缩空气送入的氧气吸收有机物，并对其进行需氧分解；生成了水、二氧化碳和其它稳定的化合物。
②接近表面的澄清水，称为上清液，它在排放时流经出水堰，沉积的淤泥从池底的泥斗中抽出。
③换句话说，微生物对废水很适应，并且如有机会，随时会通过新陈代谢吸收和分解更多的有机物。
④不是从池顶一次性地向池里添加有机物，而是采用递增或阶段式的办法添加，需氧量便会更均匀地分布于整个池体内。
⑤Contact Stabilization 接触稳定作用。
⑥这是因为在曝气池中正在稳定下来的活性淤泥的体积比废水总量要小得多。
⑦Annular 环状的。

Reading Material B

Land Treatment of Wastewater

The application of secondary effluent onto the land surface can provide an effective alternative to the expensive and complicated advanced treatment methods previously discussed. A high quality polished effluent can be obtained by the natural processes that occur as the effluent flows over the vegetated ground surface and as it percolates through the soil. [1]

An additional benefit of land treatment is that it can provide the moisture and nutrients needed for vegetation growth and it can help to recharge groundwater aquifers. [2] In effect, land treatment of wastewater allows a direct recycling of water and nutrients for beneficial use; the sewage becomes a valuable natural resource that is not simply "disposed" of. But relatively large land areas are needed for this kind of treatment. And soil type as well as climate are cirtical factors in controlling the feasibility and design of a land treatment process.

There are three basic types or modes of land treatment. These include *slow rate*, *repid infiltration*, and *overland flow*. The conditions under which they can function and the basic objectives of these types of treatment vary.

In the slow rate system, also called *irrigation*, vegetation is the critical component for the wastewater treatment process. Although the basic objective is wastewater treatment and disposal, another goal is to obtain an economic benefit from the use of the water and nutrients to produce marketable crops (i. e. , corn or grain) for animal feed. Another objective might be to conserve potable water by using secondary effluent to irrigate lawns and other landscaped areas.

Wastewater can be applied onto the land by ridge-and-furrow surface spreading or by sprinkler systems. The most common sprinkler system consists of a long spray boom that rotates on wheel supports around a center pivot. [3] In ridge-and-furrow application, the wastewater flows by gravity in small ditches. In either mode of application, most of the water and nutrients are taken up or absorbed through the roots of the growing vegetation.

Not all of the water applied to the land in a slow rate system is absorbed; some of it percolates through the soil to the groundwater zone. Uncontrolled surface runoff of the wastewater is not usually allowed, so the soil must have reasonably good drainage characteristics. The wastewater can be applied to the land at rates of up to 100 mm (4in.) per week, except during the winter months in northern climates. Of the three basic types of land treatment systems, the slow rate method provides the best results with respect to tertiary treatment levels of pollutant removal. Suspended solids and biochemical oxygen demand are significantly reduced by filtration of the wastewater and biological oxidation of the organics in the top few inches of soil. [4] Nitrogen is removed primarily by crop uptake, and phosphorus is removed by adsorption within the soil.

The rapid infiltration or "infiltration-percolation" mode of land treatment has as basic objectives to recharge groundwater aquifers and to provide advanced treatment of wastewater.⑤ A schematic diagram of the rapid infiltration method is shown in Fig. 7-2 Most of the secondary effluent percolates to the groundwater; very little of it is absorbed by vegetation. The filtering and adsorption action of the soil removes most of the BOD, TSS, and phosphorus from the effluent, but nitrogen removal is relatively poor. Soils must be highly permeable for the rapid infiltration method to work properly. Usually, the wastewater is applied in large ponds called *recharge basins*.⑥

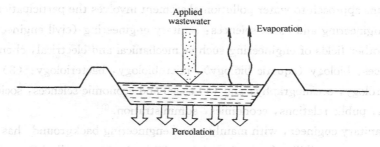

Fig. 7-2　Rapid infiltration. [EPA]

Wastewater is sprayed on a sloped terrace and allowed to flow across the vegetated surface to a runoff collection ditch. Purification is accomplished by physical, chemical, and biological processes as the wastewater flows in a thin film down the relatively impermeable surface. Overland flow can be used to achieve removal efficiencies for BOD and nitrogen comparable to other methods of tertiary treatment, but phosphorus removal is somewhat limited. The water collected in the ditch is usually discharged to a nearby body of surface water.

Notes

①通过自然的过程，即当污水流经植物生长的地面并渗入土壤，就获得了高质量的净化水。
②aquifer (s) 含水层
③最普通的洒水系统由一根固定在轮式底座上，绕着中心枢轴转动的长喷水杆组成。
④在土表几英寸厚的土壤中，废水的过滤和有机物的生物氧化使得悬浮固体和生化耗氧量显著减少。
⑤废水土壤处理的快速渗透法或称"渗透渗滤"法是把对地下含水层的补给和对废水采取先进的处理方法为基本目标的。
⑥recharge basin 回灌池

UNIT EIGHT

Text　　　　　The Role of the Engineer in
　　　　　　　Water Pollution Abatement

[1]　　Although it has been stated previously that water pollution control is not an exceedingly difficult technical problem, the field is a broad one, and of sufficient complexity to justify several different disciplines being brought together for achieving optimal results at a minimum cost. A systems approach to water pollution abatement involves the participation of many disciplines: (1) engineering and exact sciences: sanitary engineering (civil engineering), chemical engineering, other fields of engineering such as mechanical and electrical, chemistry, physics; (2) life sciences: biology (aquatic biology), microbiology, bacteriology; (3) earth sciences: geology, hydrology, oceanography; and (4) social and economic sciences: sociology, law, political sciences, public relations, economics, administration. ①

[2]　　The sanitary engineer, with mainly a civil engineering background, has historically carried the brunt of responsibility for engineering activities in water pollution control. This situation goes back to the days when the bulk of waste waters were of domestic origin. Composition of domestic wastewaters does not vary greatly. Therefore, prescribed methods of treatment are relatively standard, with a limited number of unit processes and operations involved in the treatment sequence. Traditional methods of treatment involved large concrete basins, where either sedimentation or aeration were performed, operation of trickling filters, chlorination, screening, and occasionally a few other operations. The fundamental concern of the engineer was centered around problems of structure and hydraulics, and quite naturally, the civil engineering background was an indispensable prerequisite for the sanitary engineer.

[3]　　This situation has changed, at first gradually, and more recently at an accelerated rate with the advent of industrialization. As a result of a new large variety of industrial processes, highly diversified wastewaters requiring more complex treatment processes have appeared on the scene. ② Wastewater treatment today involves so many different pieces of equipment, so many unit processes and unit operations, that it became evident that the chemical engineer had to be called to play a major role in water pollution abatement. The concept of unit operations, developed largely by chemical engineers in the past fifty years, constitutes the key to the scientific approach to design problems encountered in the field of wastewater treatment.

[4]　　In fact, even the municipal wastewaters of today are no longer the "domestic wastewaters" of yesterday. Practically all municipalities in industrialized areas must handle a combination of domestic and industrial wastewaters. Economic and technical problems involved in such treatment make it very often desirable to perform separate treatment (segregation) of industrial wastewaters, prior to their discharge into municipal sewers. ③

[5]　　Even the nature of truly domestic wastewaters has changed with the advent of a whole

series of new products now available to the average household, such as synthetic detergents and others.④ Thus, to treat domestic wastewaters in an optimum way requires modifications of the traditional approach.

[6] In summary, for treatment of both domestic and industrial wastewaters, new technology, new processes, and new approaches, as well as modifications of old approaches, are the order of the day. The image today is no longer that of the "large concrete basins", but one of a series of closely integrated unit operations. These operations, both physical and chemical in nature, must be tailored for each individual wastewater. The chemical engineer's skill in integrating these unit operations into effective processes makes him admirably qualified to design wastewater treatment facilities.

New Words and Expressions

abatement [əˈbeitmənt]	n.	减少（轻）
complexity* [kəmˈpleksəti]	n.	复杂（性）
optimal* [ˈɔptiməl]	a.	最佳的
participation [pɑːˌtisiˈpeiʃən]	n.	参与
aquatic [əˈkwætik]	a.	水生的
hydrology [haiˈdrɔlədʒi]	n.	水文学
oceanography [ˌəuʃiəˈnɔɡrəfi]	n.	海洋学
brunt [brʌnt]	n.	正面的冲击
carry the responsibility for		对……负责
go back to		追溯到
bulk [bʌlk]	n.	大量，大多数
composition [ˌkɔmpəˈziʃən]	n.	组成（物）
sedimentation [ˌsedimenˈteiʃən]	n.	沉积（作用）
trickle [ˈtrikl]	vi./n.	滴流
screening [ˈskriːniŋ]	n.	筛
hydraulics* [haiˈdrɔːliks]	n.	（复）.水力学
advent* [ˈædvənt]	n.	出现，到来
diversify [daiˈvəːsifai]	vt.	使……不同，多样化
segregation* [ˌseɡriˈɡeiʃən]	n.	分离
optimum* [ˈɔptiməm]	a./n.	最佳（的）
in summary		简言之
the order of the day		流行，风气
admirably [ˈædmərəbli]	ad.	令人羡慕地
be qualified to		胜任，适合

Notes

① A systems approach 系统方法，常见还有 systems analysis，systems design，systems engineering 等。
② "…, highly diversified wastewaters requiring more complex treatment processes." 中 wastewaters 前面的过去分词短语和其后的现在分词短语都是修饰它的。
③ 句中的 involved in such treatment 是过去分词短语，修饰 problems；句中 it 是形式宾语，to perform separate treatment (segregation) of industrial wastewaters, … 不定式短语是真实宾语。
④ now available to the average household，是后置形容词短语，修饰 new products。

Exercises

Reading Comprehension

I. Are these statements true (T) or false (F) according to the text?
 1. Water pollution abatement is a broad field involving many disciplines from natural sciences to social sciences, and it is this which makes it a hard nut to crack. (   )
 2. The sanitary engineer must have a civil engineering background for water pollution control is the most closely related to civil engineering. (   )
 3. A new large variety of industrial processes result in highly diversified wastewaters which need more complex treatment processes, so the chemical engineer is required to carry the main responsibility for water pollution abatement. (   )
 4. The traditional approach must be modified to meet the requirements in the treatment of the municipal wastewaters of today. (   )
 5. The sanitary engineer with a civil engineering background has been replaced by the chemical engineer for the "large concrete basins" are no longer used today. (   )

II. Match Column A with Column B to form meaningful sentences according to the text.

A	B
1. Water pollution control is not considered a most difficult technical problem, but a rather complicated one	a. for treatment of both domestic and industrial wastewaters.
2. The basic concern of the sanitary engineer revolves around problems of structure and hydraulics	b. and the chemical engineer has to be called to play a main role in water pollution control as a result

3. With the development of industry, wastewaters are highly diversified, which demands more complex treatment processes

4. The fact that the municipal wastewaters of today is quite different from the domestic wastewaters of yesterday requires separate treatment of industrial wastewaters

5. Nowadays, not only modifications of old approaches but also new technology, new processes, and new approaches are necessary

c. so the sanitary engineer having a civil engineering background has taken the responsibility for engineering activities in water pollution abatement

d. for it is a broad field involving the participation of many disciplines

e. before they are discharged into municipal sewers.

Vocabulary

I. Fill in the blanks with the expressions given below. Change the forms if necessary.

| admirably | as a result of | desirable | exceedingly |
| go back to | indispensable | the order of the day | |

1. It is highly _____ to know exactly what one is hoping to achieve in teaching.
2. He had behaved badly in losing his temper while she had so _____ held backhers.
3. I did not care much about his advice but now it seems _____ valuable to me.
4. Political stability is _____ for economic stability.
5. Mass production _____ the early years of industrial revolution.

II. Complete each of the following statements with one of the four choices given below.

1. After a series of experiments they have found out the _____ temperature for the growth of the plant.
   A. optimistic   B. optimal   C. optical   D. optic
2. The surface area _____ high mountains and fertile valleys and plains.
   A. is diversified of   B. diversifies of   C. is diversified with   D. diversifies with
3. We now have enough data to show that noise is a definite health hazard, and should be numbered among our more serious pollutants. And its _____ can be achieved by using available technology.
   A. modification   B. abatement   C. participation   D. segregation
4. Our merchandise must _____ the particular requirements of each overseas market.
   A. tailor for   B. tailor to   C. be tailored for   D. be tailored to
5. _____ the Revolutionary War, the United States was an English colony.

A. Prior to   B. Since   C. After   D. During

Writing   Summary writing (2)

Directions: The following is a summary of the text of Unit Eight. There are several words and/or phrases missing. Please fill in the blanks with words or phrases found from the text.

Water pollution control is not an extremely difficult technical problem but a __1__ field which involves the participation of various __2__ including engineering and exact sciences: life sciences, earth sciences and social and economic sciences.

During the days when wastewaters were mainly of __3__, the methods of treatment were limited in a number of unit processes and operations. The basic __4__ of the engineer was problems of structure and hydraulics, so the sanitary engineer with the civil engineering background took the __5__ for water pollution control.

With the arrival of industrialization, both __6__ and __7__ wastewaters are diversified. Wastewater treatment involves many unit processes and unit operations both physical and chemical in nature, so the __8__ plays a major role in water pollution abatement nowadays.

Reading Material A

Disinfection

Because of the small size of many micro-organisms it is not possible to guarantee their complete removal from water by such forms of treatment as coagulation and filtration. Some form of disinfection is therefore necessary to ensure the elimination of potentially harmful micro-organisms from potable waters. Most wastewaters and treated effluents contain large numbers of micro-organisms and it may sometimes be appropriate to disinfect such liquids although in general the routine disinfection of effluents is not to be recommended. Disinfection of an effluent before discharge will tend to retard self-purification reactions in the receiving water and the formation of reaction products from the interactions of organic compounds and disinfectants may be undesirable in waters used as sources for potable supply.[①]

It is important to appreciate the difference between sterilization (the killing of all organisms) which is rarely practised or needed, and disinfection (the killing of potentially harmful organisms) which is the normal requirement.

Chlorine

Chlorine is a powerful oxidizing agent which will rapidly combine with reducing agents and unsaturated organic compounds. [2] Chlorine (and its compounds) is widely and commonly used around the world for the disinfection of water because:

1. It is readily available as gas, liquid, or powder.
2. It is cheap.
3. It is easy to apply due to relatively high solubility (7000 mg/l).
4. It leaves a residual in solution which while not harmful to man provides protection in the distribution system.
5. It is very toxic to most micro-organisms, stopping metabolic activities.

It has some disadvantages in that it is a poisonous gas which requires careful handing and it can give rise to taste and odour problems particularly in the presence of phenols.

Ozone

Ozone (O_3) is an allotropic form of oxygen produced by passing dry oxygen or air through an electrical discharge (5000-20,000 V, 50-500 Hz). [3] It is an unstable, highly toxic blue gas with a pungent odour of new mown hay. A powerful oxidizing agent it is an efficient disinfectant and useful in bleaching colour and removing tastes and odours. Like oxygen it is only slightly soluble in water and because of its unstable form it leaves no residual. Unless cheap energy is available ozone treatment is much more expensive than chlorination but it does have the advantage of good colour removal. In these circumstances, filtration and ozonization may give a finished water similar to that produced by a more complex coagulation, sedimentation, filtration and chlorination plant. Because of the absence of ozone residuals in the distribution system, biological growths with attendant colour, taste and odour problems may result. Such growths in the distribution system can usually be prevented by adding a small dose of chlorine after ozonization. Ozone has some application in the oxidation of certain industrial wastewaters not amenable to biological oxidation.

Ozone must be manufactured on site by passing dry air through a high-voltage high-frequency electrical discharge. There are two main types of ozonizer; plate type with flat electrodes and glass dielectrics, and the tube type with cylindrical electrodes coaxial with glass dielectric cylinders. [4] The high-tension side is cooled by convection and the low-tension side by water. Air passes between the electrodes and is ozonized by the discharge across the air gap. Ozone production is usually up to about 4% by weight of the carrier air with power requirements of around 25k Wh/kg of ozone produced. Ozone will react with organic matter to form ozonides in certain conditions and the significance of the presence of these products in water is not yet fully understood.

Ultraviolet Radiation

Various forms of radiation can be effective disinfecting agents and UV radiation has been used for the treatment of small water supplies for many years. The disinfecting action of UV at a wavelength of around 254 nm is quite strong provided that the organisms are actually exposed to the radiation. [5] It is thus necessary to ensure that turbidity is absent and that the dose is increased to allow for the absorption of UV by any organic compounds present in the flow. The water to be disinfected flows between mercury arc discharge tubes and polished metal reflector tubes which gives efficient disinfection with a retention time of a few seconds although at a rather high power requirement of 10-20 $W/m^3 h$. [6] The advantages of UV disinfection include: no formation of tastes and odours, minimum maintenance, easy automatic control with no danger from overdosing. Disadvantages are: lack of residual, high cost and need for high clarity in the water.

Other Disinfectants

Various other methods have been used for water disinfection:
1. *Heat*. Disinfection by heat is very effective but is costly and impairs the palatability[7] of water by removing DO and dissolved salts. No residual effect.
2. *Silver*. Colloidal silver was used by the Romans to preserve the quality of water in storage jars since, at concentrations of about 0.05 mg/l, silver is toxic to most micro-organisms. It is of value for small portable filter units for field use where silver-impregnated gravel filter candles remove turbidity and provide disinfection. [8] The cost becomes excessive for other than very small supplies.
3. *Bromine*. A halogen like chlorine, bromine has similar disinfection properties and is sometimes used in swimming pools where the residual tends to be less irritating to the eyes than chlorine residuals.

Notes

①排放前对污水进行消毒往往会阻碍受纳水体中的自净反应。有机化合物同消毒剂的相互作用生成的反应产物对用作饮用水源的水体来说也许是不利的。
②reducing agent 还原剂。
③臭氧（O_3）是一种当干燥的氧或空气通过 5000～20 000 伏，50～500 赫兹的放电时产生的一种氧的同素异形体。
④臭氧发生器主要有两种：一为带有扁平电极和玻璃介体的板式型，另一为带有和玻璃介体圆柱同轴的圆柱电极的管状型。
⑤若把有机物置于实际辐射线下，具有约为 254 纳米波长的紫外线具有很强的消毒作用。
⑥要消毒的水，流经水银弧光放电管和抛光金属反射管之间，只需滞留几秒钟的时间，就可对水进行有效的消毒，虽然需要 10～20W/（m·3h）这样相当高的功率来完成。
⑦palatability 可口，对胃口。
⑧供野外使用的小型轻便过滤器是很有用的，其浸渍银砾石过滤棒能消除混浊并进行消毒。

Reading Material B

Nitrogen and Phosphorus Removal

Nitrogen Removal

Nitrogen can exist in wastewater in the form of organic nitrogen, ammonia, or nitrate compounds. The effluent from a conventional activated sludge plant contains mostly the ammonia nitrogen form, NH_4^+. Effluents from a trickling filter or rotating biodisc may contain more of the nitrate form, NO_3^-. This is because the nitrifying bacteria, those microbes that convert ammonia to nitrate, have a chance to grow and multiply on some of the surfaces in the trickling filter or biodisc units.① They do not survive in a mixed-growth aeration tank, where they are crowded out by the faster growing bacteria that consume carbonaceous organics.②

Nitrogen in the form of ammonia can be toxic to fish, and it exerts an oxygen demand in receiving waters as it is converted to nitrate. Nitrate nitrogen is one of the major nutrients that cause algal blooms and eutrophication.③ For these reasons, it is sometimes necessary to remove the nitrogen from the sewage effluent before discharge. This is particularly important if it is discharged directly into a lake.

One of the methods used to remove nitrogen is called *biological nitrification-denitrification*.④ It consists of two basic steps. First, the secondary effluent is introduced into another aeration tank, trickling filter, or biodisc. Since most of the carbonaceous BOD has already been removed, the microorganisms that will now thrive in this tertiary step are the so-called nitrifying bacteria, *Nitrosomoneas* and *Nitrobacter*.⑤ In this first step, called *nitrification*, the ammonia nitrogen is converted to nitrate nitrogen, producing a nitrified effluent. At this point, the nitrogen has not actually been removed, but only converted to a form that is not toxic to fish and that does not cause an additional oxygen demand.

A second biological treatment step is necessary to actually remove the nitrogen from the wastewater. This step is called *denitrification*. It is an aerobic process in which the organic chemical methanol is added to the nitrified effluent to serve as a source of carbon. The denitrifying bacteria *Pseudomonas* and other groups use the carbon from the methanol and the oxygen from the nitrates in their metabolic processes.⑥ One of the products of this biochemical reaction is molecular nitrogen, N_2, which escapes into the atmosphere as a gas.

Another method for nitrogen removal is called *ammonia stripping*. It is a physical-chemical rather than a biological process, consisting of two basic steps. First, the pH of the wastewater is raised in order to convert the ammonium ions, NH_4^+, to ammonia gas, NH_3. Second, the wastewater is cascaded down through a large tower; this causes turbulence and contact with air, allowing the ammonia to escape as a gas. Large volumes of air are circulated through the tower to carry the gas out of the system. The combination of ammonia stripping with phosphorus removal using lime as a coagulant is advantageous, since the lime can also serve to raise the pH of the wastewater. ⑦ Ammonia stripping is less expensive than biological nitrification-denitrification, but it does not work very efficiently under cold weather conditions.

Phosphorus Removal

Phosphorus is one of the plant nutrients that contribute to the eutrophication of lakes. Raw sewage contains about 10 mg/L of phosphorus, from household detergents as well as from sanitary wastes. The phosphorus in wastewater is primarily in the form of organic phosphorus and as phosphate, PO_4^{3-}, compounds. Only about 30 percent of this phosphorus is removed by the bacteria in a conventional secondary sewage treatment plant, leaving about 7 mg/L of phosphorus in the effluent.

When stream or effluent standards require lower phosphorus concentrations, a tertiary treatment process must be added to the treatment plant. This usually involves *chemical precipitation* of the phosphate ions and coagulation. The organic phosphorus compounds are entrapped in the coagulant flocs that are formed and settle out in a clarifier.

One of the chemicals frequently used in this process is aluminum sulfate, Al_2SO_4. This is called alum, the same coagulant chemical used to purify drinking water. The aluminum ions in the alum react with the phosphate ions in the sewage, to form the insoluble precipitate called aluminum phosphate. Other coagulant chemicals that may be used to precipitate the phosphorus include ferric chloride, $FeCl_3$, and lime, CaO.

Adding the coagulant downstream of the secondary processes provides the greatest overall reliability for phosphorus reduction. It not only removes about 90 percent of the phosphorus, but it removes additional TSS and serves to polish the effluent as well. But when applied in this manner, as a third or tertiary treatment step, additional flocculation and settling tanks must be built. In some cases, even filters may have to be added to remove the nonsettleable floc.

To avoid the need for construction of additional tanks and filters, in most plants requiring phosphorus removal the coagulant is added to the wastewater at some point in the conventional process. ⑧ For example, alum may be added just before the primary settling tanks. The resulting combination of primary and chemical sludge would be removed from the primary clarifiers.

Or, in activated sludge plants, the coagulant may be added directly into the aeration tanks. In this case, the precipitation and flocculation reactions occur along with the biochemical reactions. Sometimes, the coagulant may be added to the wastewater just before the secondary or final clarifiers. Regardless of the point in the process at which coagulant is added, the total volume and weight of sludge requiring disposal increases significantly.

Notes

①这是因为这些硝化微生物,即那些把氨变成硝酸的微生物,有可能在某些滴滤池或生物转盘装置的表面生长繁殖。

②在一个混合生长的曝气池里,他们无法生存;而是被那些生长更快的微生物(耗碳有机物)排挤出来。("他们"指"硝化微生物")。

③Algal blooms 藻华;Eutrophication 富营养化(作用)。

④Biological nitrification-denitrification 生物硝化—反硝化(作用)。

⑤Nitrosomoneas 亚硝化单胞菌属;Nitrobacter 硝化杆菌属。

⑥在新陈代谢的过程中,反硝化细菌,即假单胞菌和其他细菌利用了从甲醇中获得的碳和从硝酸盐中获得的氧。

⑦既然石灰也能有助于提高废水的 pH 值,那么把氨解吸法同用石灰作为助凝剂的脱磷法结合起来是有益的。

⑧为了避免建造附加曝气池、滤池,大多数工厂脱磷时,在常规工艺过程的某个步骤中在废水里加入絮凝剂。

UNIT NINE

Text   The Concept of Sustainable Development

[1]   The satisfaction of human needs and aspirations is the major objective of development. The essential needs of vast numbers of people for food, clothing, shelter and jobs are not being met, and beyond their basic needs these people have legitimate aspirations for an improved quality of life. ① A world in which poverty and inequity is endemic will always be prone to ecological and other crises②. Sustainable development requires meeting the basic needs of all and extending to all the opportunity to satisfy their aspirations for a better life. ③

[2]   Living standards that go beyond the basic minimum are sustainable only if consumption standards everywhere have regard for long-term sustainability. ④ Yet many of us live beyond the world's ecological means, for instance in our patterns of energy use. Sustainable development requires the promotion of values that encourage consumption standards that are within the bounds of the ecological possible and to which all can reasonably aspire. ⑤

[3]   Meeting essential needs depends in part on achieving full growth potential, and sustainable development clearly requires economic growth in places where such needs are not being met. Elsewhere, it can be consistent with economic growth, provided the content of growth reflects the broad principles of sustainability and non-exploitation of others. But growth by itself is not enough. High levels of productive activity and widespread poverty can coexist, and can endanger the environment. Hence sustainable development requires that societies meet human needs both by increasing productive potential and by ensuring equitable opportunities for all.

[4]   An expansion in numbers can increase the pressure on resources and slow the rise in living standards in areas where deprivation is widespread. Though the issue is not merely one of population size but of the distribution of resources, sustainable development can only be pursued if demographic developments are in harmony with the changing productive potential of the ecosystem.

[5]   A society may in many ways compromise its ability to meet the essential needs of its people in the future—by overexploiting resources, for example. The direction of technological developments may solve some immediate problems but lead to even greater ones. Large sections of the population may be marginalized by ill-considered development. ⑥

[6]   Settled agriculture, the diversion of watercourses, the extraction of minerals, the emission of heat and noxious gases into the atmosphere, commercial forests, and genetic manipulation are all examples of human intervention in natural systems during the courses of development. Until recently, such interventions were small in scale and their impact limited. Today's interventions are more drastic in scale and impact, and more threatening to life-support systems both locally and globally. This need not happen. At a minimum, sustainable development

must not endanger the natural systems that support life on Earth: the atmosphere, the waters, the soils, and the living beings.

[7] Economic growth and development obviously involve changes in the physical ecosystem. Every ecosystem everywhere cannot be preserved intact.⑦ In general, renewable resources like forests and fish stocks need not be depleted provided the rate of uses is within the limits of regeneration and natural growth.⑧ But most renewable resources are part of a complex and interlinked ecosystem, and maximum sustainable yield must be defined after taking into account system-wide effects of exploitation.

[8] As for non-renewable resources, like fossil fuels and minerals, their use reduces the stock available for future generations. But this does not mean that such resources should not be used. In general the rate of depletion should take into account the criticality of that resource, the availability of technologies for minimizing depletion, and the likelihood of substitutes being available. Thus land should not be degraded beyond reasonable recovery. With minerals and fossil fuels, the rate of depletion and the emphasis on recycling and economy of use should be calibrated to ensure that the resource does not run out⑨ before acceptable substitutes are available.

[9] Development tends to simplify ecosystems and to reduce their diversity of species. And species, once extinct, are not renewable. The loss of plant and animal species can greatly limit the options of future generations; so sustainable development requires the conservation of plant and animal species.

[10] So-called free goods like air and water are also resources. The raw materials and energy of production processes are only partly converted to useful products. The rest comes out as wastes.⑩ Sustainable development requires that the adverse impacts on the quality of air, water, and other natural elements be minimized so as to sustain theecosystem's overall integrity.

[11] In essence, sustainable development is a process of change in which the exploitation of resources, the direction of investments, the orientation of technological development, and institutional change are all in harmony and enhance both current and future potential to meet human needs and aspirations.⑪

New Words and Expressions

sustainable [sə'steinəbl]	a.	持续的
aspiration [æspə'reiʃən]	n.	渴望
legitimate [li'dʒitəmit]	a.	合法的
inequity [in'ekwity]	n.	不公平
endemic [en'demik]	a.	某地或某一人群所特有的
prone * [prəun]	a.	有……倾向的
be consistent with		与……一致
provided [prə'vaidid]	conj.	假如，倘若

coexist [kəuigˈzist]	v.	共存
equitable [ˈekwitəbl]	a.	公平的
deprivation [depriˈveiʃən]	n.	清贫
demographic [deməˈgræfik]	a.	人口（统计）的
in harmony with		与…相协调
compromise [ˈkɔmprəmaiz]	v.	危及，损害
marginalize [ˈmɑːdʒinəlaiz]	v.	无视，让靠边
ill-considered [ˈilkənˈsidəd]	a.	考虑欠周的，不明智的
diversion * [daiˈvəːʃən]	n.	转向
extraction * [ikˈstrækʃən]	n.	采掘
noxious [ˈnɔkʃəs]	a.	有害的
intervention [intəˈvenʃən]	n.	干涉
intact [inˈtækt]	a.	完整的
renewable [riˈnjuːəbl]	a.	可恢复的
regeneration * [ridʒenəˈreiʃən]	n.	再生
take … into account		考虑
criticality [kritiˈkæliti]	n.	临界（性，状态）
substitute [ˈsʌbstitjuːt]	n.	替代物
degrade [diˈgreid]	v.	退化
calibrate [ˈkælibreit]	v.	校正
diversity * [daiˈvəːsiti]	n.	多样性
extinct [ikˈstiŋkt]	a.	灭绝的
option * [ˈɔpʃən]	n.	选择
adverse [ˈædvəːs]	a.	不利的
orientation [ɔːrienˈteiʃən]	n.	定向，取向

Notes

①beyond their basic needs：除了这些基本需求以外；

"Beyond" here means "besides" or "except"。

Note：In this usage, "beyond" usually appears in a negative or interrogative sentence or a clause。

②be prone to：be liable to；be inclined to 易于……；倾向于……

Notice the fact that this phrase is followed by generally undesirable things such as accident, error, anger, idleness, superstition, etc.

③require meeting … and extending …

Here the predicate verb "require" can only be followed by a gerund, not an infinitive directly. We can never say "require to do …", but it is safe to say "require sb. or sth. to do …".

④have/show regard for: take into consideration; pay respectful attention to 考虑；关注。
⑤Sustainable development requires … within the bounds of …
within the bounds of: within the limits of 在……范围之内；(Ant.) beyond the bounds of: (反义) 在……范围之外。
Pay attention to the three attributive clauses in the sentence. They modify "values" and "consumption standards" respectively。
⑥marginalize: to omit, exclude, or ignore, especially by leaving on the fringes of society or isolating from the course of progress. 搁到一边而不予重视。
⑦Every ecosystem everywhere cannot be preserved intact。
This sentence can be paraphrased as follows:
Not every ecosystem everywhere can be preserved intact。
⑧In general: In most cases; Usually。
⑨run out: come to an end, so that there is no more. 枯竭。
⑩come out: 排出。
⑪In essence: Essentially; In its/one's nature 实质上。

Exercises

Reading Comprehension

I. Are these statements true (T) or false (F) according to the text?
1. A world in which poverty and inequity predominates will never be likely to achieve ecological perfection. ( )
2. Sustainable development has everything to do with reasonable consumption standards, those within the bounds of the ecological possible, as well as with economic growth in underdeveloped countries. ( )
3. Societies have to meet human needs both by increasing productive potential and by ensuring equitable opportunities for all so that high levels of productive activity and widespread poverty can exist together and endanger no environment. ( )
4. The direction of technological developments may solve some immediate problems but lead to even greater ones, which means that large sections of the population may benefit from ill-considered development. ( )
5. We cannot preserve any ecosystem intact at all because economic growth and development obviously involve changes in the physical ecosystem. ( )

II. Match Column A with Column B according to the text.

A | B
1. The major objective of development is. | a. a complex and interlinked ecosystem

2. Sustainable development requires
3. Living standards that go beyond the basic minimum depent on
4. In general, renewable resources need not be depleted
5. Most renewable resources are part of

b. the long-term sustainability of people's consumption standards.
c. meeting the basic needs of all and extending to all the opportunity to satisfy their as-pirations for a better life.
d. on condition that the rate of uses is within the limits of regeneration and natural growth.
e. the satisfaction of human needs and aspirations

Vocabulary

I. Fill in the blanks with the words or expressions given below. Change the form if necessary.

| degrade | genetic | calibrate | marginalize |
| deplete | recycle | orientation | |

1. A forest may be _____ in one part of a watershed and extended elsewhere, which is not a bad thing if the exploitation has been planned carefully.
2. Having been trained for one and a half years in a technical school, he has now been promoted from an office boy to a laboratory technician. His present job is _____ weighing apparatus.
3. One of the first to recognize the _____ of the environment and to voice a concern for nature was Thoreau. His solution to this eloquently stated concern was withdrawal, which was perhaps morally admirable but realistically ineffective.
4. Quite a number of schools in that country provide an _____ program for new students, which has become very popular with the parents as well as the students themselves.
5. Shopping-bag ladies in New York, who live in an isolated, mistrustful world of their own, are actually _____ by capitalist social system.

II. Complete each of the following statements with one of the four choices given below.
1. On January 1, 1970, then-President Nixon signed into law the National Environmental Policy Act, which declared a national policy to encourage productive and enjoyable harmony between people and their _____.
   A. environment
   B. encouragement
   C. institutions
   B. establishment
2. Plants and animals in their physical environment make up an _____. The study of such ecosystems is ecology.

  A. cosmos   B. ecosystem
  C. galaxy   C. universe

3. A decision is right when it tends to preserve the _____, stability, and beauty of the biotic community. It is wrong when it tends otherwise.
  A. entirety   B. entity
  C. integrity   D. unity

4. Like all vital issues, the environmental ethic will under go transformation as new data are made _____ and we humans are able to more rationally interpret and live with nature.
  A. accessible   B. advisable
  C. acceptable   D. available

5. Although this long-winded definition seems to cover all bases, it avoids classifying _____ from remotely located power plants as pollution.
  A. admission   B. mission
  C. remission   D. emission

Writing Summary Writing (3)

Direction: Read the text again and complete the following summary of the text. You need to add about 100 words.

Summary

  The satisfaction of human needs and aspirations is the major objective of development. Sustainable development requires meeting the basic needs of all and extending to all the opportunity to satisfy their aspirations for a better life. But consumption standards should be in proportion to ecological means. Sustainable development in developed countries requires the promotion of values that encourage reasonable consumption while in places where the basic human needs are not being met, it clearly requires economic growth. High levels of productive activity and wide-spread poverty can coexist, and can endanger the environment.

Reading Material A

Environmental Stress as a Source of Conflict

  Environmental stress is seldom the only cause of major conflicts within or among nations. Nevertheless, they can arise from the marginalization of sectors of the population and from ensuing violence.①

  This occurs when political processes are unable to handle the effects of environmental stress resulting, for example, from erosion and desertification. Environmental stress can thus be an important part of the web of causality associated with any conflict and can in some cases be catalytic.②

Poverty, injustice, environmental degradation, and conflict interact in complex and potent ways. One manifestation of growing concern to the international community is the phenomenon of "environmental refugees" The immediate cause of any mass movement of refugees may appear to be political upheaval and military violence. But the underlying causes often include the deterioration of the natural resource base and its capacity to support the population.

Wars have always compelled people to leave their homes and their lands, to become refugees. Also, the wars in our time have forced large numbers of people to leave their homelands, and we now have the phenomenon of environmental refugees.

In addition to the interrelated problems of poverty, injustice, and environmental stress, competition for non-renewable raw materials, land, or energy can create tension. It was the quest for raw materials that underlay much of the competition between colonial powers and the subjugation of their holdings.③ Conflicts in the Middle East inevitably contain the seeds of great power intervention and global conflagration, in part because of the international interest in oil.

As unsustainable forms of development push individual countries up against environmental limits, major differences in environmental endowment among countries, or variations in stocks of usable land and raw materials, could precipitate and exacerbate international tension and conflict. And competition for use of the global commons, such as ocean fisheries and Antarctica, or for use of more localized common resources in fixed supply, such as rivers and coastal waters, could escalate to the level of international conflict and so threaten international peace and security.

Global water use doubled between 1940 and 1980, and it is expected to double again by 2000, with two-thirds of the projected water use going to agriculture. Yet 80 countries, with 40 per cent of the world's population, already suffer serious water shortages. There will be growing competition for water for irrigation, industry, and domestic use. River water disputes have already occurred in North America, South America, South and Southeast Asia, Africa and the Middle East.

Environmental threats to security are now beginning to emerge on a global scale. The most worrisome of these stem from the possible consequences of global warming caused by the atmospheric build-up of carbon dioxide and other gases. Any such climatic change would quite probably be unequal in its effects, disrupting agricultural systems in areas that provide a large proportion of the world's cereal harvests and perhaps triggering mass population movements in areas where hunger is already endemic. Sea levels may rise during the first half of the next century enough to radically change the boundaries between coastal nations and to change the shapes and strategic importance of international waterways—effects both likely to increase international tensions. The climatic and sea-level changes are also likely to disrupt the breeding grounds of economically important fish species. Slowing, or adapting to, global warming is becoming an essential task to reduce the risks of conflict.④

Notes

①然而，重大冲突可能起因于对部分人口的漠视和由此而引起的暴力行为。
②因此，环境压力可能成为与冲突有关的因果关系网中的一个重要组成部分，并且在有些情况下还可能起了触媒作用。
③正是对原料的这种搜括导致殖民主义国家与它们所控制的殖民地之间的大量竞争。
④使全球性变暖的速度放慢或使人类对之逐步适应，这已变成一项减少冲突危险的至关重要的任务。

Reading Material B

Equity and the Common Interest

Sustainable development has been described here in general terms. How are individuals in the real world to be persuaded or made to act in the common interest? The answer lies partly in education, institutional development, and law enforcement. But many problems of resource depletion and environmental stress arise from disparities in economic and political power. An industry may get away with unacceptable levels of air and water pollution because the people who bear the brunt of it are poor and unable to complain effectively.① A forest may be destroyed by excessive felling because the people living there have no alternatives or because timber contractors generally have more influence than forest dwellers.

Ecological interactions do not respect the boundaries of individual ownership and political jurisdiction. Thus:

* In a watershed, the ways in which a farmer up the slope uses land directly affect runoff on farms downstream.

* The irrigation practices, pesticides, and fertilizers used on one farm affect the productivity of neighbouring ones, especially among small farms.

* The efficiency of a factory boiler determines its rate of emission of soot and noxious chemicals and affects all who live and work around it.

* The hot water discharged by a thermal power plant into a river or a local sea affects the catch of all who fish locally.

Traditional social systems recognized some aspects of this interdependence and enforced community control over agricultural practices and traditional rights relating to water, forests, and land.② This enforcement of the "common interest" did not necessarily impede growth and expansion though it may have limited the acceptance and diffusion of technical innovations.

Local interdependence has, if anything,③ increased because of the technology used in modern agriculture and manufacturing. Yet with this surge of technical progress, the growing "enclosure" of common lands, the erosion of common rights in forests and other resources, and the spread of commerce and production for the market, the responsibilities for decision making are being taken away from both groups and individuals.④ This shift is still under way in many developing countries.

It is not that there is one set of villains and another of victims.⑤ All would be better off if each person took into account the effect of his or her acts upon others. But each is unwilling to assume that others will behave in this socially desirable fashion, and hence all continue to pursue narrow self-interest. Communities or governments can compensate for this isolation through laws, education, taxes, subsidies, and other methods. Well-enforced laws and strict liability legislation can control harmful side effects. Most important, effective participation in decision-making processes by local communities can help them articulate and effectively enforce their common interest.

Interdependence is not simply a local phenomenon. Rapid growth in production has extended it to the international plane, with both physical and economic manifestations. There are growing global and regional pollution effects, such as in the more than 200 international river basins and the large number of shared seas.

The enforcement of common interest often suffers because areas of political jurisdictions and areas of impact do not coincide. Energy policies in one jurisdiction cause acid precipitation in another. The fishing policies of one state affect the fish catch of another. No supranational authority exists to resolve such issues, and the common interest can only be articulated through international cooperation.⑥

In the same way, the ability of a government to control its national economy is reduced by growing international economic interactions. For example, foreign trade in commodities makes issues of carrying capacities and resource scarcities an international concern.⑦ If economic power and the benefits of trade were more equally distributed, common interests would be generally recognized. But the gains from trade are unequally distributed, and patterns of trade in, say, sugar affect not merely a local sugar-producing sector, but the economies and ecologies of the many developing countries that depend heavily on this product.

Hence, our inability to promote the common interest in sustainable development is often a product of the relative neglect of economic and social justice within and amongst nations.

Notes

①get away with：(做了违章违法的事却) 逃避惩罚，逍遥法外；bear the brunt of：(在……面前) 首当其冲。
②enforce control over：对……实行强制性控制。
③if anything：说起来呢，要说呢。

④但是随着科技的迅猛发展,"圈地"趋势的日益增长,公众对森林和其他资源所拥有的权利的被侵犯,以及商业和商品生产的扩大,团体和个人都正在失去对决策所承担的责任。

⑤这意思并不是说有一帮子坏人和一群受害者。句中的 that 引导一个表示原因的从句。

⑥supranational：跨国的。

⑦… make issues of carrying capacities and resource scarcities an international concern.
…… 使承载能力和资源匮乏成为一个国际关心的问题。

UNIT TEN

Text   Assessment of Environmental Impacts

[1]   The primary goal of the EIA procedure is to predict any adverse (or beneficial) effects of a proposed project on the natural and urban environment. This is done so that measures can be taken to minimize or eliminate the harmful impacts when the project is implemented. The prediction or assessment of environmental impacts is not an easy task. It must be conducted by an interdisciplinary team, including civil engineers and technicians, urban planners, and biologists or ecologists. For large and complex projects, and particularly for sensitive environmental settings, the team may also include geologists, archaeologists, architects, and social scientists.

[2]   Certain environmental impacts can be evaluated directly and objectively. They are not really subject to conflicting subjective or personal opinions. ① For example, the expected increase in stormwater runoff due to the project can be computed and compared to the existing runoff rates and volumes. The effect of the increase on the site and on downstream properties may then be predicted. These effects might include flooding, soil erosion, and water pollution.

[3]   Air quality impacts can also be assessed using sophisticated mathematical models. Usually, emission of carbon monoxide from cars is of particular significance in land development projects; the increase in automobile traffic would contribute directly to this effect. ② Basic traffic engineering principles can be applied in order to estimate the increase in traffic, as a function of population density and land use. Using this information, along with data on existing air quality and prevailing weather conditions, the impact of the project on ambient air quality can be anticipated.

[4]   Impacts upon vegetation and wildlife are more difficult to evaluate objectively. Although it is relatively easy to estimate how many hectares or acres of woodland will be destroyed by the project, it is much more difficult to agree upon the value or importance of this impact. ③ Of course, if the project site is the last remaining woodland in an urban community, or if some of the trees are among an endangered species, the impacts would be considered more severe than otherwise. ④

[5]   It is important to distinguish between short-term impacts and longterm impacts. For example, the impacts of construction activities might include a temporary increase in neighborhood noise levels from the heavy machinery. But once the project is completed, these impacts cease; they are therefore considered short term. But the effect of the project on, say, runoff patterns and local aquifer recharge rates would not cease when construction is finished; these would be long-tern impacts. ⑤

[6]   Many procedures for conducting an environmental assessment have been developed over the years. They share the basic goal of providing a comprehensive and systematic environmental evaluation of the project, with the greatest degree of objectivity. These procedures range in

complexity from simple checklists to more complex "matrix" methods.⑥

[7]　In the checklist method, all potential environmental impacts for the various project alternatives are listed, and the anticipated magnitude of each impact is described qualitatively. For example, negative impacts can be indicated with minus signs. A small or moderate impact could be shown with, say, two minus signs (——), whereas a relatively more severe impact could be shown with three or four minus signs (————). Beneficial or positive impacts can be shown with plus (+) sign. If the environmental impact is not applicable for a particular project alternative, a zero (0) would be shown. Such a list would serve to present a visual overview of the assessment.

[8]　In the so-called matrix methods, an attempt is made to quantify or "grade" the relative impacts of the project alternatives and to provide a numerical basis for comparison and evaluation. The anticipated magnitude of each potential impact may be rated on a scale of, say, 0 to 10; the higher numbers may represent severe adverse impacts, whereas the lower numbers represent minor or negligible effects. Zero (0) would indicate no expected impact for a particular activity or environmental component.

[9]　Numerical weighting factors are also used in the matrix method, to indicate the relative importance of a particular impact. These weighting factors would be agreed upon by the assessment team, and would be site and project specific. For example, the impacts on groundwater quality may be considered more important in a particular area than impacts on air quality, particularly if the groundwater is a sole source of potable water. Groundwater quality could be assigned a relative importance or weight of, say, 0.5, compared to 0.2 for air quality.

[10]　Weighting factors can be multiplied by the respective impact magnitudes, to put each impact in perspective. For example, consider that impact on groundwater quality has a magnitude of 4 and the impact on air quality has a higher magnitude of 6.⑦ But after weighting the impacts (multiplying by the weighting factors), we see that the overall significance of the impact on water quality, $0.5 \times 4 = 2$, is more important or severe than the impact on air quality, $0.2 \times 6 = 1.2$. If the weighted impacts for all the listed items are added together, a composite score or environmental quality index can be obtained for each project alternative. The alternative with the lowest index would be the one that would cause the least harmful environmental impact, overall.

New Words and Expressions

EIA (Environmental Impact Assessment)		环境影响评价
procedure [prə'siːdʒə]	n.	程序
minimize ['minimaiz]	v.	将……减到最小程度
interdisciplinary [intə'disiplinəri]	a.	各学科之间的，多学科的
archaeologist [ɑːki'ɔlədʒist]	n.	考古学家
evaluate [i'væljuːeit]	v.	评估，评价

be subject to		受……制约
flooding ['flʌdiŋ]	n.	洪涝，水灾
prevailing [pri'veiliŋ]	a.	普遍的，主要的
anticipate [æn'tisipeit]	v.	期待
distinguish between		区分
objectivity [ˌɔbdʒek'tiviti]	n.	客观（性）
checklist ['tʃeklist]	n.	列表法
matrix * ['meitriks]	n.	矩阵
magnitude * ['mægnitjuːd]	n.	大小，数量
on a scale of		按……等级
weighting factor ['weitiŋfæktə]	n.	权重因子
specific [spe'sifik]	a.	特定的
in perspective		有透视效果的，可直观的
composite * ['kɔmpəzit]	a.	综合的
index ['indeks]	n.	索引

Notes

①be subject: be contingent or conditional upon 受制于……

②be of particular significance: be particularly significant.

③to agree upon: to have or share the same opinion about 就……取得一致意见。

④… or if some of the trees are among an endangered species, the impacts would be considered more severe than otherwise.
　be among …: be included in …; 列于……之中；归属于……
　than otherwise: than in some other way 比起其他情况下。

⑤but the effect of the project on, say, runoff patterns …
　say: suppose 假定，姑且说。

⑥range from A to B: vary from A to B 在 A 到 B 的范围内变化。

⑦consider that …: consider the fact that ….

Exercises

Reading Comprehension

Ⅰ. Are these statements true (T) or false (F) according to the text?

1. The primary goal of the EIA procedure is to determine any adverse (or beneficial) effects of a proposed project on the natural and urban environment.　　　　　　（　　）

2. The prediction or assessment of environmental impacts is not too difficult a task, for it must be conducted by an interdisciplinary team. ( )
3. Certain environmental impacts can be evaluated directly and objectively. They are not really conditional on conflicting subjective or personal opinions. ( )
4. In the matrix methods, all potential environmental impacts for the various project alternatives are listed, and the anticipated magnitude of each impact is described qualitatively. ( )
5. The numerical weighting factors in the matrix methods would be agreed upon by the assessment team, and would be site and project specific. ( )

Ⅱ. Match Column A with Column B according to the text.

A	B
1. Certain environmental impacts can be evaluated	a. from simple checklists to more complex "matrix" methods.
2. The effects of the increase in stormwater runoff on the site and on downstream properties might include	b. in a direct and objective way.
3. It is important to distinguish	c. the one that would cause the least harmful environmental impacts, overall.
4. The procedures for conducting an environmental assessment range in complexity	d. flooding, soil erosion, and water pollution.
5. The alternative with the lowest index would be	e. between short-term impacts and long-term impacts.

Vocabulary

Ⅰ. Fill in the blanks with the words or expressions given below. Change the form if necessary.

implement	be subject to	describe	evaluate
potable	function	in perspective	

1. The Council on Environmental Quality (CEQ) assists the President in _____ environmental problems and determining the best solutions to these problems.
2. The impacts on groundwater quality may be considered more important than impacts on air quality, particularly if the groundwater is a sole source of _____ water.
3. The houses don't seem to be _____ in this drawing of yours, I dare say.
4. This is done so that measures can be taken to minimize or eliminate the harmful impacts when the project _____.

5. When I say that they are taken for granted, I mean that nobody needs to _____ them or write them down or try self-consciously to teach them to children.

II. For each blank in the following sentences choose the best answer from the choices given below.

1. I have to warn you that she is playing up her strong points and _____ her weaknesses.
   A. materializing B. minimizing
   C. modernizing   D. maximizing

2. If one could _____ joy, it is likely that for me it would be a new car.
   A. beautify   B. qualify
   C. notify   D. quantify

3. When we say we are all _____ to the laws of nature, we mean that nobody can free himself from the force which controls the world independently of people.
   A. subject   B. subjective
   C. objective D. object

4. The "Environmental Impact Statement" has much to do with a project. _____, each project funded by the federal government must be accompanied with an EIS.
   A. In one respect   B. In some degree
   C. In other words   D. In a sense

5. The anticipated magnitude of each potential impact may be rated _____ 0 to 10.
   A. on a scale of   B. within the limits of
   C. in the scope of   D. in the ratio of

Writing   Summary Writing (4)

Direction: Read the text of Unit Ten again and write a summary of the text in about 200 words.

Reading Material A

Environmental Impact

On January 1, 1970, then-President Nixon signed into law the National Environmental Policy Act, which declared a national policy to encourage productive and enjoyable harmony between people and their environment.① This law established the Council on Environmental Quality (CEQ), which monitors the environmental effects of federal activities and assists the President in evaluating environmental problems and determining the best solutions to these problems. But few people realized the National Environmental Policy Act (NEPA) contained a real sleeper article: Section 102 (2) (C), which requires federal agencies to evaluate the consequences of any proposed action on the environment: ②

The Congress authorizes and directs that, to the fullest extent possible: (1) the policies, regulations, and public laws of the United States shall be interpreted and administered in accordance with the policies set forth in this chapter,③ and (2) all agencies of the Federal Government shall include in every recommendation or report on proposals for legislation and other major Federal actions significantly affecting the quality of the human environment, a detailed statement by the responsible official on—④

1. the environmental impact of the proposed action,

2. any adverse environmental effects which cannot be avoided should the proposal be implemented,⑤

3. alternatives to the proposed action,

4. the relationship between local short-term uses of man's environment and the maintenance and enhancement of long-term productivity, and

5. any irreversible and irretrievable commitments of resources which would be involved in the proposed action should it be implemented.

In other words, each project funded by the federal government must be accompanied with an "Environmental Impact Statement" (EIS). Such a published statement must assess in detail the potential environmental impacts of a proposed action and alternative actions. All federal agencies are required to prepare statements for projects and programs (a pro-grammatic EIS) under their jurisdiction. ⑥ Additionally, the agencies must generally follow a detailed and often lengthy public review of each EIS before proceeding with their projects and programs. ⑦

The original idea of the EIS is to introduce environmental factors into the decision-making machinery. The purpose of the EIS is not to provide justification for a construction project, but rather to introduce environmental concerns and have them discussed in public before the decision on a project is made. However, this objective is difficult toapply in practice. Historically, interest groups in and out of government articulated plans to their liking, the sum of which provided the engineer with a set of alternatives to be evaluated. ⑧ In many other instances, the engineer is left to create his own alternatives, or participate in a group decision-making process like the Delphi technique. ⑨ In either case there are normally one or two plans which, from the outset, seem emi-nently more feasible and reasonable, and these can be legitimatized by juggling time scales or standards of enforcement patterns just slightly and calling them alternatives (as they are in a limited sense). ⑩ As a result, non-decisions are made, i. e. , wholly different ways of perceiving the prob-lem and conceiving of solutions have been overlooked, and the primary objective of an EIS has been circumvented. Over the past few years, court decisions and guidelines by various agencies have, in fact, helped to mold this procedure for the development of environmental impact statements.

Ideally, an EIS must be thorough, interdisciplinary, and as quantitative as possible. The writing of an EIS involves three distinct phases: Inventory, assessment and evaluation. The first is a cataloging of environmentally susceptible areas, the second is the process of estimating the impact of the alternatives, and the last is the interpretation of these findings. the last is the inter pretation of these findings.

Notes

①On January 1,1970, then-President Nixon signed into law the National Environmental Policy Act, … 此句中宾语补足语 into law 置于宾语 the National Environmental Policy Act 之前。

②sleeper article：出人意料的条款。

③shall：（在条约，规章，法令等文件中表示义务或规定，一般用于第三人称）应该，必须；in accordance with：与……一致；按照。

④… all agencies of the Federal Government shall include in every recommendation or report on proposals for legislation and other major Federal actions significantly affecting the quality of the human environment, a detailed statement ….
a detailed statement 作 include 的宾语，动宾之间插入了 in 所引出的一个颇长的介词短语。

⑤should the proposal be implemented：if the proposal should be implemented.

⑥under their jurisdiction：在他们的（管辖）权限之内。

⑦proceeding with：开始着手。

⑧to their liking：合他们的心意，配他们的胃口；… the sum of which provided the engineer with a set of alternatives to be evaluated. 定语从句修饰 plans，其中 sum 义为"概要，要点"。

⑨the Delphi technique：特尔斐预测法（指在科技等领域通过归纳专家意见来预测未来的发展）。

⑪from the outset：从一开始。

Reading Material B

Environmental Assessment

The process of calculating projected effects that a proposed action or construction project will have on environmental quality is called environmental assessment.① It is necessary to develop a methodical, reproducible and reasonable method of evaluating both the effect of the proposed project and the effects of alternatives which may achieve the same ends but which may have different environmental impacts. A number of semiquantitative approaches have been used, among them the checklist, the interaction matrix, and the checklist with weighted rankings.②

Check-lists are listings of potential environmental impacts, both primary and secondary. Primary effects occur as a direct result of the proposed project, such as the effect of a dam on aquatic life. Secondary effects occur as an indirect result of the action. For example, an interchange for a highway will not directly affect a land area, but indirectly it will draw such establishments as service stations and quick food stores, thus changing land use patterns.

The checklist for a highway project could be divided into three phases: planning, construction and operation. During planning, consideration is given to environmental effects of the highway route and the acquisition and condemnation of property.[3] The construction phase checklist will include displacement of people, noise, soil erosion, water pollution and energy use. Finally, the operation phase will list direct impacts due to noise, air pollution, water pollution due to runoff, energy use, etc., and indirect impacts due to regional development, housing, lifestyle, and economic development.

The checklist technique thus simply listststs all of the pertinent factors; then the magnitude and importance of the impacts are estimated. The estimation of impact is quantified by establishing an arbitrary scale,[4] such as

0 = no impact
1 = minimal impact
2 = small impact
3 = moderate impact
4 = significant impact
5 = severe impact

This scale can be used to estimate both the magnitude and the importance of a given item on the checklist. The numbers can then be combined, and a quantitative measurement of the severity of environmental impact for any given alternative estimated.[5]

Example:

A landfill is to be placed in a floodplain of a river. Estimate the impact using the checklist technique.

First the items impacted are listed, then a judgment concerning both importance and magnitude of the impact is made. In this example, the items are only a sample of the impacts one would normally consider. The numbers in this example are then multiplied and the sum obtained. Thus:

Potential Impact	Importance × Magnitude
Groundwater contamination	5 × 5 = 25
Surface water contamination	4 × 3 = 12
Odor	1 × 1 = 1
Noise	1 × 2 = 2
Total	40

This total of 40 can then be compared to totals calculated for alternative courses of action. In the checklist technique most variables must be subjectively judged. Further, it is difficult to predict future conditions such as land-use pattern changes or changes in lifestyle. Even with these drawbacks, how-ever, this method is often used by engineers in governmental agencies and consulting firms, mainly due to its simplicity.

The interaction matrix technique is a two-dimensional listing of existing characteristics and conditions of the environment and detailed proposed actions which may impact the environment. For example, the characteristics of water might be defined as:

* surface
* ocean
* underground
* quantity
* temperature
* groundwater rechange
* snow, ice and permafrost

Similar characteristics must also be defined for air, land, and other important considerations.

Opposite these listings in the matrix are lists of possible actions.⑥ In our example, one such action is labeled resource extraction, which could include the following actions:

* blasting and drilling
* surface extraction
* subsurface extraction
* well drilling
* dredging
* timbering
* commercial fishing and hunting

The interactions, as in the checklist technique, are measured in terms of magnitude and the importance.⑦ The magnitudes are represented by the extent of the interaction between the environmental characteristics and the proposed actions, and typically can be measured.⑧ The importance of the interaction, on the other hand, is often a judgment call on the part of the engineer.

If an interaction is present, for example, between underground water and well drilling, a diagonal line is placed in the block. Numbers can then be assigned to the interaction, with 1 being a small and 5 being a large magnitude or importance, and these placed in the blocks with magnitude above and importance below. Appropriate blocks are filled in, using a great deal of judgment and personal bias, and then are summed over a line, thus giving a numerical grade for either the proposed action or environmental characteristics.

Notes

①projected effects: 预测的影响。

②weighted rankings：权重等级。
③the acquisition and condemnation of property：地产的获得和征用。
④an arbitrary scale：一张任意的级别表。
⑤在 estimated 前省略了 can then be。
⑥本句为倒装句，表语 Opposite these listings in the matrix 被置于句首予以突出。
⑦in terms of：根据……；用……的措辞（话语，字眼）。
⑧typically：一般地，通常。

UNIT ELEVEN

Text Man and His Environment

[1]   Man is an animal. We are similar in anatomy and physiology to our mammalian cousins and, like all other animals, we must eat food and breathe air to survive. ① Nevertheless, we are different, but this difference lies in accomplishment and behaviour. ② We possess not only a genetic inheritance which determines our animal nature, but also a cultural inheritance of knowledge and custom transmitted by language and symbols. As with other animals, however, we occupy a habitat which exists in both space and time and forms our environment. ③ Although this is a physical, chemical and biological environment, it is also a cultural environment with social, political, economic and technological dimensions.

[2]   This twofold distinction is reflected in a dichotomy in the study of Man-environment relationships, with the natural sciences concerned with the natural environment, and the social sciences and applied sciences concerned with the cultural environment. ④ Geography—the study of Man's interaction with his environment—reflects this dichotomy. In reality these two components of environment cannot be fully under-stood in isolation from Man and his interactions with it. But natural environment can be considered in anything but a superficial way, we must understand that environment and, for this reason, this book is concerned mainly with the natural environment—its physical, chemical and biological components, the relationships between these components and those between them and Man. ⑤

[3]   How should we begin this formidable task? We could start by taking the environment to pieces to see what it is composed of and how it works, much as we might dismantle a piece of machinery. ⑥ This process can be called the analysis of the environment. It is one of the traditional approaches of science, whereby different sciences (or different branches of a science) separate different types of pieces and study them in isolation. ⑦ Thus, oceanography is concerned with the sea, meteorology with the air, hydrology with water, geology with rocks, and biology with organisms; physics and chemistry take in all of these things but in terms of smaller, more fundamental pieces.

[4]   The problem with this approach becomes apparent when trying to put the environment back together again: when turning from analysis to synthesis, the selected pieces have been looked at in different ways, with different degrees of rigour, and different terminologies have been developed, so we may no longer recognise the pieces as being part of the original whole. The process of reassembling the pieces becomes more difficult because we can no longer remember how they fitted together, or we failed to find out before we dismantled the environment. Also, some of the pieces may have been overlooked in the process of analysis, because none of the specialist sciences regarded them as their concern. The real problem, therefore, is the lack of any true integration. What are the links between a kingfisher, a developing thunder

cloud, a breaking wave and a landslide? Much may be known about each of these pieces, but how do they fit together into the environmental jigsaw puzzle? You might ask whether it really matters. ⑧ Is it necessary to synthesise, to reassemble the pieces, as long as our knowledge of them is pursued in sufficient depth?⑨ These questions can perhaps best be answered visually.

[5]   Our finite natural environment represents not only living space and resources for Man and his animal needs but, because Man is a cultural animal, it must also provide for our developing cultural needs. As our cultural complexity, social organisation and technological capacity have increased through time, we have made progressively greater demands on the environment. Also, as cultural development has made us progressively less dependent on our immediate environment, so the nature of our perception of it, and of our interactions with it, have changed. We have exploited, modified and damaged or destroyed it to an extent not equalled by any other animal. In the 20th century our demands have begun to outstrip the capacity of the environment, and it is our ability to manage intelligently, protect and conserve the environment that has become paramount. It is also the recognition of this need that has precipitated the increased awareness of, and support for, conservation policies at all levels. However, before we can manage our environment we must understand it. It is this urgent need more than any philosophical consideration that has given added impetus to the integrated study of Man's natural environment. More than this, it has emphasised the fact that the separation of the natural from the cultural is not only unreal, but also dangerous. Our interaction with the natural environment can only be understood with reference to our perception of it and behavioural response to it, both of which are conditioned by our complex cultural environment.⑩

New Words and Expressions

anatomy [ə'nætəmi]	n.	解剖
physiology [fizi'ɔlədʒi]	n.	生理学
mammalian [mæ'meiliən]	a.	哺乳类的
cousin ['kʌzən]	n.	堂（表）兄（妹）
accomplishment [ə'kɔmpliʃmənt]	n.	成就
inheritance [in'heritəns]	n.	继承，遗产（传）
dichotomy [dai'kɔtəmi]	n.	二分法，二歧法
component [kəm'pəunənt]	n.	成分
isolation * [aisə'leiʃən]	n.	孤立，分离
superficial [sju:pə'fiʃəl]	a.	表面的
formidable * ['fɔ:midəbl]	a.	可怕的，棘手的
take ... to pieces		拆开，拆散
be composed of		由……组成
dismantle [dis'mæntl]	v.	拆开，拆散

whereby [wɛə'bai]	ad.	藉以，由此	
oceanography [ˌəuʃjə'nɔgrəfi]	n.	海洋学	
rigour ['rigə]	n.	精确，严密	
overlook [əuvə'luk]	v.	忽视	
integration * [inti'greiʃən]	n.	集成	
kingfisher ['kiŋfiʃ]	n.	翠鸟	
landslide ['lændslaid]	n.	滑坡	
jigsaw puzzle ['dʒigsɔːpʌzl]	n.	拼板玩具	
finite ['fainait]	a.	有限的	
perception [pə'sepʃən]	n.	感知	
paramount ['pærəmaunt]	a.	至高无上的	
impetus ['impitəs]	n.	动力，刺激	

Notes

①We are similar in anatomy and physiology to our mammalian cousins and … "be similar in some respect to sb. or sth. else"：在某个方面与其他人或物有相似之处。

②lie in：exist in 存在。

③As with other animals：As in the case of other animals 就如其他动物的情况一样。

④… with the natural sciences concerned with the natural environment, and the social sciences and applied sciences concerned with the cultural environment.

分词独立结构（nominative absolute），作补充说明。

⑤anything but：not at all; far from 根本不，决不，远非。

⑥to take sth. to pieces：dismantle; separate sth. into parts 拆开，拆散。

⑦whereby：by means of which; according to which 藉此，由此。

⑧matter：be important 重要的，举足轻重的。

⑨… as long as our knowledge of them is pursued in sufficient depth?

This sentence can be paraphrased as follows：

"… if our knowledge of them is gained through continual efforts and in sufficient depth ? "

⑩with reference to：in connection with 与……相关联。

Exercises

Reading Comprehension

Ⅰ. Are these statements true (T) or false (F) according to the text?

1. We possess both a genetic and a cultural inheritance, which respectively determines our animal nature and develops our knowledge and custom. （　）

2. This twofold distinction is reflected in a dichotomy in the study of Man-environment relationships, with the social and applied sciences concerned with the natural environment,

and the natural sciences concerned with the cultural environment. ( )
3. Our infinite natural environment not only represents living space and resources for Man and his animal needs, but provides for his developing cultural needs. ( )
4. We can take the environment to pieces to see what it is composed of and how it works. And the process of reassembling the pieces is a piece of cake because we can well remember how they fitted together. ( )
5. It is this urgent need rather than any philosophical consideration that has given added impetus to the integrated study of Man's natural envi- ronment. ( )

II. Match Column A with Column B according to the text.

A	B
1. The problem with this appraoch becomes apparent	a. and this difference lies in accomplishment and behaviour.
2. Some of the pieces may have been overlooked in the process of analysis	b. when trying to put the environment back together again.
3. It is our ability to manage, protect and conserve the environment	c. with reference to our perception of it and behavioural response to it.
4. Our interaction with the natural environment can only be understood	d. that has become paramount.
5. We are similar in anatomy and physiology to our mammalian cousins. Nevertheless, we are different,	e. because none of the specialist sciences regarded them as their concern.

Vocabulary

I. Fill in the blanks with the words or expressions given below. Change the form if necessary.

lie in	more than	take to pieces	dismantle
outstrip	interaction	transmit	

1. As we know, the power which the engine develops _____ to the wheels of the car.
2. In studies of the consequences of air pollution there is a general tendency to treat the living systems which they affect as though they were discrete and separate rather than _____.
3. A great deal of effort goes into determining how much and what type of pollution _____ the atmosphere.
4. If one considers the real world where atmospheric pollutants nearly always exist _____ as mixturesas single chemicals, the list of possible consequences upon different biological systems expands alarmingly.

5. With the rising of the living standards of the people, the demand for household electrical appliances _____ supply last year in our country.

II. For each blank in the following sentences choose the best answer from the choices given below.

1. The branch of science which is concerned with the sea is _____.
   A. hydrology   B. oceanography
   C. geology   D. meteorology

2. In the United States _____ problems affecting asthmatics have been reported in New Orleans.
   A. same   B. similar
   C. single   D. alike

3. Before we can _____ our environment, we must understand it.
   A. do away with   B. succeed
   C. ignore   D. manage

4. Scientists have _____ the fact that the separation of the natural from the cultural is not only unreal, but also dangerous.
   A. emphasized   B. sympathized
   C. synthesized   D. synchronized

5. We failed to find out how they fitted together before we _____ the environment.
   A. dismounted   B. disposed
   C. dismantled   D. dispossessed

Writing   Abstract Writing (1)

An abstract is a greatly condensed version of a piece of writing. An abstract is different from a summary in that it is much shorter than a summary and so is called "summary of a summary". An abstract only lists the topics without supplying detailed information. Be sure to include the following items if there are any.

   a. The problems/processes/phenomena/mechanism involved or described;
   b. The scope of work;
   c. Major conclusions/recommendations.

Directions: The following is an abstract of the text of Unit Eleven (no more than 140 words) and there are eight words missing. Please fill in the blanks with some of the words given. (12 words given, and 8 blanks to be filled)

Abstract

Man is an animal, and a cultural animal at that. We possess a cultural __1__ of knowledge and custom. Thus ours is an environment cultural as well as physical, chemical and biological. This __2__ distinction is reflected in dichotomy in the study of Man-environment __3__.

We are concerned mainly with the natural environment and taking it to __4__, we start to see what it is composed of and how it works. The real problem with this traditional __5__ is the lack of any true __6__. We can't see clearly the relationships between its components and those between them and Man.

Therefore, before we can __7__ our environment we must understand it. It is this urgent need that has given added impetus to the integrated study of Man's natural environment, which is __8__ by our complex cultural one.

| manage | interaction | integration | attitude | inheritance | conditioned |
| approach | relative | twofold | relationships | slices pieces | |

Reading Material A

A Preface to Air Pollution and Acid Rain

Pollution has always been an emotive topic irrespective of whether it occurs in the air, on land or at sea.① In the latter half of this century much attention has been drawn to air pollution caused by modern methods of communication although some cradles of the Industrial Revolution must have experienced local levels of high pollution quite unimaginable by present standards and we must never forget that such progress upon which our society is built was bought at great cost to the health and the immediate surroundings of those involved.②

Campaigns against the more widespread effects of atmospheric pollution are constantly mounted by the media, of which the printed word is only a part; meanwhile scientific knowledge still advances on all fronts. This greater appreciation allows a more fundamental understanding of the consequences of pollution upon the whole environment and all those who live in it, which includes the polluters, the polluted, the media and the researchers—hence the emotion.③

If one turns to books for information on the subject the problem is not the lack of it but the abundance.④ On the topics of air pollution, library shelves in centres of learning are full of scientific journals and perhaps a hundred books of expert opinion on one or more of the various aspects involved.⑤ The difficulty is making out what it all means and what the consequences are to all of us and to the world in which we live. One could turn to oppreciations by journalists who thrive on sensationalism to make their points, valid though some of them may be.⑥ This may be suitable for socio-politico-economic appreciations which avoid the scientific fundamentals. If on the other hand a scientific understanding of the background mechanisms, without the need to become an expert in each area, is desired then there are very few sources to rely upon. Very often texts tend to concentrate on one aspect of air pollution without linking them together. This book attempts to do this and at the same time show how acid rain is a part of atmospheric pollution, how the complicated chemistry of the atmosphere is a series of interrelated reactions, and how the components involved interact with others, with vegetation, with microbes and with ourselves at the molecular level.

In studies of the consequences of air pollution there is a general tendency to treat the living systems which they affect as though they were discrete and separate rather than interactive. A great deal of effort goes into determining how much and what type of pollution exists in the atmosphere, by what means it moves around and in describing the outward changes of living systems: how much they change colour or show leaf defects if they are plants, or what types of lung ailments they have if they are humans. ⑦ One then is left with an immense catalogue of ills and ailments which gets longer as time passes. Indeed, if one considers the real world where atmospheric pollutants nearly always exist as mixtures rather than as single chemicals, the list of possible consequences upon different biological systems expands alarmingly. ⑧ The only sensible course of action is to delve into the basic mechanisms by which each of the different pollutants enters and attacks living systems, to examine how they in turn resist change and, if they fail, to assess the nature and consequences of metabolic changes within all living systems. To do this, even as an expert, one needs to be a combination of a physicist, chemist, biochemist, physiologist, microbiologist, animal toxicologist and plant pathologist. ⑨ Nevertheless, there are a number of broad principles that govern the effects of atmospheric pollutants upon living systems which can be gathered together and that is what this book is all about. It attempts to examine these mechanisms in plants and animals in rather more detail than other books on air pollution. This is the only way to make sense of the mass of information concerning the visible and outward changes upon the variety of living systems which have been ascribed to atmospheric pollutants—especially if we are ever to progress to an understanding of how combinations of pollutants interact with each other in the real world. ⑩ It is therefore unavoidable that a prior understanding of basic chemistry is necessary in order to appreciate these mechanisms.

The major harm caused by air pollutants, locally and globally, is ulti-mately shown as a lack of growth of plants or poorer health of animals. This may mean many different things have happened because of difficulties with the regulation of normal events that go on in living cells. It has been said that "the cell is a self-centered comfort machine" which might be an overstatement but the principle of regulatory events acting in concert together to maintain a balance of cellular activities within pre-set limits has been well known to physiologists for a long time as "homeostasis" or "the wisdom of the body". ⑪

Notes

①irrespective of: 不论，不顾；whether 引出的是介词 of 的宾语从句。
②at great cost to the health and the immediate surroundings of those involved.

at great cost to: at great cost of 以……为代价; of those involved: of those people involved 所涉及到的人们的……

③appreciation: 评定, 判断。

④turn to: 求助于, 求教于, 查阅。

⑤centres of learning: 学术中心 (指科学院, 高等院校, 研究机构等)。

⑥… valid though some of them may be.

倒装句, 意为"虽然他们的某些论点可能是站得住脚的"。

⑦A great deal of effort goes into determining …

动名词 determining 后跟 4 个由连接代词 what 或连接副词 how 所引出的宾语从句。

⑧rather than: more than 而不(是)。

⑨To do this: 作目的状语。

⑩to make sense of: 理解, 弄懂。

⑪be known as …: 被称为……。

Reading Material B

Effects of Air Pollution on Health

Much of our knowledge of the effects of air pollution on people comes from the study of acute air pollution episodes. As previously noted, the two most famous episodes occurred in Donora, Pennsylvania, and in London, England. In both episodes the illness appeared to be chemical irritation of the respiratory tract. The weather circumstances were also similar in that a high pressure system with an inversion layer was present.① An inversion is a layer of warm air aloft which prevents the pollutants from escaping and diluting vertically. In addition, inversions are usually accompanied by low surface winds leading to reduced horizontal dilution of pollutants.

In both episodes, the pollutants affected a specific segment of the public—those individuals already suffering from diseases of the cardio-respiratory system. Another observation of great importance is that it was not possible to blame the adverse effects on any one pollutant.② This observation puzzled the investigators (industrial hygiene experts) who were accustomed to studying industrial problems where one could usually relate health effects to a specific pollutant.③ Today, after many years of study, it is thought that the health problems during the episodes were attributable to the combined action of a particulate matter (solid or liquid particles) and sulfur dioxide, a gas. No one pollutant by itself, however, could have been responsible.

Another episode of historical significance is one involving the accidental release of hydrogen sulfide gas from a refinery at Poza Rica, Mexico, in November 1950. Although the Poza Rica episode is not community air pollution in its usual sense, it is an important example of air pollution which resulted from an industrial accident. The accident occurred when the processes in a refinery went astray and a large quantity of hydrogen sulfide gas escaped. ④ H_2S is a heavy, poisonous gas, and when it. escaped, it hugged the ground around the refinery and crept into nearby homes In all, 22 persons died and 320 became ill.

Another historically important air pollution health effect is "Yokohama Asthma."⑤ Following the Second World War an unusual number of American military personnel and their dependents residing in the Yokohama area of Japan required treatment for attacks of an "asthma-like" condition. These attacks were first noted in the winter of 1948. Investigation showed that the attacks were coincident with conditions of low wind velocity and resulting high pollution levels. Interestingly, only people who were heavy smokers were affected, and the only solution to the problem was reassignment of the victims to another location.

In the United States similar problems affecting asthmatics have been reported in New Orleans. Studies of patients admitted for emergency treatment for asthma attacks were conducted over a period of years at New Orleans' Charity Hospital. These studies indicated that a sharply increased number of asthmatics required emergency treatment when winds of low speed from the south and southwest prevailed. Investigation further showed that the occurrence of these attacks was associated with a burning dump southwest of New Orleans. A measure of the severity of this problem is illustrated by the October 1962 episode which caused the deaths of nine asthmatics and required emergency treatment for 300.

Recently, several air pollution episodes have taken place in New York City and other metropolitan areas. The first well documented episode occurred in November 1953, and air pollution alerts occur every year. The Morbidity and mortality data from these episodes have demonstrated a statistical association between public health and the occurrence of temperature inversions and the resulting increased levels of particulate matter and sulfur dioxide.⑥

Except for these episodes, scientists have very little information from which to evaluate the health effects of air pollution. ⑦ Laboratory studies with animals are of some help, but the step from a rat to a man (anatomically speaking) is quite large.

Notes

①in that：because 因为。
②to blame A on B：把 A 归咎于 B。
③… who were accustomed to studying industrial problems where one could usually relate health effects to a specific pollutant.
　　be accustomed to：习惯于……（注意：后跟名词，代词或动名词）；to relate A to B：将 A 与 B 联系起来。
④go astray：出差错。
⑤"Yokohama Asthma"：（日本）"横滨哮喘"。
⑥The morbidity and mortality data …：有关发病率和死亡率的数据（资料）。
⑦… from which to evaluate the health effects of air pollution.
　　介词 from 引出的动词不定式短语，在这里用作定语修饰前面的名词 information.

UNIT TWELVE

Text Biological Design of Activated Sludge

[1] The purpose of activated sludge or any biological waste treatment process is to remove the organic matter as completely as possible from the raw wastes with the least expenditure of time and funds. The nature of the raw wastes and their flow characteristics are set and the treatment process must be designed around them. Only in a few industrial situations can the wastes be discharged to a surge tank for leveling out the organic strength and flow. ①

[2] One of the basic problems with conventional activated sludge has been the variable predomination of the microorganisms. The organic matter in the raw wastes stimulates certain bacteria species in the aeration tank. As the organic matter is removed and the microorganisms pass into the endogenous phase, the primary group of microorganisms which were responsible for stabilizing the organic matter die off and lyse. ② A second group of bacteria utilize the lysed products of the primary group and predominate at the end of the aeration tank. When the sludge is returned to the head end of the aeration tank, the primary group of bacteria have to grow all over again. With a long aeration period the number of primary bacteria can drop off to a level that requires a long recovery period to handle sudden increases in waste flow or strength. This is very important in activated sludges treating strange industrial wastes, and it is one of the reasons activated sludge is slow in responding to shock loadings.

[3] The only way to keep the bacteria species uniform is to keep the organic level uniform. ③ This is impossible to do with a variable waste, but the variations can be kept to a minimum. ④ The F : M ratio is the key to bacterial growth. A high F : M ratio has been shown to yield rapid growth while a low F : M ratio depresses the apparent growth. In conventional activated sludge, both F and M are constantly changing, with the F : M ratio going from a maximum to a minimum with each cycle. If the raw wastes were diluted with the entire contents of the aeration tank as in complete mixing, the aeration tank would become a large surge tank, damping out wide fluctuations in F. With complete mixing in the aeration tank, F becomes a minimum value with minimum fluctuations and the microbial activity at any point in the tank is the same as at any other point. The microbial variation over the normal growth cycle tends to approach a point function rather than a wide band as in conventional activated sludge. ⑤ Thus it is that the complete mixing system offers the most advantages from a microbiological standpoint and the least disadvantages. ⑥

[4] In any waste disposal problem the organic load is fixed so that the F : M ratio can be varied only by adjusting M. It is possible to operate at any point on the bacterial growth curve by adjusting the F : M ratio. It has already been pointed out that certain phases of the growth curve do not yield satisfactory operations as far as waste treatment is concerned. With complete mixing systems the operations will range at some point in the declining growth phase.

[5]   One of the most recent innovations has been the operation of complete mixing systems at the lower end of the declining growth phase where sludge increase is minimal. The excess sludge is allowed to be discharged with the effluent without causing nuisance conditions. The ratio of act-ive solids to inactive solids in the effluent would have to be the same as it is in the mixed liquor. It is doubtful if total oxidation will have much application to the disposal of domestic sewage unless the solids are removed at periodic intervals, as they cannot be discharged with the effluent.

[6]   On the other hand, a soluble industrial waste can be operated close to total oxidation with only a slow build-up of inert solids. The excess solids in the effluent would be in direct proportion to the organic matter being treated with approximately 10 to 13 percent of the organic matter appearing in the effluent as inert solids.

[7]   In most instances activated sludge must have a means of solids separation and wasting. One of the major problems still to be solved with activated sludge is the efficient removal and concentration of the sludge from the liquid. Current methods depend upon gravity separation and are limited in their ability to concentrate the sludge.

[8]   If the sludge is predominantly active, it will require further stabilization before it can be ultimately disposed of.⑦ Normally, anaerobic digestion is used for sludge stabilization but recently in small systems aerobic digestion has accomplished the same purpose. Once again economics determines which process should be used since both will produce a stable material which can be dewatered by filtration. If the sludge is predominantly inactive, there is no need for further stabilization and the sludge can be dewatered directly.

New Words and Expressions

expenditure [iks'pendiʃə]	n.	花费
surge tank ['sə:dʒtæŋk]	n.	调节池
level out	v.	平衡，衡定
conventional [kən'venʃənl]	a.	常规的，传统的
variable ['vɛəriəbl]	a.	变化的，可变的
predomination [pridɔmi'neiʃən]	n.	支配，优势
predominantly [pri'dɔminəntli]	ad.	占优势地，据支配地位地
aeration tank [ɛə'reiʃən tæŋk]	n.	曝气槽
aeration period [ɛəreiʃən piəriəd]	n.	曝气周期
endogenous [en'dɔdʒənəs]	a.	内源的，内部产生的
endogenous phase [en'dɔdʒənəs feiz]	n.	内源期
die off	v.	衰减，相继死亡
lyse [lais]	v.	细胞衰败
drop off	v.	减少，下降
respond to	v.	对……作出反应

shock loadings [ˈʃɔk ləudiŋz]	n.	冲击荷载
cycle [ˈsaikl]	n.	周期
growth cycle [ˈgrəuθ saikl]	n.	生长周期
growth curve [ˈgrəuθ kə:v]	n.	生长曲线
damp out	v.	减少
standpoint [ˈstændpɔint]	n.	立足点
as far as … be concerned		就……而言
decline [diˈklain]	v.	衰败
in direct proportion to		与……成正比
gravity [ˈgræviti]	n.	重力
gravity separation [ˈgræviti sepəˈreiʃən]	n.	重力分离
stabilization [steibilaiˈzeiʃən]	n.	稳定（性）

Notes

①若 only 引出的状语置于句首，则该句须用倒装语序。
②be responsible for：作为……的原因；对……应负责任。
③to keep sth. uniform：保持……均匀。在此结构中 uniform 作宾语补足语。
④to do with：to deal with 处理，处置。
⑤tends to …：倾向于……；有助于……。
⑥Thus it is that the complete mixing system offers the most advantages …
　在上述结构中，代词 it 为无具体意义的主语，可理解为泛指的"情况"，"事实"等。
⑦be disposed of：被处理（置）。

Exercises

Reading Comprehension

I. Are these statements true (T) or false (F) according to the text?

1. The purpose of activated sludge or any biological waste treatment process is to remove the inorganic matter as completely as possible from the raw wastes.　　　　　　　　　　　　　(　)
2. One of the basic problems with conventional activated sludge has been the changeable predomination of the microorganisms.　　　　　　　　　　　　(　)
3. In any waste disposal problem the organic load is fixed so that the F∶M ratio can be varied only by adjusting F.　　　　　　　　　　　　(　)
4. The excess sludge is allowed to be discharged with the effluent without causing inconvenient conditions.　　　　　　　　　　　　(　)
5. If the sludge is predominantly active, it will require further stabilization after it can be ul-

timately disposed of.

II. Match Column A with Column B according to the text.

A

1. The primary group of microorganisms were
2. The only way to keep the bacteria species uniform is
3. One of the most recent innovations has been
4. A soluble industrial waste can be operated close to total oxidation
5. Both anaerobic and aerobic will produce a stable material which can be dewatered by filtration, so which process should be used depends on

B

a. with only a slow build-up of inert solids
b. the operation of complete mixing system at the lower end of the declining growth phase where sludge increase is minimal.
c. economics.
d. responsible for stabilizing the organic matter.
e. is to keep the organic level uniform.

Vocabulary

I. Filling in the blanks with the words or expressions given below. Change the form if necessary.

| level out | die off | in direct proportion to | decline |
| surge | respond to | as far as ··· be concerned | |

1. To people's great delight, the cost of living _____ in Septem- ber after going up for six months.
2. A water shortage had struck the area and the wild life _____ alarmingly in the intense heat.
3. He was sick in bed, looking miserable and wondering how long it would be before the fever began _____.
4. The excess solids in the effluent would be _____ the organic matter being treated with approximately 10 to 13 percent of the organic matter appearing in the effluent as inert solids.
5. It has already been pointed out that certain phases of the growth curve do not yield satisfactory operations _____ waste treatment _____.

II. For each blank in the following sentences choose the best answer from the choices given below.

1. If the sludge is predominantly inactive, there is no need for further _____ and the

118

sludge can be dewatered directly.
   A. stereotyping   B. stabilization
   C. sterilization   D. statistics
2. Current methods depend upon gravity separation and are limited in their ability _____ the sludge.
   A. to concentrate   B. to contaminate
   C. to concrete   D. to constitute
3. With complete mixing in the aeration tank, F becomes a minimum value with minimum _____.
   A. frictions   B. frustrations
   C. fractions   D. fluctuations
4. The gases which do not act chemically with other substances are labelled as _____.
   A. initial   B. inactive
   C. innate   D. inert
5. In most instances activated sludge must have _____ solids separation and wasting.
   A. a form of   B. a type of
   C. a means of   D. a kind of

Writing   Abstract Writing (2)

Directions: The following is an abstract of the text of Unit Twelve and there are 8 words missing. Please fill in the blanks with the words found from the text or with your own words.

Abstract

The purpose of activated sludge __1__ process is to remove the organic matter as completely as possible from the raw wastes with the least expenditure of time and funds. One of the basic problems with __2__ activated sludge has been the variable predomination of the microorganisms. Another problem still to be solved is the efficient removal and __3__ of the sludge from the liquid. The only way to keep the bacterial species uniform is to keep the organic level __4__. The F : M ratio is the key to bacterial growth.

A most recent __5__ has been the operation of complete mixing systems at the lower end of the declining growth phase where sludge increase is minimal.

In most cases activated sludge must have a __6__ of solids separation and wasting. Current methods __7__ on gravity separation and are limited in their ability to concentrate the sludge.

Either anaerobic or aerobic digestion is used for sludge stabilization. The __8__ is determined by economics.

Reading Material A

Landfills

Landfills must be adequately designed and operated if public health and environment are to be protected. The general components that go into the design of these facilities, as well as the correct procedure to follow during the operation and post-closure phase of the facility's life are discussed below.

Three levels of safeguard must be incorporated into the design of a hazardous landfill. The primary system is an impermeable liner, either clay or synthetic material, coupled with a leachate collection and treatment system.① Infiltration can be minimized with a cap of impervious material overlaying the landfill, and sloped to permit adequate runoff and to discourage pooling of the water.② The objectives are to prevent rainwater and snow melt from entering the soil and percolating to the waste containers and, in case water does enter the disposal cells, to collect and treat it as quickly as possible.③ Side slopes of the landfill should be a maximum of 3 : 1 to reduce stress on the liner material. Research and testing of the range of synthetic liners must be viewed with respect to a liner's strength, compatibility with wastes, cost, and life expectancy. Rubber, asphalt, concrete and a variety of plastics are available, and such combinations as polyvinyl chloride overlaying clay may prove useful on a site-specific basis.

A leachate collection system must be designed by contours to promote movement of the waste to pumps for extraction to the surface and subsequent treatment. Plastic pipes, or sand and gravel, similar to systems in municipal landfills and used on golf courses around the country, are adequate to channel the leachate to a pumping station below the land-fill. One or more pumps direct the collected leachate to the surface, where a wide range of waste-specific treatment technologies are available, including:④

* sorbent material: carbon and fly ash arranged in a column through which the leachate is passed.

* packaged physical-chemical units, including chemical addition andndnd flash mixing, controlled flocculation, sedimentation, pressure filtration, pH adjustment, and reverse osmosis.

The effectiveness of each method is highly waste-specific and tests must be conducted on a site-by-site basis before a reliable leachate treatment system can be designed. All methods produce waste sludges which must reach ultimate disposal.

A secondary safeguard system consists of another barrier contoured to provide a backup leachate collection system. In the event of failure of the primary system, the secondary collection system conveys the leachate to a pumping station, which in turn relays the wastewater to the surface for treatment.⑤

A final safeguard system is also advisable. This system consists of a series of discharge wells up-gradient and down-gradient to monitor groundwater quality in the area and to control leachate plumes if the primary and secondary systems fail. Up-gradient wells act to define the background levels of selected chemicals in the groundwater and to serve as a basis for comparing the concentrations of these chemicals in the discharge from the down-gradient wells. This system thus provides an alarm mechanism if the primary and secondary systems fail.

As waste containers are brought to a landfill site for burial, specific precautions should be taken to ensure the protection of public health, worker safety and the environment. Wastes should be segregated by physical and chemical characteristics and buried in the same cells of the landfill. Three-dimensional mapping of the site is useful for future mining of these cells for resource recovery purposes. Observation wells with continuous monitoring should be maintained, and regular core soil samples should be taken around the perimeter of the site to verify the integrity of the liner materials.

Once a site is closed and does not accept more waste, the operation and maintenance of the site must continue. The impervious cap on top of the landfill must be inspected and maintained to minimize infiltration. Surface water runoff must be managed, collected and possibly treated. Continuous monitoring of surface water, groundwater, soil and air quality is necessary, as ballooning and rupture of the cover material may occur if gases produced and/or released from the waste rise to the surface. Waste inventories and burial maps must be maintained for future land use and waste reclamation. A major component of post-closure management is maintaining limited access to the area.

Notes

① … coupled with a leachate collection and treatment system.

… 同时配有沥出液的收集和处理装置。

② … with a cap of impervious material overlaying the landfill, and sloped to permit adequate runoff and to discourage pooling of the water.

overlaying … 和 sloped … 为现在分词短语和过去分词短语，分别修饰 a cap of impervious material。

③ in case …：如果，假如。

④ One or more pumps direct the collected leachate to the surface, where a wide range of waste-specific treatment technologies are availa-ble, including …

where 引出的定语从句修饰 the surface；including 引出的现在分词短语修饰 a wide range of waste-specific treatment technologies。

⑤ in the event of：如果。

⑥ to serve as …：用作……。

Reading Material B

Disposal of Sludge Containing Heavy Metals

Introduction

The municipal sewage is usually mixed with wastewater containing heavy metals from factories. The heavy metals can be concentrated in sludge of primary or secondary sedimentation when treatment plants provide primary or secondary treatment. If sludge containing heavy metals is abandoned directly or used as fertilizer, they will return to sources of water, and corps, and finally enter into the human body by food chain, thus causing various diseases and seriously harming the health of human beings.[①] The minamata and ouch-ouch diseases are both caused by heavy metals, mercury and cadmium respectively, in Japan.

In 1980's, in order to abate environmental pollution, developed countries have studied methods for treating and recovering heavy metals in municipal wastewater sludge. In 1981, British experts reported the process of using sulphuric acid leaching and lime precipitation to recover heavy metals in sludge. This process reduced the volume of the sludge to be treated. In 1983, Japanese experts reported the use of magnetic separation tech-nology for treating heavy metals contained in the sludge. The methods des-cribed above are not cost-effective.[②]

The rate of treatment of municipal wastewater is very low in China; from available references about the contents of heavy metals in the sludge of wastewater treatment plants in China, some of the sludge could not be used as fertilizer because of high concentration of heavy metals in it.

Research Methods

There exists a certain amount of sulphur compounds in municipal sludge, which contain mainly sulphate and protein containing sulfide, etc. The two forms of sulphur could be changed into S^{2-} ion by means of controlling them under anaerobic condition. The S^{2-} ion could make the instable combining forms of heavy metals (exchangeable ionic form, combined form as hydroxides and carbonates, combined form as hydrous Fe and Mn oxide) change into the combining forms of stable sulphides.

Test sludge was the fresh one taken from the primary sedimentation tank of the Beijing Gaobeidian Municipal Wastewater Treatment Plant where the volume ratio of domestic wastewater to industrial wastewater was 48∶52. The characteristics of the sludge were similar to those of average sewage sludge.

The main testing equipment was a set of simulative anaerobic sludge digesters. It consisted of five metallic digesters with 0.2 meter in diameter and 0.24 meter in height. The digesters were put into a heated rectangular water tank with a thermostat to control the temperature at 35℃±1℃. Each digester was equipped with a mini-motor-driven mixer.

The test was to control the various concentrations of certain metals in wet sludge, so as to observe the poisoning effect of heavy metals on sludge digestion and the ability of stabilizing heavy metals. The resolu-tion test of digested sludge releasing heavy metals was made.[3] For simulat-ing the acid rain, adjusting the pH of leaching water to 3.35 and 5.6 with nitric acid, keeping leaching rate at 0.106cm/hr (simulating the filtration rate through clay), we made the digested sludge leached for 85 days, then found that the concentrations of various heavy metals and pH value of effluents all reached the stable state after 10 days.

Conclusion

1. S^{2-} ion played an important role in heavy metals stability. Allow-able concentrations of heavy metals in sludge would be raised by adding sulfide which can form S^{2-} ion in the sludge.[4] When S^{2-} ion was added, the concen-trations of heavy metals in sludge reached Cu: 5.08g/kg dry sludge, Zn: 6.17g/kg dry sludge, Pb: 5.63g/kg dry sludge, Cd: 5.72g/kg dry sludge. Each value was 10 times the value by adding no sulfide, and had no poisoning effect on the digesting process.

2. For simulating the acid rain (pH=3.35), we made the anaerobic digested sludge leached for 85 days, then found that the leaching percentage of heavy metals in it were Cu: 2×10, Pb: 2×10, Zn: 3×10, Cd: 14. The sta-bility of various metals in sludge decreased in the order of Cu> Zn> Cd. The sludge containing high cadmium is not suitable for land use.

3. The digested sludge can be used as fertilizer and this can save a large amount of money for disposal. The cost of sludge for landfill can be saved by one million yuan per annum in a city which has a population of one million, if 0.3 liter of dry sludge is produced by each a day.

Notes

①… thus causing various diseases and seriously harming the health of human being
　thus 引出的现在分词短语作结果状语。
②cost-effective: cost-efficient 有成本效益的，划算的。
③resolution test: 解析实验。
④play an important role in …: 在……起着重要的作用。

UNIT THIRTEEN

Text   Energy, Economy and Environment

[1]   The growth of energy demand in response to industrialization, urbanization, and societal affluence has led to an extremely uneven global distribution of primary energy consumption. The consumption of energy per person in industrial market economies, for example, is more than 80 times greater than in sub-Saharan Africa.① And about a quarter of the world's population consumes three-quarters of the world's primary energy.

[2]   In 1980, global energy consumption stood at around 10TW. ②If per capita use remained at the same levels as today, by 2025 a global population of 8.2 billion would need about 14TW (over 4TW in developing and over 9TW in industrial countries) —an increase of 40 per cent over 1980. But if energy consumption per head became uniform worldwide at current industrial country levels, by 2025 that same global population would require about 55TW.

[3]   Neither the 'low' nor the 'high' figure is likely to prove realistic, but they give a rough idea of the range within which energy futures could move, at least hypothetically. ③ Many other scenarios can be generated in-between, some of which assume an improved energy base for the developing world. For instance, if the average energy consumption in the low-and middle-income economies trebled and doubled, respectively, and if consumption in the high-income oil-exporting and industrial market and non-market countries remained the same as today, then the two groups would be consuming about the same amounts of energy. The low- and middle-income categories would need 10.5TW and the three 'high' categories would use 9.3TW-totalling 20TW globally, assuming that primary energy is used at the same levels of efficiency as today.

[4]   How practical are any of these scenarios? Energy analysts have conducted many studies of global energy futures to the years 2020-2030. Such studies do not provide forecasts of future energy needs, but they explore how various technical, economic, and environmental factors may interact with supply and demand. In general, the lower scenarios require an energy efficiency revolution. The higher scenarios aggravate the environmental pollution problems that we have experienced since the Second World War.

[5]   The economic implications of a high energy future are disturbing. A recent World Bank Study indicates that for the period 1980-95, a 4.1 per cent annual growth in energy consumption would require an average annual investment of some $130 billion (in 1982 dollars) in developing countries alone. About half of this would have to come from foreign exchange and the rest from internal spending on energy in developing countries.

[6]   The environmental risks and uncertainties of a high energy future are also disturbing and give rise to several reservations. Four stand out:

   * the serious probability of climate change generated by the 'greenhouse effect' of gases

emitted to the atmosphere, the most important of which is carbon dioxide (CO_2) produced from the combustion of fossil fuels

* urban-industrial air pollution caused by atmospheric pollutants from the combustion of fossil fuels
* acidification of the environment from the same causes; and
* the risks of nuclear reactor accidents, the problems of waste disposal and dismantling of reactors after their service life is over, and the dangers of proliferation associated with the use of nuclear energy.

[7]　Along with these, a major problem arises from the growing scarcity of fuelwood in developing countries. If trends continue, by the year 2000 around 2.4 billion people may be living in areas where wood is extremely scarce.

[8]　These reservations apply at even lower levels of energy use. The study indicated that a realistic fuel mix—a virtual quadrupling of coal and a doubling of gas use, along with 1.4 times as much oil—could cause significant global warming by the 2020s. No technology currently exists to remove CO_2 emissions from fossil fuel combustion. The high coal use would also increase emissions of oxides of sulphur and nitrogen, much of which turns to acids in the atmosphere.④ Technologies to remove these latter emissions are now required in some countries in all new and even some old facilities, but they can increase investment costs by 15-25 per cent. ⑤If countries are not prepared to incur these expenses, this path becomes even more infeasible, a limitation that applies much more to the higher energy futures that rely to a greater extent on fossil fuels. A near doubling of global primary energy consumption will be difficult without encountering severe economic, social, and environmental constraints.

[9]　This raises the desirability of a lower energy future, where GDP growth is not constrained but where investment effort is switched away from building more primary supply sources and put into the development and supply of highly efficient fuel-saving end-use equipment. In this way, the energy services needed by society could be supplied at much reduced levels of primary energy production.⑥ By using the most energy-efficient technologies and processes now available in all sectors of the economy, annual global per capita GDP growth rates of around 3 per cent can be achieved. This growth is at least as great as that regarded in this assay as a minimum for reasonable development.⑦But this path would require huge structural changes to allow market penetration of efficient technologies, and it seems unlikely to be fully realizable by most governments during the next 40 years.

[10]　The crucial point about these lower, energy-efficient futures is not whether they are perfectly realizable in their proposed time frames. Fundamental political and institutional shifts are required to restructure investment potential in order to move along these lower, more energy-efficient paths.

[11]　The Commission believes that there is no other realistic option open to the world for the 21th century.⑧ The ideas behind these lower scenarios are not fanciful. Energy efficiency has already shown cost- effective results. In many industrial countries, the primary energy re-

quired to produce a unit of GDP has fallen by as much as a quarter or even a third over the last 13 years, much of it from implementing energy efficiency measures. Properly managed, efficiency measures could allow industrial nations to stabilize their primary energy consumption by the turn of the century. They would also enable developing countries to achieve higher levels of growth with much reduced levels of investment, foreign debt, and environmental damage. But by the early decades of the 21st century they will not alleviate the ultimate need for substantial new energy supplies globally.

New Words and Expressions

in response to		为了响应
urbanization [ə:bənai'zeiʃən]	n.	都市化
affluence ['æfluəns]	n.	丰富，富裕
stand at		（数量）为
hypothetically [haipou'θetikəli]	adv.	假设地，有前提地
treble ['trebl]	vi.	成为三倍，增加两倍
scenario [si'nɑːriou]	n.	情况，方案
aggravate ['ægrəveit]	vt.	使恶化，使更严重
probability [ˌprɔbə'biləti]	n.	可能性，概率
combustion * [kəm'bʌstʃən]	n.	燃烧
acidification [ə'sidifikeiʃən]	n.	酸化
proliferation [prouˌlifə'riʃn]	n.	扩散，激增
scarcity ['skɛəsəti]	n.	缺乏，稀少，供不应求
virtual ['vəːtʃuəl]	a.	实际上的，现实的
quadrupling [ˌkwɔ'druplɪŋ]	n.	四倍
emission * [i'miʃən]	n.	放射，散发
incur * [in'kəː]	v.	遭受，惹起，承担
infeasible [in'fiːzəbl]	a.	不能实行的，办不到的，不可能的
constraint [kən'streint]	n.	制约，压抑
constrain * [kən'strein]	vt.	限制，制约
switch away		转移，移动
assay [ɛə'sei]	n./v.	分析，化验
crucial * ['kruːʃəl]	a.	决定性的，关键的
frame [freim]	n.	框架，计划
institutional [ˌinsti'tjuːʃənəl]	a.	公共机构的，制度上的
restructure ['riː'strʌktʃə]	vt.	调整
move along		向前走
fanciful ['fænsiful]	a.	奇异的，空想的

Notes

①sub-Saharan Africa 撒哈拉沙漠以南的非洲。
②TW 单位名：太瓦（10^{12}W）。
③… within which energy futures could move，… 定语从句，within which 在定语从句中作状语。
④… much of which turns to acids in the atmosphere 定语从句。
⑤to remove these latter emissions 动词不定式短语作定语，修饰 technologies。
⑥… needed by society 过去分词短语作定语，修饰 the energy services。
⑦regarded in this assay as a minimum for reasonable development 过去分词短语作定语修饰 that。
⑧The Commission 指的是世界环境和发展委员会。

Exercises

Reading Comprehension

Ⅰ. Are these statements true (T) or false (F) according to the text?

1. About a quarter of the world's population consumes half of the world's primary energy. (　)
2. In 1980, global energy consumption reached at about 10TW. (　)
3. Energy analysts have conducted many studies of global energy, which provide forecasts of future energy needs. (　)
4. The environmental risks and uncertainties of a high energy future are also causing worry and some other problems. (　)
5. By the early decades of the 21st century they will not lessen the ultimate need for substantial new energy supplies globally. (　)

Ⅱ. Match Column A with Column B to form meaningful sentences according to the text.

A	B
1. If the average energy consumption in the low-and middle-income economies made three times and two times as many respectively, and if consumption in the high-income oil-exporting and industrial market and non-market countries remained the same as today,	a. that we have experienced since the Second World War

2. In general, the higher scenarios make worse the environmental pollution problems
3. About half of the annual investment would have to come from foreign exchange,
4. A big problem arises from the growing scarcity of fuelwood in developing countries
5. The Commission believes

b. and the rest from internal spending on energy in developing countries
c. then the two groups would be consuming about the same amounts of energy.
d. that there is no other realistic choice open to the world for the 21st century.
e. by the year 2000 about 2.4 billion people may be living in areas where wood is extremely scarce

Vocabulary

I. Match Column A with Column B according to their definitions.

A	B
1. treble	a. unable to be done; impossible
2. scenario	b. to arrange (a system or organization) in a new way
3. acidification	c. make three times as many
4. infeasible	d. a description of possible course of action or events
5. restructure	e. making into or becoming an acid

II. Fill the blanks with the words and the expressions given below. Change the form where necessary.

> atmospheric   institutional   proliferation
> substantial   emission   alleviate   penetration

1. The result of the experiment showed the superior _____ of this kind of light oil.
2. The government tried its best to _____ the economic crisis.
3. We must strictly protect us from nuclear _____.
4. The _____ control device is very important for a paper mill.
5. The _____ pollution is increasingly becoming more dangerous than ever to the people.

III. Complete each of the following sentences with one of the four choices given below.
1. His scientific remark _____ a considerable amount of speculation.
   A. gives raise to   B. gives rise to
   C. gets rise to   D. gets raise to
2. The quick recovery was truly in response _____ medication.

    A. for   B. at
    C. to   D. in

3. The flood level _____ three feet above usual for several weeks.
    A. stood at   B. stood for
    C. stood by   D. stood out

4. Edison's talents _____ in comparison with the others.
    A. stood for   B. stood in
    C. stood by   D. stood out

5. The ore _____ high in gold.
    A. assays   B. tries
    C. experiments   D. tests

Writing   Abstract Writing (3)

Directions: Read the text of Unit Thirteen again and write an abstract of the text using the words and phrases given below.

    relationship   energy demand
    air pollution   acidification
    increase investment lower scenarios

Reading Material A

The Growth of Cities

    This is the century of the 'urban revolution'. In the 35 years since 1950, the number of people living in cities almost tripled, increasing by 1.25 billion. In the more developed regions, the urban population nearly doubled, from 447 million to 838 million. In the less developed world, it quadrupled, growing from 286 million to 1.14 billion.

    Over only 60 years, the developing world's urban population increased tenfold, from around 100 million in 1920 to close to 1 billion in 1980. At the same time, its rural population more than doubled.

    * In 1940, only one person in eight lived in an urban center, while about one in 100 lived in a city with a million or more inhabitants (a 'million city').①

    * By 1960, more than one in five persons lived in an urban center, and one in 16 in a 'million city'.

    * By 1980, nearly one in three persons was an urban dweller and one in 10 a 'million city' resident.

    The population of many of sub-Saharan Africa's larger cities increased more than sevenfold between 1950 and 1980-Nairobi, Dar es Salaam, Nouakchott, Lusaka, Lagos, and Kinshasa among them. During these same 30 years, populations in many Asian and Latin American cities (such as Seoul, Baghdad, Dhaka, Amman, Bombay, Jakarta, Mexico City, Manila, Sao Paulo, Bogota, and Managua) tripled or quadrupled. In such cities, net immigration has usually been a greater contributor than natural increase to the population growth of recent decades.②

In many developing countries, cities have thus grown far beyond anything imagined only a few decades ago-and at speeds without historic precedent.③ But some experts doubt that developing nations will urbanize as rapidly in the future as in the last 30-40 years, or that megacities will grow as large as UN projections suggest.④ Their argument is that many of the most powerful stimuli to rapid urbanization in the past have less influence today, and that changing government policies could reduce the comparative attractiveness of cities, especially the largest cities, and slow rates of urbanization.

The urban population growth rate in developing countries as a whole has been slowing down—from 5.2 per cent per annum in the late 1950s to 3.4 per cent in the 1980s. It is expected to decline even further in the coming decades. Nevertheless, if current trends hold, Third World cities could add a further three-quarters of a billion people by the year 2000. Over the same time, the cities of the industrial world would grow by a further 111 million.

These projections put the urban challenge firmly in the developing countries. In the space of just 15 years (or about 5,500 days), the developing world will have to increase by 65 per cent its capacity to produce and manage its urban infrastructure, services, and shelter—merely to maintain present conditions. And in many countries, this must be accomplished under conditions of great economic hardship and uncertainty, with resources diminishing relative to needs and rising expectations.

Few city governments in the developing world have the power, resources, and trained staff to provide their rapidly growing populations with the land, services, and facilities needed for an adequate human life: clean water, sanitation, schools, and transport. The result is mushrooming illegal settlements with primitive facilities, increased overcrowding, and rampant disease linked to an unhealthy environment.⑤

In most Third World cities, the enormous pressure for shelter and services has frayed the urban fabric. Much of the housing used by the poor is decrepit. Civic buildings are frequently in a state of disrepair and advanced decay. So too is the essential infrastructure of the city; public transport is overcrowded and overused, as are roads, buses and trains, transport stations, public latrines, and washing points, water supply systems leak, and the resulting low water pressure allows sewage to seep into drinking water. A large proportion of the city's population often has no piped water, storm drainage, or roads.

A growing number of the urban poor suffer from a high incidence of diseases; most are environmentally based and could be prevented or dramatically reduced through relatively small investments. Acute respiratory diseases, tuberculosis, intestinal parasites, and diseases linked to poor sanitation and contaminated drinking water (diarrhoea, dysentery, hepatitis, and typhoid) are usually endemic; they are one of the major causes of illness and death, especially among children.⑥ In parts of many cities, poor people can expect to see one in four of their children die of serious malnutrition before the age of five, or one adult in two suffering intestinal worms or serious respiratory infections.

Air and water pollution might be assumed to be less pressing in Third World cities because of lower levels of industrial development. But in fact hundreds of such cities have high concentrations of industry. Air, water, noise, and solid waste pollution problems have increased rapidly and can have dramatic impacts on the life and health of city inhabitants, on their economy, and on jobs. Even in a relatively small city, just one or two factories dumping wastes into the only nearby river can contaminate everyone's drinking, washing, and cooking water. Many slums and shanties crowd close to hazardous industries, as this is land no one else wants. This proximity has magnified the risks for the poor, a fact demonstrated by great loss of life and human suffering in various recent industrial accidents.

The uncontrolled physical expansion of cities has also had serious implications for the urban environment and economy. Uncontrolled development makes provision of housing, roads, water supply, sewers, and public services prohibitively expensive. Cities are often built on the most productive agricultural land, and unguided growth results in the unnecessary loss of this land. Such losses are most serious in nations with limited arable land, such as Egypt. Haphazard development also consumes land and natural landscapes needed for urban parks and recreation areas. Once an area is built up, it is both difficult and expensive to re-create open space.

In general, urban growth has often preceded the establishment of a solid, diversified economic base to support the build-up of housing, infrastructure, and employment.⑦ In many places, the problems are linked to inappropriate patterns of industrial development and the lack of coherence between strategies for agricultural and urban development. The world economic crisis of the 1980s has not only reduced incomes, increased unemployment, and eliminated many social programs.

Notes

①1940 年，8 个人中有 1 人居住在城市中心，而 100 人中有 1 人居住在人口在 100 万以上的城市中（百万人口城市）。
②在这些城市中，向城市移居的居民净数量的增长是比近几十年来城市人口自然增长更为重要的导致城市人口增长的因素。
③… far beyond anything imagined ……令人难以想象的。
④megacities 百万人口城市，大都市。
⑤其所导致的结果将是如雨后春笋般地出现非法的条件极其落后的新住宅区，人口拥挤与日俱增，由不利于健康的环境所导致的疾病将到处蔓延。
⑥由不良的卫生条件和受污饮用水所引起的急性呼吸道疾病。结核病、肠道寄生虫病及其

它疾病（腹泻、痢疾、肝炎和伤寒）通常是地方性流行病，它们是疾病和死亡的主要原因之一，对儿童而言尤其如此。

⑦一般而言，城市发展常常是一种固定的、多样化的经济基础的建立的先导，以作为建造住房、基础设施和提供就业机会的支持。

Reading Material B

The Situation in Industrial World Cities

The commission's focus on the urban crisis in developing countries is not meant to imply that what transpires in the cities of the industrial world is not of crucial importance to sustainable development globally.① It is. These cities account for a high share of the world's resource use, energy consumption, and environmental pollution. Many have a global reach and draw their resources and energy from distant lands, with enormous aggregate impacts on the ecosystems of those lands.

Nor is the emphasis on Third World cities meant to imply that problems within the cities of industrialized countries are not serious.② They are. Many face problems of deteriorating infrastructure, environmental degradation, inner-city decay, and neighborhood collapse. The unemployed, the elderly, and racial and ethnic minorities can remain trapped in a downward spiral of degradation and poverty, as job opportunities and the younger and better-educated individuals leave declining neighborhoods.③ City or municipal governments often face a legacy of poorly designed and maintained public housing estates, mounting costs, and declining tax bases.

But most industrial countries have the means and resources to tackle inner-city decay and linked economic decline. Indeed, many have succeeded in reversing these trends through enlightened policies, cooperation between the public and private sectors, and significant investments in personnel, institutions, and technological innovation. Local authorities usually have the political power and credibility to take initiatives and to assess and deploy resources in innovative ways reflecting unique local conditions. This gives them a capacity to manage, control, experiment, and lead urban development. In centrally planned economies, the ability to plan and implement plans for urban development has been significant. The priority given to collective goods over private consumption may also have increased the resources available for urban development.④

The physical environment in many cities of the industrial world has improved substantially over the decades. According to the historical records of many major centers—like London, Paris, Chicago, Moscow, and Melbourne—it was not too long ago that a major part of their population lived in desperate circumstances amid gross pollution. Conditions have improved steadily during the past century, and this trend continues, although the pace varies between and within cities.

In most urban areas, almost everyone is served by refuse collection today.⑤ Air quality has generally improved, with a decline in the emission of particles and sulphur oxides. Efforts to restore water quality have met with a mixed record of success because of pollution from outside of cities, notably nitrates and other fertilizers and pesticides. Many coastal areas, however, close to major sewage outlets, show considerable deterioration. There is rising concern about chemical pollutants in drinking water and about the impacts of toxic wastes on groundwater quality. And noise pollution has tended to increase.

Motor vehicles greatly influence environmental conditions in the cities of the industrial world. A recent slowdown in the growth rate of vehicle numbers, stricter emission standards for new vehicles, the distribution of lead-free gasoline, improvements in fuel efficiency, improved traffic management policies, and landscaping have all helped reduce the impacts of urban traffic.

Public opinion has played a critical role in the drive to improve urban conditions.⑥ In some cities, public pressure has triggered the abandonment of massive urban development projects, fostered residential schemes on a more human scale, countered indiscriminate demolition of existing buildings and historic districts, modified proposed urban highway construction, and led to transformation of derelict plots into playgrounds.⑦

The problems that remain are serious but they affect relatively limited areas, which makes them much more tractable than those of Cairo or Mexico City, for example. Certain aspects of urban decline even provide opportunities for environmental enhancement. The exodus of population and economic activities, while creating severe economic and social difficulties, reduces urban congestion, allows new uses for abandoned buildings, protects historic urban districts from the threat of speculative demolition and reconstruction, and contributes to urban renewal. The de-industrialization of these cities is often counterbalanced by the growth of the services sector, which brings its own problems.⑧ But this trend creates opportunities to remove heavy industrial pollution sources from residential and commercial areas.

The combination of advanced technology, stronger national economies, and a developed institutional infrastructure give resilience and the potential for continuing recovery to cities in the industrial world. With flexibility, space for manoeuvre, and innovation by local leadership, the issue for industrial countries is ultimately one of political and social choice. Developing countries are not in the same situation. They have a major urban crisis on their hands.

Notes

①此委员会对发展中国家城市危机的重视并不意味着在发达国家城市中所发生的一切对全球的持续发展是根本不重要的。
②同样对第三世界的重视并不是说发达国家中所存在的问题就不严重的。
③… remain trapped in a downward spiral of degradation and poverty。处在不断恶化和贫困

的境况中。… leave declining neighborhoods 离开不断萎缩的聚居区。

④优先考虑集体消费胜于个人消费也可能会增加用于城市发展所需要的资源。

⑤refuse collection 垃圾收集。

⑥公众舆论在推动改善城市环境的过程中起着非常关键的作用。

⑦… fostered … 公众压力促使住宅区的规划更合乎人类需求。

⑧工业化程度的减少经常与第三产业的发展持平。

UNIT FOURTEEN

Text Ecology—Its Relation to Other Sciences and Its Relevance to Civilization

[1]   The word "ecology" is derived from the Greek " oikos", meaning "household," and "logos", meaning "study ". Thus, the study of the environmental house includes all the organisms in it and all of the functional processes that make the house habitable. Literally, then, ecology is the study of "life at home" with emphasis on "the totality or pattern of relations between organisms and their environment," to cite one of the definitions in Webster's Unabridged Dictionary.①

[2]   The word "economics" is also derived from the Greek root" oikos". Since nomics means "management", economics translates as "the management of the household, " and accordingly, ecology and economics should be companion disciplines. Unfortunately, many people view ecologists and economists as adversaries with antithetical visions.② Later, this text will consider the confrontation that results because each discipline takes too narrow a view of its subject and the special effort made to bridge the gap between them. ③

[3]   Ecology was of practical interest early in human history. To survive in primitive society, all individuals needed to know their environment, i. e. the forces of nature and the plants and animals around them. Civilization, in fact, began coincidentally with the use of fire and other tools to modify the environment. Because of technological achievements, we seem to depend less on the natural environment for our daily needs; we forget our continuing dependence on nature. Also, economic systems of whatever political ideology value things made by human beings that primarily benefit the individual, but place little value on the goods and services of nature that benefit us as a society. Until there is a crisis, we tend to take for granted natural goods and services; we assume they are unlimited or somehow replaceable by technological innovations, despite evidence to the contrary.

[4]   The great paradox is that industrialized nations have succeeded by temporarily uncoupling humankind from nature through exploitation of finite, naturally produced fossil fuels that are rapidly being depleted. Yet civilization still depends on the natural environment, not only for energy and materials but also for vital life-support processes such as air and water cycles. The basic laws of nature have not been repealed; only their complexion and quantitative relations have changed, as the world's human population and its prodigious consumption of energy have increased our power to alter the environment. Accordingly, our survival depends on knowledge and intelligent action to preserve and enhance environmental quality by means of harmonious rather than disruptive technology.

[5]   Like all phases of learning, the science of ecology has had a gradual, if spasmodic, development during recorded history. The writings of Hippocrates, Aristotle, and other philoso-

phers of ancient Greece clearly contain references to ecological topics.④ However, the Greeks did not have a word for ecology. The word "ecology" is of recent origin, having been first proposed by the German biologist Ernst Haeckel in 1869.⑤ before this, many great men of the biological renaissance of the eighteenth and nineteenth centuries had contributed to the subject, even though the word "ecology" was not in use. For example, in the early 1700s, Anton van Leeuwenhoek, best known as the premier microscopist, also pioneered the study of food chains and population regulation (Egerton, 1968).⑥ and the writing of the English botanist Richard Bradley revealed that he had a good understanding of biological productivity (Egerton, 1969). All three of these subjects are important areas of modern ecology.

[6]　　As a recognized, distinct field of science, ecology dates from about 1900, but only in the past decade has the word become part of the general vocabulary. At first, the field was rather sharply divided into plant and animal ecology, but the biotic community concept of F. E. Clements and V. E. Shelford, the food chain and material cycling concepts of Raymond Liderman and C. E. Hutchinson, and the whole lake studies of E. A. Birge and Chauncy Juday, among others, helped establish basic theory for a unified field of general ecology.

[7]　　What can best be described as a worldwide environmental awareness movement burst upon the scene during two years, 1968 to 1970. Suddenly, it seemed, everyone became concerned about pollution, natural areas, population growth, and food and energy consumption, as indicated by the wide coverage of environmental concerns in the popular press. The increase in public attention had a profound effect on academic ecology. Before the 1970s, ecology was viewed largely as a subdivision of biology. Ecologists were staffed in biology departments, and courses were generally found only in the biological science curricula. Although ecology remains strongly rooted in biology. it has emerged from biology as an essentially new integrative discipline that links physical and biological processes and forms a bridge between the natural sciences and the social sciences.

New Words and Expressions

ecology [i(:)'kɔlədʒi]	n.	生态学
relevance * ['relivəns]	n.	关联
have relevance to		和…有关
discipline ['disiplin]	n.	科学；科目
adversary ['ædvəsəri]	n.	对手；敌方（手；人）
antithetical [ænti'θetikl]	a.	对立的；相反的
confrontation [kɔnfrʌn'teiʃn]	n.	比较；冲突
primitive ['primitiv]	a.	原始的
paradox ['pærədɔks]	n.	奇论；疑题
uncouple ['ʌn'kʌpl]	vt.	分开；分离
humankind [hju:mən'kaid]	n.	（用作单或复）人类

repeal [ri'pi:l]	vt.	废除；否定
complexion [kəm'plekʃən]	n.	情况
quantitative * [kwɔntitətiv]	a.	定量的；数量的
prodigious [prə'didʒəs]	a.	巨大的；惊人的
harmonious [hɑ:'məunjəs]	a.	协调的；相称的
disruptive [dis'rʌptiv]	a.	破坏性的；分裂的
spasmodic [spæ'mɔdik]	a.	间歇的；一阵阵的
premier ['premjə]	a.	首位的；最早的
microscopist [mai'krɔskəpist]	n.	显微镜学家
botanist ['bɔtənist]	n.	植物学家
biotic [bai'ɔtik]	a.	生命的；生物的
burst upon		突然来到；突然发现
curricula [kə'rikjulə]	n.	（curriculum 的复数）课程
integrative ['intigreitiv]	a.	综合的

Notes

①to cite one of the definitions in Webster's Unabridged Dictionary 动词不定式短语作状语。
②to view … as … 把……视作……。
③that results 定语从句，修饰 confrontation。
④Hippocrates [hi'pɔkrætiz] 希波克拉底（460？～377？BC.），古希腊医师，被称为"医学之父"。现存《希波克拉底文集》，内容涉及解剖、临床、妇女疾病等。Aristotle [eristɔtl] 亚历士多德（384～322 BC.），古希腊哲学家和科学家，柏拉图的学生，亚历山大大帝的教师，雅典逍遥派创始人，著作涉及当时所有知识领域，尤以《诗学》、《修辞学》等著称。
⑤Ernst Haeckel ['ernst 'hekəl]（1834-1919）爱仑斯特·海克尔，德国动物学家，达尔文主义支持者，提出生物发生律，为进化论提供了有力证据，主要著作有《人类发展史》、《生命的奇迹》等。
⑥Anton van Leeuwenhoek ['æntən vain 'leivənhu:k] 安东·范·列文虎克（1632～1723），荷兰生物学家，显微镜学家，一生磨制 400 多块透镜，最早用于透镜观察细菌和原生动物，发现精子、血红细胞和水中微生物。

Exercises

Reading Comprehension

I. Are these statements true (T) or false (F) according to the text?
  1. Ecology and economics should not be companion disciplines.   (   )

2. Civilization still depends on the natural environment not only for energy and materials but also for vital life-support processes such as air and water cycles. (   )
3. The word 'ecology' was first put forward by the German biologist Ernst Haeckel in 1869. (   )
4. Shelfod pioneered the study of food chains and population regulation. (   )
5. Before the 1970s, ecology was considered largely as a subdivision of biology. (   )

II. Match Column A with Column B to form the meaningful sentences according to the text.

A	B
1. Unfortunately, many people view ecologists and economists	a. their environment, i.e. the forces of nature and the plants and animals around them
2. Civilization, in fact, started coincidentally with	b. that links physical and biological processes and forms a bridge between the natural sciences and the social sciences.
3. To survive in primitive society, human beings needed to know	c. as adversaries with antithetical visions
4. Yet civilization still depends on	d. the use of fire and other tools to modify the environment
5. Ecology has emerged from biology as an basically new integrative discpline	e. the natural environment, not only for energy and materials but also for vital life-support processes such as air and water cycles

Vocabulary

I. Match Column A with Column B according to their definitions.

A	B
1. ecology	a. a living being
2. organism	b. a specialist in studying plants
3. disruptive technology	c. a comprehensive subject of knowledge
4. botanist	d. the technology which brings into disorder
5. integrative discipline	e. the scientific study of the pattern of relations of plants, animals, and people to each other and to their surroundings

II. Fill in the blanks with the words or the expressions given below. Change the form where necessary.

| repeal | spasmodic | uncouple | burst upon |
| antithetical | delete | derive from | |

1. These two ideas are strongly _____.
2. They will _____ the old locomotive from the carriages and use a new one.
3. The unjust law was finally _____.
4. The fire had _____ the wild game in the forest.
5. In the middle of his experiment, the scientist _____ the truth.

Ⅲ. Complete each of the following statements with one of the four choices given below.
1. What you said has no relevance _____ what we are talking about.
   A. on   B. to
   C. at   D. in
2. His interest in science fiction is _____.
   A. regular   B. irregular
   C. spasmodic   D. continual
3. It is a _____ that in such a rich country there should be so many poor people.
   A. problem   B. question
   C. paradox   D. puzzle
4. The President started a _____ with congress over the budget issue.
   A. fighting   B. battle
   C. quarrel   D. confrontation
5. These plans must be _____ if they are to be used unsuccessfully
   A. modified   B. changed
   C. practised   D. implied

Writing   Abstract writing (4)

Directions: Read the text of Unit Fourteen again and write an abstract of the text using the words and phrases given below.

ecology   economics   the natural environment
paradox   origin   development

Reading Material A

Elements of Ecology

Plants and animals in their physical environment make up an ecosystem. The study of such ecosystems is ecology. Although we often draw lines around a specific ecosystem in order

139

to be able to study it more fully (e.g. a farm pond) and in so doing assume that the system is totally self-contained, this obviously is not true, and we must remember that one of the tenets of ecology is that "everything is connected with everything else."①

Within an ecosystem there exist three broad categories of actors. ② The producers take energy from the sun, nutrients such as nitrogen and phosphorus from the soil, and through the process of photosynthesis produce high-energy chemicals. The energy from the sun is thus stored in the chemical structure of their organic molecules. These organisms are often referred to as being in the first trophic level and are called autotrophs.

A second group of organisms are the consumers who use some of this energy by ingesting the high-energy molecules. These organism are in the second trophic level in that they directly use the energy of the producers. There can be several more trophic levels as the consumers use the level above as a source of energy.

The third group of organisms, the decomposers or decay organisms, use the energy in animal wastes and dead plants and animals, and in so doing covert the organic molecules to stable inorganic compounds. The residual inorganics then become the building blocks for new life, using the sun as the source of energy.

Ecosystems exhibit a flow of both energy and nutrients. ③ Energy flow is in only one direction: from the sun and through each trophic level. Nutrient flow, on the other hand, is cyclic. Nutrients are used by plants to make high-energy molecules, which are eventually decomposed to the original inorganic nutrients, ready to be used again.

The entire food web, or ecosystem, stays in dynamic balance, with adjustments being made as required. Such a balance is called homeostasis. For example, a drought one year may produce little grass, thus exposing field mice to predators such as owls. The mice, in turn, spend more time in burrows, thus not eating as much, and allowing the grass to reseed for the following year. External perturbations, however, can upset and even destroy an ecosystem. ④ In the previous example, the use of a herbicide to kill the grass might also destroy the field mouse population, and in turn diminish the number of owls. It must be recognized that although most ecosystems can absorb certain amount of insult, a sufficiently large perturbation can cause irreparable damage.

The amount of perturbation a system is able to absorb without being destroyed is tied to the concept of the ecological niche. ⑤ The combination of function and habitat of an organism in an ecological system is its niche. A niche is not a property of a type or organism or species, but is its best accommodation with the environment. In the example above, the grass is a producer which acts as food for the field mouse, which in turn is food for the owl. If the grass were destroyed, both the mice and owls might eventually die out. But suppose there were two types of grass, each equally acceptable as mouse food. Now if one died out, the ecosystem would not be destroyed because the mice would still have food. This simple example demonstrates an important ecological principle: the stability of an ecosystem is proportional to the number of organisms capable of filling various niches.

Problems associated with pollutants which affect the dissolved oxygen levels can not be appreciated without a fuller understanding of the concept of decomposition or biodegradation, part of the total energy transfer system of life.

Notes

①draw lines：划定界线。
②… three bread categories of actors：三大类作用；actors 指有机物。
③a flow of both energy and nutrients：能量流和营养流。
④external perturbations：外部干扰。
⑤… a system is able to absorb without being destroyed …：定语从句，修饰 the amount of perturbation。

Reading Material B

Role of Consumers in Food Web Dynamics

Animals and other consumers are not just passive "eaters" along the food chain. In satisfying their own energy requirements, they often exert a positive feedback on "upstream" trophic levels.① Through natural selection, predators and parasites become adapted not only to avoid destroying their food sources but also in many cases to ensure or even increase continued will-being of their prey. In theory, then, there are not only negative feedback controls, but also positive feedback effects. However, only during the past decade have specific cases been documented to show that consumers can positively affect primary production.② Several examples will suffice to illustrate.

McNaughton (1976) has demonstrated that the grazing of the great herds of migratory East African antelopes, coupled with dry-season fires, increases the rate of return of nutrients to the soil. Regrowth is enhanced, and production of grass is increased during the subsequent rainy season. These interactions thus facilitate energy flow through all of the system. This beautiful symbiosis between grass and grazers that has evolved in what Sinclair and Norton-Griffiths (1976) call the Serengeti Ecosystem unfortunately works only on a large scale, since the most numerous grazers migrate long distances. This efficiency plant-animal partnership will be difficult to preserve in the face of rapid growth of the human population in Africa. Restricting the animals to game parks will disrupt the symbiosis and likely produce overgrazing.

In an experimental greenhouse study, Dyer and Bokhari (1976) compared grass plants whose leaves were eaten by grasshoppers with plants from which the same number of leaves were removed by clipping. Regrowth was more rapid in plants grazed by the grasshoppers. Apparently, a substance in the insect's saliva stimulates root growth and thus increases the plant's ability to regenerate new leaves.

The length of food chains is of some interest. Reducing the energy available to successive links obviously limits the length of food chains.③ However, availability of energy may not be the only factor, since long food chains often occur in infertile systems, such as oligotrophic lakes, and short ones are often found in very productive or eutrophic situations. Rapid production of nutritious plant material may invite heavy grazing, resulting in concentration of energy flow in the first two or three trophic levels. Eutrophication of lakes also shifts the planktonic food web from a phytoplankton-large zooplankton—game fish sequence to a microbial-detrital microzooplankton system not so conducive to support of recreational fisheries.④

Pimm and Lawton (1977) suggest that living at the higher trophic levels increases the risk of extinction (uncertain food supply), a contention challenged by Saunders (1978) who reports that the longest food chains are found at the sea-land interface.

In 1960, Hairston, Smith, and Slobodkin proposed a "balance of nature" hypothesis that caused discussion and controversy among ecologists. They argued that since plants by and large accumulate a lot of biomass (the world is green), something is inhibiting grazing. That something, they theorized, is predators. Accordingly, primary consumers are limited by secondary consumers, and primary producers are thus resource rather than grazer-limited. Subsequently, Smith (1969) and Fretwell (1977) suggested that odd-length and even-length chains differ in how primary production is controlled by the food chain exploiting it.⑤ Thus, if only plants and herbivores (primary consumers) are present, the plants will be limited and controlled by the grazing pressure, whereas the herbivores will be food-limited. If a predator level is present (resulting in an odd length chain), then herbivores become predator-limited, and plants no longer being heavily grazed become resource-limited (i.e., limited by nutrients and water). If a fourth level (i.e., secondary predator of parasite) is added, plants again become grazer-limited. If this theory holds, a plot of standing crop biomass by trophic level should have peaks and valleys; the valleys (i.e., consumer-controlled levels) are 1, 3, 5- levels in even-numbered chains and 2, 4, 6-levels in odd-numbered chains. Such a situation has been reported for fish ponds.

Mechanisms other than consumers help control the use of primary production, for example, allelopathic chemicals produced by plants that inhibit heterotrophic consumption themselves. All of these theoretical control mechanisms are operating in the real world, but no one theory can explain everything.

Notes

① "upstream" trophic level: "上游"营养级，意指高一层次的营养级。
② Only … have … Only 后面引出倒装语序。
③ available to successive links: 作定语，修饰 the energy。
④ 湖泊的富营养化也改变了浮游生物的食物网，使其从浮游植物群落般大的浮游动物鱼类

向生产力不足于维持娱乐性捕渔业的微观浮游动物系统转化。
⑤odd-length and even-length chains：奇数长链和偶数长链。

UNIT FIFTEEN

Text   The Environmental Ethic

[1]   More and more citizens are considering questions not only from the standpoint of economics, but also from that of environmental quality. Lawyers, economists and politicians are finding it more difficult to answer such questions as "Is growth really necessary?" or "Should the gross national product always increase?" or "Should we consider the benefits and costs of public projects solely on the basis of dollars?" A few years ago such questions would have been brushed aside as foolish.① They weren't foolish, and they deserve straight answers.

[2]   In fact, ecology and economics are on a collision course. Man cannot continue to grow in numbers and output (and use of resources) without eventual self-destruction. Present economic systems do not have a feedback loop which slows down the processes detrimental to survival.

[3]   The conflict between ecologists and economists has been boiled down to this ditty:
   Ecology's uneconomic,
   But with another kind of logic,
   Economy's unecologic.

Technical economists notwithstanding, the environmental ethic has become a permanent part of our lives. It is in its infancy, a new and bold concept which must be given time to mature and develop.② Legal principles, economic calculations and engineering considerations are all evolving rapidly, some perhaps prematurely.

[4]   The word "ethic" derives from the Greek "ethos," meaning the character of a person as defined by his actions. This character has been developed during the evolutionary process and has been influenced by the need for adapting to the environment. The "ethic" in short, governs our way of doing things, and this is a direct result of our environment.

[5]   When people talk of a "crisis in the environment," they really mean that our way of thinking about and doing things (our ethic) is not adapted to the environment. Humans at one time lived in harmony with the environment, but somehow the species, either as an accident or as a colossal practical joke by some unknown power, changed its lifestyle to the point where it no longer adapted.③ There is thus no "environmental crisis," but rather a crisis in the recognition that somehow over the years of development we are no longer adapted to our environment.

[6]   In the ecological context, such maladaptation results in two options:
   1. The organism dies out.
   2. The organism evolves to a form and character where it once again is compatible with the environment.

[7]   The birth of the environmental ethic as a force is partly a result of our concern for our

own long-term survival, as well as our realization that humans are but one form of life, and that we should share our earth with our fellow travelers. It is not a religion, since the ethic is based not only on faith, but also on hard facts and thorough analyses.

[8]　One of the first to recognize the degradation of the environment and to voice a concern for nature was Thoreau. His solution to this eloquently stated concern was withdrawal, which was perhaps morally admirable but realistically ineffective. What we have experienced in the last decade has been the coupling of Thoreau's concern with activism. It is one thing to be concerned, but it's much more effective to take action in order to promote your concern.

[9]　One powerful and original attempt at defining an environmental ethic was made by Aldo Leopold, a naturalist and writer. He proposed that:

[10]　A decision is right when it tends to preserve the integrity, stability, and beauty of the biotic community. It is wrong when it tends otherwise.

[11]　Leopold argued convincingly toward the adoption of environmental values other than economic, and his writings have had a major impact on the growth of environmental awareness.

[12]　The environmental ethic is very new, and none of the doctrine is cast in immutable decrees and dogma. On the contrary, like all vital issues, the environmental ethic will undergo transformation as new data are made available and we humans are able to more rationally interpret and live with nature.

[13]　Some critics have mistaken this maturation of the ethic for transience. The problem is so immense that to think of it as a fad is ludicrous.④ But herein is the dilemma: Unless there is public awareness as to the true nature of the problems and realistic solutions, public concern may rapidly fade. For the impetus to survive there must be public confidence and the environmental scientist or engineer must engender this trust by analyzing and interpreting environmental problems correctly and proposing and developing constructed facilities that are compatible with our ecosystem. Sensationalism and the bandwagon tactics of some "environmentalists", politicians and other well-meaning citizens can easily destroy the public sentiment so necessary for a successful assault on our common problems.

[14]　Education of the public to environmental problems and the solutions is of prime importance. It is necessary for people to be critical, and to be literate in the scientific, technological, economical and legal aspects of controlling environmental pollution.

[15]　But that is not enough. We must also live the environmental ethic recognize the power of nature and feel humble in the realization that we are just one small cog in a wonderful and still mysterious system.⑤

New Words and Expressions

ethic ['eθik]	n.	伦理学
gross [grəus]	a.	总的

brush aside		漠视；扫除（障碍）
deserve [di'zə:v]	vt.	应受；值得
collision [kə'liʒən]	n.	冲突
feedback ['fi:dbæk]	n.	反馈
loop [lu:p]	n.	圈；回路
boil down to		归结起来是
ditty ['diti]	n.	小曲；歌谣
uneconomic ['ʌn,i:kə'nɔmik]	a.	不经济的，浪费的
unecologic ['ʌn,i:kə'lɔdʒik]	a.	不主张生态保护的
notwithstanding * [nɔtwiθ'stændiŋ]	ad.	尽管；还是
infancy ['infənsi]	n.	初期
evolutionary [i:və'lju:ʃənəri]	a.	发展的；进化的
colossal [kə'lɔsl]	a.	异常的，非常的
maladaptation [,mælədæp'teiʃən]	n.	不适应；适应不良
compatible * [kəm'pætəbl]	a.	可和谐共存的；适合的（with）
coupling ['kʌpliŋ]	n.	结合；连接
activism ['æktivizəm]	n.	（主张为政治目的采取有力行动的）行动主义
integrity * [in'tegriti]	n.	完整
doctrine ['dɔktrin]	n.	学说
cast [kɑ:st]	vi.	预测；估计
immutable [i'mju:təbl]	a.	不可改变的；永远不变的
decree [di'kri:]	n.	法令
dogma ['dɔgmə]	n.	教条；教义
rationally ['ræʃənəli]	ad.	合理地
maturation [mætju'reiʃən]	n.	成熟
transience ['trænziəns]	n.	短暂；无常
fad [fæd]	n.	一时的风尚，一时的爱好
ludicrous ['lju:dikrəs]	a.	荒唐得滑稽的；荒谬可笑的
dilemma [di'lemə]	n.	困难，困境
engender [in'dʒendə]	vt.	产生；造成；引起
sensationalism [sen'seiʃənlizm]	n.	危言耸听
bandwagon ['bænd'wægən]	n.	潮流；浪头
assault [ə'sɔ:lt]	n.	攻击；冲击
cog [kɔg]	n.	不重要但又不可少的人（或物）；（齿轮的）轮齿

Notes

① … such questions would have been brushed aside as foolish。虚拟语气，与事实情况相反。
② It is in its infancy … which … 强语势，为了加强语气。
③ either as an accident or as a colossal practical joke by some unknown power 状语，说明原因；
  where it no longer adapted 定语从句，修饰 point。
④ to think of it as a fad 是结果状语从句中的主语。
⑤ that we are just one small cog in a wonderful and still mysterious system 同位语从句，补充说明 the realization。

Exercises

Reading Comprehension

I. Are these statements true (T) or false (F) according to the text?

1. The "ethic" guides our way of doing things, this is a direct result of our environment.
   ( )
2. Alde Leopold was one of the first to discover the degradation of the environment and to voice a concern for nature.
   ( )
3. The environmental ethic will experience a great change as new data are obtained.
   ( )
4. Some critics have a wrong idea about this maturation of the ethic for transience.
   ( )
5. Education of the public to environmental problems and the solutions is of no importance.
   ( )

II. Match Column A with Column B to form meaningful sentences according to the text.

A	B
1. More and more citizens are considering questions not only from the standpoint of economics,	a. that our way of thinking about and doing things is not adapted to the environment
2. The word "ethic" comes from the Greek "ethos",	b. of prime importance.
3. The "crisis in the environment" really means	c. but also from that of environmental quality
4. Leopold argued convincingly toward the adoption of environmental values	d. meaning the character of a person as defined by his actions

5. Education of the public to environmental problems and the solutions is   e. other than economic

Vocabulary

I. Match Column A with Column B according to their definitions.

A	B
1. doctrine	a. a difficult choice to be made between two courses of action, both undesirable
2. cog	b. unchangeable
3. dilemma	c. at the start of development or growth
4. immutable	d. principles in a branch of knowledge or system of belief
5. infancy	e. one of the teeth round a wheel that turns another wheel in a machine

II. Fill the blanks with the words or expressions given below. Change the form where necessary.

> standpoint   compatible   brush aside   feedback
> bandwagon   notwithstanding   coupling

1. A great economic reform _____ sweeps across China.
2. _____ Let's look at this great event from a historical _____.
3. The computer company welcomes _____ from people who use the goods it produces.
4. He tried to prevent the accident but it took place _____.
5. All these chemical reactions were _____ with its properties.

III. Complete each of the following statements with one of the four choices given below.

1. The whole matter _____ a power struggle between two parties.
   A. boils down   B. boils away
   C. boils down to   D. boils over
2. _____ the enemy, we swept the next town.
   A. Brushing aside   B. Brushing down
   C. Brushing of   D. Brushing up
3. The ship is reported to have been _____ with an oil tanker.
   A. in accident   B. at collision
   C. in collision   D. at accident
4. No one plays that game any more, it was only a _____.
   A. sport   B. ball
   C. interest   D. fad

5. With our hard work the experiment was a _____ success.
   A. large   B. colossal
   C. wonderful   D. huge

Writing   Abstract Writing (5)

Directions: Read the text of Unit Fifteen again and write an abstract of the text in about 120 words.

Reading Material A

Resolution of Environmental Conflicts
(Part I)

The development of various systems of ethics stems from the human need to create a unified and universally applicable method of "getting along."① The major concern with many ethical theories is first to determine what is good, and second, what is right. In addition, it becomes necessary, if the ethical theory is to have any utility, to strive toward what has been determined to be good and right; once we decide that a system is correct, then we should live by the conclusions we derive from the system.②

Many so-called systems of ethics have been proposed over the years. One of the oldest systems is hedonism, espoused by the sophists with whom Socrates debated.③ Hedonism seeks to maximize pleasure. Whatever gives you pleasure is therefore right. In isolation, this may be a workable philosophy, but not in a society which depends on the general acceptance of the golden rule.

Plato's arguments against hedonism included the concept of a person being governed by reason, and that "good" decisions can only be made in the face of well-considered arguments.④ He extrapolated this to the idea that since not all people have the opportunity to study philosophy, decisions for the society should be made by a "philosopher-king." In Plato's system, therefore, the decisions are taken out of the hands of the masses and the power given to a benign dictator who, Plato argued, would make the "correct" decisions.

Immanuel Kant proposed a third alternative: establish a set of rules that everyone agrees to and then follow these no matter what.⑤ The categorical imperative commits each person to a set of consistent and universally shared required action (e.g., do not lie under any circumstances; or "dioxin" is bad, so don't allow any dioxin out of a municipal waste incinerator). In this system, the focus is on the act itself, not its consequences.

An opposing view holds that consequences are the major concern. Utilitarianism, developed in eighteenth century England by Jeremy Bentham, John Stuart Mill and others, holds that one's actions should strive for the greatest good, defined as individual happiness. Under this system, one could construct a happiness-benefit/cost ratio for every action, and the options with the highest ratio would clearly be the ones of choice. Extending this idea to the social level, we have the concept that governmental actions should follow the dictum of "the greatest good for the greatest number." This concept blends directly into socialism, developed to a large extent by Karl Marx and Friedrich Engels, in which the society is the prime instrument and the individual is no longer very important. Under socialism, decisions are made on the basis of maximizing production, of increasing the average wealth of the society.

There are other systems of ethics worth noting, none of which have attained the historical stature of the ones discussed above.

A major problem with the application of any of the ethical theories is that they were all developed as means of resolving conflicts among people. Our concerns, however, are problems between people and animals, people and plants and people and places. This severely complicates the issue, since now the conflict exists between two parties, each having a different value. As long as the actors are people, the value of a human life is a given constant. Now we have an inequality, and we must seek to place a value on nature.

Notes

①"getting along": "前进"。
②live by: 靠……生活。
③One of the oldest systems is hedonism, espoused by the sophists with whom Socrates debated. with whom Socrates debated 为定语从句，全句可译为：最古老的体系之一是被苏格拉底所辩驳的诡辩家信奉的享乐主义。苏格拉底（469～399 BC.）：古希腊哲学家。
④Plate: 柏拉图（427～347 BC.）古希腊哲学家。
⑤Immanuel Kant: 以马内利·康德（1724～1804）德国哲学家。

Reading Material B

Resolution of Environmental Conflicts
(Part Ⅱ)

The concept that nature has a value is fairly modern. With a few noteworthy exceptions, nature has not been considered through the development of human civilization as an entity possessing value, and has thus not entered into the development of ethical theories.

In the past, only dominance and perpetual progress have shaped our relationship with the natural environment.① In fact, this has been for years a substitute for an environmental ethic, and these exploitative notions have guided our behavior toward a nature which by itself did not possess value.②

But simply stating that nature is valuable is not adequate. Why and how is it valuable?

This question has emerged as a major point of discussion in philosophical literature. The two primary views that seem to be emerging in this debate can be classified as instrumental and intrinsic.

The instrumental view considers nature for its real value to humans, in terms of life support, material wealth, recreational and aesthetic beauty, etc. This view was first popularized by Ralph Waldo Emerson, who witnessed the wholesale destruction of nature during the nineteenth century "rape of the land," and proposed that in the use of nature's bounty, one should be grateful for the blessings and material wealth nature provides.③ This is, of course a utilitarian and anthropocentric view of nature, but it nevertheless represented a first recognition that nature has value.

The second view holds that nature has intrinsic value above and beyond what we might be able to measure in dollars. This, however, is a difficult argument to tie down.④ In a way the belief in the intrinsic value of nature represents a faith—one has to feel that it is right. This feeling has been even translated to legalistic terms, most notably in a work entitled Should Trees Have standing? - Toward Legal Rights for Natural Objects. The question we face is whether nature is here for the welfare of mankind, or does nature have its independent claims to exist.

The problem is further complicated by what we mean by nature.⑤ It's not difficult to get people upset over the senseless slaughter of whales, or of baby seals. Why? Simply because whales are too much like humans; they have many of our own most admirable characteristics and lead a placid, peaceful life, and baby seals are so cute!

Can you imagine an equal outcry raised against the destruction of the polio virus, or the rattlesnake? Do these two species also have standing, a right to left alone and not destroyed?

The issue is of course complex. But to not face it is unacceptable. There is in the intrinsic approach to the value of nature a germ of a positive and intuitively desirable notion. By not striving to develop and foster this idea, might we be freezing our environmental ethic at too low a level? Many widely accepted principles of the past, such as slavery and the divine right of monarchs, have fallen. Albert Schweitzer noted that Europeans long considered people with darker skins to be subhuman. It was at one time stupid to think of them as equals, and to treat them humanely.

Notes

①在过去，唯有控制和不断进步形成了我们与自然环境的关系的形式。
②which by itself did not possess value：作定语从句，修饰 nature，意思为：它本身并不具有价值。
③Emerson：爱默生（1803～1882）美国思想家，散文家，诗人，超验主义运动的主要代表，

强调人的价值，提倡个性绝对自由和社会改革。rape of the land：大地的严重破坏。
④tie down：束缚；约束。
⑤根据我们对大自然所下的定义，这个问题就变得为更加复杂了。

UNIT SIXTEEN

Text   EPA Must Look to the Future

[1]   The oceans, noncancer human health effects, ecosystems sustainability, "nontraditional environmental stressors." and total air pollution loading are likely to be major environmental concerns of the next 30 years, according to an EPA Science Advisory Board committee charged with mapping the environmental landscape of the future. ①

[2]   In a report approved by the Board in January, the SAB Environmental Futures Committee recommends that EPA incorporate long-range, anticipatory thinking into its day-to-day activities and place more emphasis on understanding societal activities that drive environmental change. This approach, the report notes, has not been regular part of Agency operations.

[3]   "The bottom line is that EPA give as much attention to avoiding future environmental problems as it does to controlling current ones," says Raymond Loehr, committee chairman and civil engineering faculty member at the University of Texas. ②"In a sense we are asking for a form of 'generational equity', where we do not pass on to future generations what we can avoid today."

[4]   Looking to the future, Loehr says, is what EPA is supposed to do and was the intent when EPA was established.

[5]   This report follows two other future oriented SAB policy reports: Future Risk Research Strategies for the 1990s released in 1988 and Reducing Risk: Setting Priorities and strategies for Environmental Protection, published in 1990. The SAB formally took up the project in July 1993 after a request from EPA.

[6]   Strategy for the future:

[7]   The Science Advisory Board's report Beyond the Horizon: Protecting the Future with Foresight recommends that EPA take the following steps to prepare for the environmental challenges of the future:

 * Emphasize avoiding future environmental problems as much as controlling current ones.

 * Establish an "early warning system" to identify emerging future environmental risks and, on a pilot basis, subject one or two difficult problems to rigorous analysis by EPA and other organizations.

 * Stimulate greater cooperation among federal agencies and the private sector to anticipate and respond to environmental change.

 * Concentrate initial research on five key environmental areas: ecosystem sustainability, noncancer human health effects, total air pollution loading, nontraditional environmental stressors, and health of the oceans.

 * Recognize global environmental quality as a matter of strategic national interest and

adopt policies that link security, foreign relations, environmental quality, and economic growth.

[8] In preparing the report, committee members examined the work of futurists, and they surveyed SAB standing committees and EPA policy staff, asking them to identify issues of future significance.

[9] The five initial research areas of future concern were selected by the committee because of their potential impact on human health and the environment.

[10] Ecosystem sustainability. Ecosystems are at risk from toxic chemicals, heightened competition for land use, and growing population pressure. EPA should develop ecological risk assessment guidelines and endpoints.

[11] Noncancer human health effects. Scientific studies suggest that estrogen-mimicking compounds cause reproductive problems as well as birth defects and a host of developmental and noncancer problems in animals and humans. These may be weak signals of human health effects, but EPA should broaden its approach to examining noncancer diseases resulting from chronic environmental exposures of susceptible populations.

[12] Total air pollutant loading. Rather than focus on the effects of individual pollutants, EPA should examine the synergism of multiple air pollutants, which may lead to new and unforeseen human health and ecological problems.

[13] Nontraditional environmental stressors. EPA should broaden its concerns to consider less well understood stressors, begin monitoring new stressors (such as control resistant bacteria, plants, and insects; new water-borne pathogens; and accidental or misguided introduction of exotic species), and look further into the cumulative effects of better understood stressor.

[14] Health of oceans. Oceans face increasing stress from a growing global population, and although only weak signs of deterioration are evident now, stress to the sea should be recognized quickly and deserves immediate attention because of the scope and value of the resources at risk.

[15] The report, Loehr says, also recommends establishing a cross-cutting office within EPA to look at future issues. EPA, Loehr says, is the proper place for such an operation. He estimates a future approach would cost a few million dollars and help avoid much more costly cleanups.

[16] The EPA's concern will bring about what is often termed the "environmental ethic", a new concern and awareness of our world. More and more citizens will consider questions not only from the stand-point economics, but also from that of environmental quality. It will also bring about an ethic in education of the public to environmental problems and the solutions and make the public think it necessary to be literate in scientific, technological, economical and legal aspects of controlling environmental pollution.

New Words and Expressions

incorporate ... into ...		包含，吸收
anticipatory [æn'tisipeitəri]	a.	预见的
oriented ['ɔ:rientid]	a.	以……为方向的，以……为目的的
on a pilot basis		在实验室的基础上
sector ['sektə]	n.	机构，组织
defect ['di:fekt]	n.	缺点，不完美
synergism ['sinədʒizm]	n.	协同作用
exotic * [eg'zɔtik]	a.	外来的，外国种的
cumulative ['kju:mjulətiv]	a.	累积的，渐增的
cleanup [kli:mʌp]	a.	净化环境，清除

Notes

①EPA：Envirtonmental Protection Agency（美国）环境保护局；SAB：Science Advisory Board 科学咨询部。

②… as … as it does to controlling current ones … as 后是一个从句，does 是代动词，代 "gives attention"，"to" 是 attention to 中的 to，为介词。

Exercises

Reading Comprehension

I. Are these statements true (T) or false (F) according to the text?

1. According to Science Advisory Board, it is likely that the oceans, cancer human health effects, ecosystems sustainability, traditional environmental stressors and total air pollution loading will be major environmental problems in the next 30 years. ( )
2. "Generational equity" in the text means what we can avoid today will never pass on to future generations. ( )
3. EPA should pay as much attention to avoiding future environmental problems as it does to controlling current ones. ( )
4. Looking to the future is what EPA should do now and was also the purpose of setting up EPA. ( )
5. Do initial research on five major environmental concerns is one of the strategies for the future. ( )

II. Match Column A with Column B to form meaningful sentences according to the text.

A	B
1. What endanger ecosystems are	a. examining noncancer diseases resulting from chronic environmental exposures of susceptible populations
2. The SAB Environmental Futures Committee recommends	b. from the growth of global population
3. EPA should broaden its approach to	c. that EPA incorporate long-range, anticipatory thinking into its day-to-day activities
4. Oceans face increasing stress	d. what is often termed the "environmental ethic".
5. The EPA's concern will bring about	e. toxic chemicals, competition for land use and population pressure

Vocabulary

I. Match column A with Column B according to their definitions.

A	B
1. synergism	a. balance
2. sustainability	b. cooperative action of discrete agencies such that the total effect is greater than the sum of the two effects taken independently
3. sector	c. equitable claim or right
4. global	d. an area of operation or activity
5. equity	e. world-wide

II. Fill in the blanks with the words or expressions given below. Change the form where necessary.

> exotic   initial   defect   rigorous
> societal   susceptible   anticipatory

1. The _____ intent of EPA is to look to the future.
2. EPA and other organization's analysis of the environmental problems is usually quite _____.
3. _____ people should not expose to noise for too long.
4. There is no one who has no _____.
5. He likes growing flowers and has introduced some _____ species.

III. Complete each of the following statements with one of the four choices given below.
1. They unreservedly _____ to their technical know-how.
   A. passed through   B. passed on
   C. passed over   D. passed by
2. Many factories in Shanghai are developing _____ industry rapidly.
   A. export-oriented   B. export-orientating
   C. export-oriental   D. export-orient
3. The _____ effects of many illnesses made her a weak lady.
   A. collective   B. cumulative
   C. communicative   D. commutative
4. The government is launching a big _____ campaign against bribery and corruption.
   A. clearcut   B. clearup
   C. cleancut   D. cleanup
5. They _____ his new ideas into their plans which will be carried out next week.
   A. corporated   B. inconsiderated
   C. incorporated   D. considered

Writing Abstract Writing (6)

Directions: Read the text of Unit Sixteen again and write an abstract of the text in about 120 words

Reading Material A

EMAP Shifts Focus to Research①

The scope of EPA's Environmental Monitoring and Assessment Program (EMAP) is being scaled back, says Robert Huggett, head of the Office of Research and Development (ORD), which houses the program, EMAP has been under a cloud for the past year as critical reviews by the National Research Council (NRC) and EPA's Scientific Advisory Board raised concerns about the scientific underpinnings of the project.②

"The germ of a new program should be in place in April," states Huggett.

EMAP was originally billed as an ongoing nationwide effort to monitor changes in selected indicators, by using a probabilistic data sampling design, that would assess ecological resources on a regional scale.③ As indicators changed they would be traced back to human or natural stresses on the environment; these data then would be used for risk management as well as policy decisions. Demonstration projects have been under way since 1990, and a major new effort looking at the mid-Atlantic region of the United States is scheduled to be peer reviewed soon.

    Huggett says that EMAP does not currently receive enough funds to allow monitoring at the national level. Rick Linthurst, director of EMAP center within ORD at Research Triangle Park, NC, estimates that it would cost $100 million annually to run a national program.④ EMAP's budget is now less than $40 million. That number is likely to shrink and given Congress' budget-cutting mood, the program could be eliminated if scientific criticisms are not answered, warn a number of EMAP observers.⑤

    "I think EMAP is an extremely important program, but we have to change it," states Huggett, According to Huggett, the new EMAP will research what should be monitored, why. and at what frequency.⑥ "There will probably be a decrease in the thrust of extrapolating EMAP data over broad areas. We are looking at ways to leverage the EMAP money.⑦" During this reassessment, Huggett says programs are on hold.

    Robert Fisher (Texas A&M University), who chairs NRC's EMAP review committee, says that NRC reviewers are especially concerned about the poor understanding of the cause-and-effect relationship of many of EMAP's indicators. "if you can't reach that level of understanding, what is the value of the data?"

    Privately, EMAP researchers complain that the scientific reviews have been unduly harsh and that most of the criticisms have been answered. Fisher says that the differences centered on what the program was mandated to achieve.

    According to Fisher, "Collecting information on certain indicators could be as valuable as census or weather data." However, what EMAP showed researchers was that they had a poor understanding of the cause-and-effect connections for these indicators. Gaining an understanding of these connections, says Fisher, would be a valuable research effort, but expecting that the indicators could be understood well enough to unequivocally make policy decisions was "ill founded in the first place."⑧

    Other concerns expressed by NRC about EMAP include the management of the huge database of information, the level of understanding of how stresors at various ecological levels affect the environment, and what scale to monitor. We need a lot of research before we can go into large-scale monitoring, " adds Fisher.

Notes

①环境监测和估价计划的重点转移到研究方面。
②under a cloud 是指"受怀疑"。
③环境监测和估价计划原本是通过运用可能性数据样品设计,在全国范围内监测选定指标的变化,用以估价在某一地区内的生态资源。
④NC North Carolina（美国）北卡罗来纳州。
⑤… given Congress's budget-cutting mood, the program could be eliminated if scientific criticisms are not answered,… 考虑到国会削减预算的倾向性,如果科学性的批评得不到答复

的话，环境监测和估价计划有可能会落空……

⑥… the new EMAP will research what should be monitored, why, and at what frequency. why, and at what frequency 是省略句，=why it should be monitored, and at what frequency it should be monitored.

⑦leverage 意指"举债经营"。

⑧… but expecting that the indicators could be understood well enough to unequivocally make policy decisions was "ill founded in the first place".
但是指望能透彻地理解这些指标，以正确无误地作出决策，"起码也是不正确的"。句中 was 之前的部分是主语。

Reading Material B

States Try Out "Pollution Prevention Permits"

Pollution prevention and swifter introduction of innovative environmental technologies are key goals of a demonstration project getting under way in New Jersey. Because of a state law, regulators will issue 18 companies facility-wide "pollution prevention permits," rather than separate, media-specific operating permits, according to Jeanne Herb, director of the New Jersey Office of Pollution Prevention. ①

Along with maximizing opportunities for pollution prevention and source reduction, Herb says, the program also helps companies by streamlining the permitting process because one permit will be issued instead of a half-dozen or more. With the pollution prevention focus, the program moves manufacturers toward process changes and away from traditional end-of-pipe controls, Herd stresses. ②

EPA is also looking into trying permitting to pollution prevention, but the lead is up to the states, says Lance Miller, executive director of an EPA permit improvement team and a former New Jersey environmental official. After holding meetings around the country last year on general permitting problems, EPA learned that "stakeholders" thought there were plenty of other things to fix before the Agency embarked on a multimedia, facility-wide permitting program, Miller says, Nonetheless, Miller embraces the approach as a spur to encourage better technologies. ③ "pollution prevention and innovative technologies are almost two sides of the same coin, " he says.

In New Jerey, Herb says, new facility-wide permits look like a book with a chapter for each production process in the manufacturing chain and a pollution prevention analysis and material accounting matrix for each chapter. ④ An emissions limit is set for each process, but the company is left to find ways to meet those limits and comply with regulations. " As long as companies don't exceed those limits, they have a lot of operational flexibility to make business decisions and do whatever they want," she adds.

So far, a pharmaceutical manufacturer in Kenilworth, owned by Schering-Plough, Corp, has been issued a permit, and three others are expected to be permitted in April. A final report on the program will be issued to the legislature in 1996. In the course of doing the analysis for the permit, Schering phased out a production process that used the hazardous solvent trichloroethane and replaced it with a water-based solvent. ⑤ Company engineers also installed a closed loop recycling system to reuse Freon, reducing use of the ozone- depleting chemical by 140, 000 lb a year. ⑥ Schering saved $ 300, 000 a year by these changes, according to the states.

"We are starting to see new technologies, " Herb says, "but not technologies in terms of slapping on a new piece of equipment. Rather, we are seeing operational changes and equipment modifications that cut hazardous materials and combine pollution prevention and efficiency. "

Other states have looked into similar programs, but none is as far along as New Jersey. ⑦ Last year Washington states passed legislation calling for facility-wide permitting on a demonstration basis, and Weyerhaeuser Corp. , and two aluminum manufacturers are considering the program, says Hugh O'Neill, an official with the state's Department of Ecology.

Massachusetts has looked into the value of facility-wide permits but recently backed away. Instead, as part of a reorganization of the environmental office, the state is encouraging a multimedia permitting approach by requiring state environmental regulators responsible for specific media to" at least talk to each other" when issuing permits, according to Deborah Gallagher of the Massachusetts Department of Environmental Protection. ⑧ The state is holding training sessions to help staff understand how permitting requirements can sometimes block innovative technologies.

The state of Oregon, EPA, and Intel, Corp. , have developed a permit that encourages the company to conduct pollution prevention analyses in return for the state's acceptance of minor air permit modifications. The plant makes literally daily production changes that affect air emissions and normally might lead to a lengthy regulatory permit review, says Phil Berry, small business advocate and pollution prevention coordinator for the state. So an agreement was struck in which Intel can make production changes without modifying its permit as long as actual emissions are not increased. ⑨ In return, Intel agreed to a pollution prevention program, including training and the requirement that equipment vendors and chemical suppliers develop low-pollution technologies for Intel.

The program is voluntary, Berry notes, which is one of the biggest difficulties in pollution prevention solutions. "We searched throughout the Clean Air Act and there is no pollution prevention requirement in the law where we could hang the program. "⑩

Notes

①Because of a state law, regulators will issue 18 companies facility-wide "pollution prevention permits," rather than separate, media-specific operating permits …

由于州的一条法律，管理方面的官员将向 18 家公司颁发了公司范围的污染防治许可证，而不是独立的，新闻媒体特有的营业许可证，……

② With the pollution prevention focus, the program moves manufacturers toward process changed and away from traditional end-of-pipe controls, …

由于以污染防治为核心，该计划建议制造商们把目标转向工艺技术的改造，改变传统的排放管末端的控制方法，……

③ stakeholders 原指"赌金保管人"，文中指"美国各州"。

④ matrix 数学上的"矩阵"。

⑤ trichloroethane 三氯乙烷。

⑥ 公司工程师还安装了闭合环路收回系统，用以回收氟利昂，每年节省利用了这种消耗臭氧层的化学物达十四万磅。

句中"lb"=pound 磅。

⑦ … but none is as far along as New Jersey

句中"along"是指（距离）远，到相当的程度。

⑧ … the state is encouraging a multimedia permitting approach by requiring state environmental regulators responsible for specific media to "at least talk each other" when issuing permits。

……马萨诸塞州鼓励准许多媒体的办法，即通过要求负责特定传播媒介的州环境管理员在颁发许可证的时候，"至少要互相交谈"

⑨ So an agreement was struck in which …

为了保持句子的平衡，which 引导的定语从句后置。

⑩ "我们阅遍了"清洁空气条例"也难以找出防止污染的要求，使我们能把这个计划与之挂起钩来。"

Appendix I Vocabulary

a plate count 平皿读数		03
abatement *n.* 减少（轻）		08
absorbent *a.* 有吸收作用的		03
abstraction *n.* 引水		01
accomplishment *n.* 成就		11
acidification *n.* 酸化		13
activism *n.* （主张为政治目的采取有力行动的）行动主义		15
administrative *a.* 管理的，行政的		04
admirably *ad.* 令人羡慕地		08
adsorption * *n.* 吸附（作用）		02
advent * *n.* 出现，到来		08
adversary *n.* 对手；敌方（手；人）		14
aeration period *n.* 曝气周期		12
aeration tank *n.* 曝气槽		12
aesthetically *ad.* 美（学）地		02
affluence *n.* 丰富，富裕		13
agar *n.* 琼脂		03
agency *n.* 部门，机构		04
agglomerate *n.* 烧结块		05
aggravate *vt.* 使恶化，使更严重		13
alum *n.* 明矾		07
aluminium sulphate 硫酸铝		05
amenity *n.* 愉快		06
anatomy *n.* 解剖		11
anticipate *v.* 期待		10
anticipatory *a.* 预见的		16
antithetical *a.* 对立的；相反的		14
appalling *a.* 令人震惊的，骇人的		01
apply to 运用，应用		05
aquatic *a.* 水生的		08
archaeologist *n.* 考古学家		10
armament *n.* 武器，器械		01
as far as … be concerned 就……而言		12
aspiration *n.* 渴望		09
assault *n.* 攻击；冲击		15
assay *n./v.* 分析，化验		13
assimilate *vt.* 同化，吸收		06
atmospheric * *n.* 大气中的，空气的		13
augment * *vt.* 扩大，增加，加强		01
bandwagon *n.* 潮流；浪头		15
bank *n.* 堆		06
barren *a.* 荒芜的，贫瘠的		06
be composed of 由……组成		11
be consistent with 与……一致		09
be open to 可利用的，容易受到		04
be qualified to 胜任，适合		08
be subject to 受……制约		10
binding *n./a.* 粘合（的），束缚（的）		05
biotic *a.* 生命的；生物的		14
boil down to 归结起来是		15
botanist *n.* 植物学家		14
break-up 分离，分解		05
bridging *n./a.* 桥接（的）		05
brunt *n.* 正面的冲击		08
brush aside 漠视；扫除（障碍）		15
build-up *n.* 产生，形成		06
bulk *n.* 大量，大多数		08
burst upon 突然来到；突然发现		14
calcium *n.* 钙		07
calibrate * *v.* 校正		09
carbonate *n.* 碳酸盐		02
carbonate *n.* 碳酸钙		07
carry the responsibility for 对……负责		08
cast *vi.* 预测；估计		15
catchment *n.* 流域，集水处		06
cesspit *n.* 粪坑，污水坑		01
chamber *n.* 小室		03

词汇	词性	释义	编号
charge	n.	电荷,负荷	05
charge	vt.	使承担责任	04
checklist	n.	列表法	10
chloride *	n.	氯化物	02
chloroform	n.	氯仿,三氯甲烷	02
chlorophenol	n.	氯(苯)酚	02
clean up		清除	16
coexist	v.	共存	09
cog	n.	不重要但又不可少的人(或物);(齿轮的)轮齿	15
coliform	n.	大肠杆菌	02
collision	n.	冲突	15
colloid	n./a.	胶体(的),胶质(的)	03
colony	n.	菌落,群体	03
colossal	a.	异常的,非常的	15
combustion *	n.	燃烧	13
communal	a.	公有的,公用的	01
compatible *	vt.	可和谐共存的;适合的(with)	15
complexion	n.	情况	14
complexity *	n.	复杂(性)	08
complicate	vt.	使复杂	05
component	n.	成分	11
composite *	a.	综合的	10
composition	n.	组成(物)	08
compromise	v.	危及,损害	09
confirmatory	a.	起确定作用的	03
confrontation	n.	比较;冲突	14
constant	n.	恒量	07
constrain *	vt.	限制,制约	13
constraint	n.	制约,压抑	13
consumptive	a.	消耗性的,消费的	06
contaminate *	vt.	污染,弄脏	01
contribute to		对……产生影响	07
conventional	a.	常规的,传统的	12
convert … to		转变成	07
conveyance	n.	运送,输送	01
corrosive *	a.	腐蚀的	02
coupling	n.	结合;连接	15
cousin	n.	堂(表)兄(妹)	11
crevice	n.	缝隙	07
critical	a.	挑剔的	02
criticality	n.	临界(性,状态)	09
crucial *	a.	决定性的,关键的	13
cumutative	a.	累积的,渐增的	16
curricula	n.	(curriculum 的复数)课程	14
cyanide	n.	氰化物	02
cycle	n.	周期	12
damp out	v.	减少	11
decide on		决定,选定	04
decline	v.	衰败	11
decree	n.	法令	15
defect	n.	缺点,不完美	16
deficient	a.	缺乏的,不足的	06
deficit	n.	缺乏,不足	06
degrade *	vt.	降低,减少	07
demise	n.	死亡,灭亡,终止	01
demographic	a.	人口(统计)的	09
denitrification	n.	脱硝(作用)	07
depict *	vt.	描绘	07
depress	vi.	降低,减少	07
depression *	n.	低压	03
deprivation	n.	清贫	09
derive from		由…得出	04
deserve	vt.	应受;值得	15
designat … as … *		指定,指派	01
destabilization	n.	脱稳(作用)	05
dichotomy	n.	二分法,二歧法	11
die off	v.	衰减,相继死亡	12
differentiate *	vt.	区分,分别	03
dilemma	n.	困难	15
discharge permit		排污许可证	04
discipline	n.	科学;科目	14
dismantle	v.	拆开,拆散	11
disruptive	a.	破坏性的;分裂的	14
distinguish between		区分	10
ditty	n.	小曲;歌谣	15
diversify	vt	使…不同,多样化	08

diversion *	n. 转向		09
diversity *	n. 多样性		09
doctrine	n. 学说		15
dogma	n. 教条；教义		15
dominant *	a. 显性的,显著的		05
drop off	v. 减少,下降		12
dwelling	n. 住宅,住所		01
ecology	n. 生态学		14
EIA (Environmental Impact Assessment) 环境影响评价			10
electrostatic *	a. 静电的		05
emission *	n. 放射,散发		13
enamel	n. 珐琅质		02
enclosed	a. 封闭式的		07
endemic	a. 某地或某一人群所特有的		09
endogenous	a. 内源的,内部产生的		12
endogenous phase	n. 内源期		12
endrin	n. 异狄氏剂（一种杀虫剂）		02
engender	vt. 产生；造成；引起		15
enmeshment	n. 吸附,包入作用		05
enrichment	n. 富集		06
enteric	a. 肠的		01
enumeration	n. 计数		02
equitable	a. 公平的		14
eradicate	vt. 根除,消灭,杜绝		01
etch *	vt. 刻蚀		03
eutrophic	a. 富营养的		06
eutrophication	n. 富有养分		06
evaluate	v. 评估,评价		10
evidence	vt. 证明,作为……的依据		04
evolution	n. 进化,发展		04
evolutionary	a. 发展的；进化的		15
evolve	vi. 发展,演变		04
excrete	vt. 排泄,分泌		03
excretion	n. 排泄（物）,分泌（物）		06
expel	vt. 排出		07
expenditure *	n. 花费		12
extinct	a. 灭绝的		09
extract *	n. 提取物		02
extraction *	n. 采掘		09
extreme	n. 极端		04
facultative	a. 兼生的		07
fad	n. 一时的风尚；一时的爱好		15
faecal	a. 粪便的,排泄物的		03
fall into	陷入,陷于		01
fanciful	a. 奇异的,空想的		13
feedback	n. 反馈		15
ferment	vt./n. 发酵		03
fishable	a. 有鱼可捕的		04
fishing	n. 鱼场		06
flocculation	n. 絮凝		05
flooding	n. 洪涝,水灾		10
flow	n. 流量（速）		07
fluoride	n./a. 氟化物（的）		02
focus	vt./n. 集中		04
formidable *	a. 可怕的,棘手的		11
foul *	a. 污浊的,腐烂的		01
frame	n. 框架,计划		13
function	n. 依据,随……变化		04
gadget	n. 小装置		07
genus	n. 类,种类		03
give rise to	引起,导致		06
go back to	追溯到		08
gravity	n. 重力		12
gravity separation	n. 重力分离		12
grid *	n. 格子,格栅		03
gross	a. 总的		15
growth curve	n. 生长曲线		12
growth cycle	n. 生长周期		12
harmonious	a. 协调的；相称的		14
have relevance to	和……有关		14
heterogeneous *	a. 非均匀的,异类的		05
hindrance	n. 障碍,妨碍		06
humankind	n. （用作单数或复数）人类		14
hydraulics *	n. （复）水力学		08
hydrology	n. 水文学		08
hydrolyse	v. 水解		05

hydrolysis	n.	水解(作用)	05
hydrophobic	a.	恐水的,蔬水的	05
hydroxyapatite	n.	碱式磷酸钙	07
hypothetically	ad.	假设地,有前提地	13
identification *	n.	识别,鉴别	03
ill-considered	a.	考虑欠周的,不明智的	09
immutable	a.	不可改变的;永远不变的	15
impart *	vt.	给予,传递	02
implement	vt.	实施,执行	04
impoundment	n.	贮水	01
in attempt to		试图	05
in contact with		与……有联系的	03
in direct proportion to		与……成正比	12
in harmony with		与……相协调	09
in perspective		有透视效果的,可直观的	10
in practice		实际上	04
in response to		为了响应	13
in summary		简言之	08
in the case of		就……而论,那……来说	05
in the context		在……方面	06
in the way of		关于	06
in this role		在这项工作中	04
inclusion *	n.	包括,内含	02
incompatible	a.	不相容的,不一致的	06
incorporate … into …		含,吸收	16
incubate	vt.	(细菌)培养	03
incur *	v.	受,惹起,承担	13
index	n.	索引	10
inequity	n.	不公平	09
inevitably	ad.	不可避免地	06
infancy	n.	初期	15
infeasible	a.	不能实行的,办不到的,不可能的	13
inheritance	n.	继承,遗产(传)	11
inoculate	vt.	移植,培养	03
inorganic *	a.	无机的,人造的	06
insoluble *	a.	不溶解的	05
institutional	a.	公共机构的,制度上的	13
intact *	a.	完整的	09
integration *	n.	集成	11
integrative	a.	综合的	14
integrity *	n.	完整	15
intercept *	vt.	截流	01
interdisciplinary	a.	各学科之间的,多学科的	10
intervention	n.	干涉	09
intestine	n.	肠	03
isolation *	n.	孤立,分离	11
issue	vt.	配给,发行	04
jelly	n.	胶冻,胶状物	03
jigsaw puzzle	n.	拼板玩具	11
justification	n.	以……为理由	04
kingfisher	n.	翠鸟	11
lactose	n.	乳糖	03
landslide	n.	滑坡	11
latrine	n.	(沟形、坑形的)厕所	01
laxative	a.	致轻泻的	02
legitimate	a.	合法的	09
level out	v.	平衡,衡定	12
life expectancy		估计寿命,平均寿命	01
lime	n.	石灰	07
lindane	n.	高丙体六六六,林丹	02
liquefy	vt.	液化,稀释	03
long-chain		一系列,一连串	05
loop	n.	圈;回路	15
ludicrous	a.	滑稽的;荒谬可笑的	15
lyse	v.	细包衰败	12
magnesium *	n.	镁	02
magnification *	n.	放大(率)	03
magnitude *	n.	大小,数量	10
maladaptation	a.	不适应;适应不良	15
malformation	n.	畸形(体)	02
mammalian	a.	哺乳类的	11
marginalize	v.	无视,让靠边	09
marketable	a.	有销路的	07
matrix *	n.	矩阵	10

165

英文	词性	中文	编号
maturation	n.	成熟	15
mechanism *	n.	机理	05
metabolic	a.	新陈代谢的	03
methaemoglobinaemia	n.	高铁血红蛋白血（症）	02
microscopist	n.	显微镜学家	14
microstrainer	n.	微应变器	07
minimal *	a.	最低限度的，最小的	01
minimize	v.	将……减到最小程度	10
molecular *	a.	分子的	05
motile	a.	运动的	03
motility	n.	运动	03
mottling	n.	斑驳状，杂色	02
mount	n.	载片	03
move along		向前走	13
moving	a.	移动的，活动的	07
mutagenic	a.	致突变的	02
mutation	n.	突变	02
navigable	a.	可通航的	04
neutralization	n.	中和	05
nitrification	n.	氮的硝化（作用）	07
nitrobacter	n.	硝化杆菌	07
nitrogen	n.	氮	02
not ... but rather		不是……而是	04
notwithstanding *	ad.	尽管；还是	15
noxious	a.	有害的	09
objectionable *	a.	令人讨厌、作呕的	01
objectivity	n.	客观（性）	10
oceanography	n.	海洋学	08
oligotrophic	a.	贫营养的	06
on a pilot basis		在实验室的基础上	16
on a scale of		按……等级	10
optimal *	a.	最佳的	08
optimum *	a./n.	最佳（的）	08
option	n.	选择	09
organism	n.	生物体，有机物	03
organophosphate	n.	有机磷酸盐	02
orientation *	n.	定向，取向	09
oriented	a.	以……为方向的，以……为目的的	16
originate from		来源于	03
outcry	n.	强烈抗议或反对	01
overlap *	n.	复叠，部分相同	02
overlook	v.	忽视	11
paradox	n.	奇论；疑题	14
paramount	a.	至高无上的	11
partially	ad.	部分地	05
participation	n.	参与	08
penetration *	n.	穿透	07
perception	n.	感知	11
petri	n.	皮氏培养皿	03
phenolic	a.	苯酚的	02
phosphorus *	n.	磷	06
physiology	n.	生理学	11
plate	n.	平皿	03
population	n.	总数，全体	03
pose *	vt.	提出，形成	01
potential	n.	电位，电势	05
predomination	n.	支配，优势	12
premier	a.	首位的；最早	14
prerequisite *	n.	先决条件，前提	01
prevailing	a.	普遍的，主要的	10
primitive	a.	原始的	14
probability	n.	可能性概率	13
procedure	n.	程序	10
prodigious	a.	巨大的；惊人的	14
productivity *	n.	生产率	06
professional	n.	专业人员，行家	04
profound	a.	深远的，深刻的	06
proliferation	n.	扩散，激增	13
prolific	a.	多产的，有生殖力的	06
prone *	a.	有…倾向的	09
provided	conj.	假如，倘若	09
provision	n.	设备，装置	01
pseudomonas	n.	假单胞菌属	07
quadrupling	n.	倍	13
quantitative *	a.	量的；数量的	14
quantitatively	adv.	定量地	04

英文	词性	中文	页
rampant	a.	蔓延的,猖獗的	01
random *	a.	随机的,不规则的	03
range … from … to		从……到……不等	04
rationally	ad.	合理地	15
recreation	n.	消遣娱乐	06
regarding	prep.	关于,就……而论	01
regenerate	vt.	还原,再生	07
regeneration *	n.	再生	09
relevance *	n.	关联	14
removal	n.	清除	05
renewable	a.	可恢复的	09
repeal	vt.	废除;否定	14
repulsion *	n.	排斥	05
repulsive	a.	排斥的	05
resolution	n.	晰象,分辨	03
respond to	v.	对……作出反应	12
restabilization	n.	再稳定	05
restriction	n.	限制	06
restructure	vt.	调整	13
retain	vt.	残留	03
retention *	n.	保持,停留	07
reversal *	n.	改变,反向	05
rigour	n.	精确,严密	11
rot	vi.	腐朽	06
scarcity	n.	缺乏,少,供不应	13
scenario	n.	情况,方案	13
screening	n.	筛	08
sector	n.	机构,组织	16
sedimentation	n.	沉积(作用)	08
segregation *	n.	分离	08
sensationalism	n.	危言耸听	14
serial	a.	系列的	03
set to		转化	03
sheen	n.	光泽,光彩	03
shock loadings	n.	冲击载荷	12
shooting	n.	直射	03
significant	a.	相当数量的	07
slake	vt.	熟化	07
soluble	a.	可溶的	02
sophisticated *	a.	采用先进技术的	04
spasmodic	a.	间歇的;一阵阵的	14
specific	a.	特定的	10
specification *	n.	说明	02
specify	vt.	详细说明	05
spectrum *	n.	范围	04
spell out		详细说明	04
stabilization	n.	稳定(性)	12
stain	vt./n.	着色,染色	03
stand at		(数量)为	13
stand out		引人注目,醒目	03
stoichiometric	a.	化学计量的	07
straightforward *	a.	明确的,肯定的	04
strategy	n.	战略,策略	04
strenuous	a.	奋发的,努力的	01
subculture	vt.	再次培养	03
subsequently	ad.	后来,接着	04
substitute	n.	替代物	09
sulphate	n.	硫酸	05
superficial	a.	表面的	10
surge tank	n.	调节池	12
suspension *	n.	悬浮液(体)	03
sustainable	a.	持续的	09
switch away		转移,移动	13
synthetic detergent		合成洗涤剂	06
sysnergism	n.	协同作用	16
take a view of		抱…观点	06
take … to pieces		拆开,拆散	11
take … into account		考虑	09
tend to		往往,趋向于	04
teratogenic	a.	畸形形成的	02
term	vt.	把……叫做	06
the order of the day		流行,风气	08
thoroughly	ad.	彻底地	07
toxin	n.	毒素	02
transience	n.	短暂;无常	15
treble	vi.	成为三倍,增加两倍	13
trickle	vi./n.	滴流	08
uncouple	vt.	分开;分离	14

unecologic	a. 不主张生态保护的	15
uneconomic	a. 不经济的,浪费的	15
unsightly	a. 不雅观的,难看的	07
upheaval	n. 动乱,剧变	01
urbanizaton	n. 都市化	13
variable	a. 变化的,可变的	12
vegetation	n. 植被,草木	06
vibrational *	a. 振动的	03
virtual	a. 实际上的,现实的	13
washout	n. 冲洗	07
weighting factor	n. 权重因子	10
whereby *	ad. 藉以,由此	11
whilst=while	conj. 尽管,虽然	03
wilderness	n. 荒野	06
workable *	a. 切实可行的	04
wriggle	vt. 蠕动,扭动	03
yield	n. 效率	07
zeta potential	ζ电位	05

Appendix Ⅱ　Translation for Reference

第1单元

给水排水设备介绍

　　水或许是世界上最重要的自然资源，因为没有水就没有生命，没有工业。和其他各种原料不同，在水的多种用途中是找不到代用品的。由于可靠的供水是建立永久性居民区的先决条件，所以水在居民区的发展中起着至关重要的作用。遗憾的是一个永久性居民区所产生的废水和垃圾是引起环境污染潜在的重要因素。原始文明时期，解决污染问题的办法十分简单，只需把居民区迁移到另一合适的居住地。到了较为先进的文明时期，此类兴师动众的搬迁是行不通的，必须采取措施保护和扩大供水，妥善处理废物。随着人口的日益增长，工业的不断发展，需水量逐渐增大，必须认识到水作为自然资源务须审慎管理。

　　给水排水设备的重要性在古代文明的前数百年中就为人们所认识。考古资料表明新石器时代的居室里安装有厕所及排水道；公元前2000年的克里特岛的米诺斯文明时期，民居中修建了陶土给排水管道和抽水马桶。罗马人建造了非常发达的给排水系统，他们的城市使用连续作业的喷水池作为主要供水水源，为大多数居民提供饮用水，而有钱人家则使用自家安装的管道供水。当时建造的距离超过80km的大型高架渠为城市提供了充足的优质水，有些至今依然存在。街道上用石块敷设的污水管用于排除地表水、收集厕所的排出物并运送到城外。随着罗马帝国的灭亡，他们建造的大部分市政工程设施被废弃了。几百年中，几乎没有任何给排水设施。中世纪时期，在河流的重要交汇处，城镇发展起来了，这些河流通常成为取之便利的水源，又是排污纳废的好去处。尽管较大的城镇里修建了下水道，但主要用于排除地面水。特别是英国，在1815年以前，法律规定禁止把污水秽物排入下水道。那时卫生设备只是凤毛麟角而已：例如，在1579年，伦敦某街六十幢房屋共用三个厕所。从窗户向大街上泼污水扔垃圾司空见惯。所以毫不奇怪，当时人们的平均寿命还不到目前发达国家寿命的一半。为了改善当时的状况，1847年通过了一项法律：规定在伦敦必须把粪坑和厕所粪便排入下水道。伦敦的下水道向泰晤士河排放污水，同时该河又是伦敦供水的主要水源。加之，由于许多下水道长年失修，造成污水泄漏至供取水的另一主要地下蓄水层。这种状态必然导致水源污染愈来愈严重，泰晤士河成了臭气冲天，令人不快的都市景观；更严重的是饮水传染的疾病在市内猖獗一时。1854年，布罗德大街抽水泵引发的霍乱暴发事件导致一万人死亡。该事件为约翰·斯诺博士提供了充足的材料，证明污水污染的水源与诸如霍乱、伤寒一类肠道疾病之间的关系。公众强烈的抗议促成了建造现代第一项重大的公共卫生工程设施：贝泽尔格特截流污水管。这些管道把收集的污水输送到伦敦下游排入泰晤士河的入海口，而从不受潮汐影响的特迪顿河段引水供伦敦使用。因此到1870年时，在英国，饮水传染的疾病已经在很大程度上得到控制，同时在西欧和美国的一些城市也在采取类似的解决措施。始于英国的工业革命大大增加了城市的需水量，因而19世纪后期建造了多项重大的供水工程，其中包括大型高地贮水池，例如为伯明翰供水的艾伦谷工程，为纽约建造的克罗顿水库和卡特思基尔水库。

通过坚持不懈地大量投资解决水质控制问题，才使饮水传染的疾病在发达国家里几乎根除绝迹。然而这些成就决不能因此而掩盖了许多发展中国家里给排水设施方面的骇人状况。1975年进行的调查表明：世界农村人口的80%和城市人口的23%不能正常享用安全可靠的饮用水。排水设施情况更加糟糕：85%的农村人口和25%的城市人口根本没有卫生设备。由于高出生率，根据发展中国家人口增长的情况，如果不竭尽全力增加给排水设施，那么未来拥有符合给排水设施标准的世界人口的百分率实际上是在下降。因此联合国把1981年至1990年这个时期定名为"世界饮用水供给和排水设施十年"，以达到为全球所有人提供安全饮用水和充足的排水设施的目标。实现这样的目标谈何容易，必须投入大量的财力和人力。不过，据估计，要达到十年目标的费用仅是全球同期军备开支的约5%。

发达国家中现在的需水量是比较稳定的，基本的水质控制措施也已完备。然而，许多现有的供水和污水工程已经比较陈旧了，因而重建这些设施又给将来提出了许多新问题。除此以外，随着人们对各种环境污染后果的了解的不断增加，又出现了潜在的新危险。例如，目前人们关注的是水中存在一些低浓度有机化合物可能有致癌的危险。总之，对水质进行各方面的控制将仍然是全世界保护公共卫生首当其冲的问题。

第2单元

水 质 标 准

城市用水有多种用途——洗涤、饮用、废弃物处理以及工业用水。水质标准由这些用途中对水质要求最高的饮用水确定。该标准反映了所生产的水须满足以下要求：
 (a) 合乎卫生，即病菌和毒素含量最低；
 (b) 外观令人满意并可饮用；
 (c) 对配水系统无腐蚀作用；
 (d) 生产成本低廉。

为满足这些要求，人们已经提出了多项标准，并在不断修改之中。所提出的特定浓度是指那些不会影响水质的浓度标准。饮用水的一般标准用以下参数表示：微生物学指标、卫生及毒性指标和水体的感官性质。

饮用水的微生物学标准

饮用水的微生物学标准被认为是最重要、最常用的标准。因为水中病原体总量很少，但种类很多，所以直接监测十分困难。水体的常规微生物学检验是取决于水中非病原体大肠杆菌的数量。一般标准是每100毫升水样中大肠杆菌的平均数小于1，该平均数是根据不同的统计方法和取样次数确定的。

饮用水的卫生和毒性标准

有几种化合物被认为是对人体有害的，其中有有机物，也有无机物。如铅、铬、镉等金属是有毒物质，它们在水中的最大允许浓度一般每升低于 0.1 毫克，而且通常是每升低于 0.01 毫克。这种浓度标准同样也适用于氰化物。最近才提出有毒有机化合物的标准，其主要原因是水中各种物质种类繁多而且分析难度大。但是越来越多的物质被纳入饮用水标准之中。诸如活性炭氯仿提取物（一般小于 1 毫克/升），这样的一般参数可用来估算出有机物的含量。有些类型的物质，如有机磷酸盐和碳酸盐可归为一类（小于 0.1 毫克/升），而其它化学药品则需分别确定它们的标准。例如，异狄氏剂（农药）（小于 0.001 毫克/升），高丙体六六六（小于 0.056 毫克/升）和 DDT（小于 0.042 毫克/升）。由于许多有机化合物很可能是致癌物（导致癌症），诱变物（诱发突变）或畸变物（导致畸形），其不良影响可能要若干年后才会表现出来，所以标准得不断修改。但水质标准中包括了这些物质后，促使人们越来越多地采用像活性炭吸附的工艺来清除水中的有机分子。

人们对水中其它一些化学物质制定了标准，因为它们对人体有害。首当其冲的是硝酸盐离子和氟化物离子。硝酸盐离子（NO_3^-）可能引起婴儿（6 个月以下的儿童）高铁血红蛋白血症。饮用水中硝酸盐的浓度常控制在小于 10～50 毫克/升；如果不能满足这个条件，应改用其他供水方式作为幼儿的饮用水。如果水中氟化物离子过量（大于 1.5 毫克/升），会引起牙斑釉，严重时则导致牙齿变黑并损坏其结构。某些其它化学物质对人体也有特别的影响，如硫酸盐离子，尤其是当它与镁离子同时存在于饮用水中时，会导致初饮者轻度腹泻。

饮用水的感官标准

一般认为，生产的饮用水必须合乎感官要求，使饮用者对其卫生质量放心。对水的浊度、色度、味臭进行物理测定，目的在于确保所生产的水可以饮用并具有良好的感官性质。一般标准要求所生产的水，其性质指标应控制在一定限值内，例如色度小于 5 个单位并无异味和异臭。某些特殊的化学物质则有额外的限制。氯离子浓度大于 200 毫克/升时，水会有咸味，而限制酚类化合物的原因之一是它容易产生具有强烈气味的氯酚物质。

饮用水水质标准和原水水质

因为分类的重叠，任何一种水质标准的分类都具有随意性。有毒物质标准之所以最容易分类，是因为可以以饮用后不产生副作用的含量为其浓度标准。然而，毒性对人体的长期影响却很难确定，不同毒素的相互作用也会导致毒性总量的增加。同时，由于水的消耗量极大，即使像氯离子那样的无毒物质也会产生副作用。

一般而言，选择能提供最佳水质和/或所花费的处理成本最低的水体作为原水水源。由于传统的水处理工艺对许多物质的清除能力差，这就意味着原水中这些物质的浓度必须与建议的饮用水标准接近。由于水污染常常和水中的病原体、有毒物质和高浓度的可溶性物质有关，因而原水中所含有的会导致污染的物质浓度必须很低。原水的需氧量（化学需氧量小于 10 毫克/升，5 天生化需氧量小于 6 毫克/升），油脂（小于 1 毫克/升），氨（小于 0.5 毫克/升），活性炭氯仿提取物（小于 0.5 毫克/升），以及含氮总量标准的制定旨在使污染减小到最低程度。

第 3 单元

微生物检验

由于微生物十分微小，所以用肉眼是看不见的；而那些较为初级的微生物，其外貌特征并没有提供识别它们的确凿依据。人们必须利用细菌的生化性质或代谢性质帮助识别微生物的种类。因为活标本接近无色，在液体底色上不显眼，所以观察时十分困难。在有些情况下，给死标本着色是十分有效的方法，但进行着色和制作载片本身可能会改变细胞的一些特征。

光学显微镜的最高放大倍数为 1,000 倍，分辨能力限度约为 0.2 微米。因此使用光学显微镜时，大多数病毒是观察不到的，只能观察到细菌细胞结构的有限情况。如果要进行更详细的观察，必须使用电子显微镜，其放大倍数约为 50,000 倍，分辨能力限度约为 0.01 纳米。

研究活标本必须测定生物体是否是移动的，而且只能使用光学显微镜完成。在这种情况下须使用悬滴液载片，关键在于分清究竟是布朗运动还是真实移动，布朗运动是一种常见于胶体的随意振动，而真实移动是一种急速运动或蠕动运动。

在许多观察研究中，需要估计出水样中的微生物数。对于像水藻那样较大的微生物，在进行计数和实际辨别微生物种类时，可以使用一种具有已知容积的凹槽式专用显微镜载片，上面蚀刻了格子，通过数出载片室里适量的微生物数，就能获得所需的数据。

要计算出水样中活细菌数（活细胞计数），可采用琼脂营养培养基的平皿计数法。把一毫升水样（必要时，水样要先期稀释）和盛放在皮氏培养皿中摄氏 40℃ 的液化琼脂培养基混合在一起，琼脂培养基开始呈胶状，这样使细菌细胞固定位置。然后把培养皿置于合适的条件下（天然水细菌在 22℃ 下培养 72 小时，来自动物或人体的细菌在 37℃ 下培养 24 小时）培养。培养结束时，每个细菌会繁殖出肉眼可以观察到的菌落，而菌落的数量被认为是原水样中活细胞的函数。实际上，这类平皿计数法并不能给出水样中的细菌总数，因为单种培养基和单一温度的条件组合无法繁殖出所有的细菌。然而，假如在两种温度下，采用大范围培养基进行活菌计数，那么就能全面地了解水样中细菌的质量和污染史。

为了确定某一特定菌属或种类的存在，就需要利用它的特性行为，而这可以通过采用只适合所研究细菌的专用的选择性培养基和（或者）培养条件来达到。许多严重的疾病和水中的微生物污染有关，其中大多数疾病是由那些患病者或携带者排出的病原菌所引起的。虽然我们能够检验出水样中某种病原体的存在，但是，有一种更加灵敏的试验方法是采用指示生物大肠杆菌，这是常年栖居人体肠内的寄生菌，并且大量排出人体。水中有大肠杆菌，表明有人粪尿的污染，因此这种水样的潜在危险在于，很可能水样中还有病原粪便菌的存在。一般大肠菌会使乳糖发酵而产生酸和气体，因此使用在连续多次稀释的水样中的乳糖培养基就能发现大肠菌。在 37℃ 下经过 24 小时的培养，如果有酸和气体放出，就认为是大肠杆菌类的阳性显示，可以根据统计表格查出每 100 毫升水样中大肠菌的最大可能数。作为大肠杆菌的确认试验，阳性试管在 44℃ 下置于新鲜培养基中再次培养 24 小时，在这种情况下，只有大肠杆菌能生长，从而产生酸和气体。

另一种现在常用的细菌分析法是使用特殊的薄膜滤纸，其孔径可以使细菌和悬浮液分开。然后，留在滤纸上的细菌被直接置于吸水衬垫上进行培养，这种盛在小塑料皮氏培养皿中的吸水衬垫里含有合适的营养培养基。鉴定细菌的类别是根据所使用的营养培养基的种类和通常是根据形成的菌落的外观（颜色、光泽）确定的。菌落的计数提供了必要的定量资料。薄膜过滤法在进行现场试验中十分方便，但材料的费用比常规分析法要高一些。

第4单元

水质管理中监测的作用

各种水质管理的策略都因法规而生，其中每一种策略都按各自独特的方式利用水质监测的结果。这些策略包括从"危机管理"到"无污染物排放"，范围很广。危机管理法一般是在专门研究的基础上进行监测，这种方法经常在资源有限的情况下使用。危机管理法也属水质管理中较早期的方法，由此衍生发展而成为后来更先进的方法。另一方面，无污染物排放法把监测的重点放在排放水上，而不是来水水质上。

实际上，大部分水质管理部门在操作时，采取介于上述两个极端之间的方法。所需要的水质资料的确切特性是根据行政部门对法规的解释而定的。因为在有关理解水质性能变化的某一特定法规中可能有多种含义，所以监测中的侧重点是由每一个水质管理部门的工作人员决定的。解释水质性能变化的要求可能包含在法定目标中，以及为达到目标而授予的管理职责和权限中，也可能作为监测要求直截了当地阐明。为了更充分地理解这些含义，我们首先看一下水域可垂钓可游泳这个法定目标。一个水质管理部门，特别是属全州性或全国性的部门，如何获取水质资料以使其能够就是否达到这个法定目标得出结论？在目标和所获得的数据之间是否存在着一种明确的关系，以衡量是否已成功达到目标？

其次，要考虑的是，大多数水质管理法规都规定了的在水质管理中可供行使的一些管理职责和权限（即管理"工具"）。要能够有效且恰如其分地使用每一种管理工具，都必须获得水质资料。每种工具需要的准确信息通常在法规中没有详加叙述，而是由负责实施的工作人员规定的。这些水质管理专业人员常常须解决诸如下列难题：一个部门如何准确地确认需要什么样的资料方能有效地行使其管理工具？需要什么样的资料才能从定量角度说明达到了河流标准？需要什么样的水质资料才可以签发排水许可证？需要什么样的水质资料才可以提供贷款建造废水处理厂？

上述问题的切实可行的解决办法可以从为实施水质管理法而选定的管理策略中得到。为了设计支持水质管理的水质监测系统，必须首先确定管理策略及其所需要的资料。通过监测收集的数据及其在管理部门内部的使用这两者之间的关系是成功地设计任何水质监测系统的重要因素。

最后，在水质管理部门内部，除了上述水质监测法规中的含义外，在许多水质管理法中都有明确的监测要求。例如，联邦清洁水法中的第305（b）条款要求各州准备一份其州界内所有的通航水道的水质情况报告。对于环境水质的监测所提出的这种明确无误的要求经常成为各州进行定点监测的理由。在此项工作中，使用评价监测以确定法定目标是否得以实现。然而，大部分环境监测系统和目标评价之间没有明确的设计上的关系。因此，用环境监测数据评估目标进展情况是十分困难的。通过美国环境保护局不断修改联邦清洁水法的第305(b)条款的报告指南及美国地质勘查局正在重新设计国家河流质量统计网计划，证明了这个领域内需要进行最新的研究和发展。

鉴于建立管理机构的法规不够明确，管理中监测的作用也就在很大程度上任凭实施法规的工作人员进行解释。明确工作人员愿意承担的监测职责是设计有效的水质监测（信息）系统的第一步，该系统将有助于以定量的方式作出管理决策。

第5单元

混凝机理

水中自然含有的悬浮泥沙颗粒清除十分困难，这是因为它们非常小，常常只有胶体粒子大小，并带有负电荷。因此无法相互聚结形成易于沉淀的较大颗粒。通过沉淀清除这些微粒的步骤首先要中和负电荷，其次是促进微粒相互碰撞。电荷的中和法通常称为混凝，而使微粒形成较大的颗粒的过程则被称为絮凝。现在让我们较详细地研究这个机理。

虽然化学混凝是一种广泛使用的方法，但是，尽管进行了大量的研究工作，其作用原理至今未被完全了解。目前认为，混凝中碱性胶体的稳定性可以解释所观察到的结果。如图5-1所示，疏水胶悬体的稳定性被认为是作用在微粒上的各种力所致。微粒相互排斥是由静电的表面电荷引起的，但可以通过增加带有相反电荷的离子，减少排斥力，使分子之间的引力呈显性（优势），达到胶粒脱稳。在这种情况下，ζ电势值，即颗粒结块边缘的电势是比较重要的。从理论上说，零ζ电势时，混凝条件为最佳。然而，在处理水中非均匀（多相）悬浮物时，似乎由于多种复杂因素，操作过程中测定ζ电势并不总是很重要的。

在悬浮固体浓度较低的情况下，通常，在水中加入混凝剂（絮凝剂）发生反应，形成不溶水解物，通过吸附聚结，完成混凝处理。在这种扫络混凝中，原悬浮物质的性质无足轻重，水解物的特性决定了整个反应过程。遗憾的是，混凝剂加入水中时，其变化是十分复杂的。水处理最常用的混凝剂为硫酸铝，当加入水中后，发生一系列复杂的反应，常常简化成：

$$Al_2(SO_4)_3 + 6H_2O \rightarrow \underline{2Al(OH)_3} + 3H_2SO_4$$

$$3H_2SO_4 + 3Ca(HCO_3)_2 \rightarrow 3CaSO_4 + 6H_2CO_3$$

$$6H_2CO_3 \rightarrow 6CO_2 + 6H_2O$$

即总式为：

$$Al_2(SO_4)_3 + 3Ca(HCO_3)_2 \rightarrow \underline{2Al(OH)_3} + 3CaSO_4 + 6CO_2$$

人们知道这些简化了的反应式跟实际反应情况相去甚远。铝的水解物是十分复杂的,其性质受到如混凝溶液的熟化和强度的影响。铝的水解物包括化合物:

$$[Al(H_2O)_5OH]^{2+} \text{ 和 } [Al_6(OH)_{15}]^{3+}$$

而且会产生硫酸盐的络合物。因此详细说明实际发生的反应是十分困难的。

如果悬浮固体浓度较高时,胶体学说提供了解释观察到的反应的依据。因此胶体悬浮物的脱稳是由于吸附了部分水解后带强电荷的金属离子所致。连续的吸附导致电荷逆转,并在混凝剂高剂量时引起悬浮物的再稳定。在这种情况下,胶体颗粒的性质因此会影响混凝的过程。

当混凝用来清除水的色度时,反应似乎取决于可溶性有机物和混凝剂结合生成的沉淀物。因此,一般来说,色度与清除色度所需要的混凝剂剂量之间直接相关。

助凝剂的作用与形成长链结构的大分子的能力有关,这种大分子能为相邻的悬浮颗粒提供交联和连接的作用,从而促使结块,防止在剪力作用下发生絮凝物破碎。如果用离子助凝剂,就如使用主混凝剂那样也会发生电荷的中和,尽管使用正常剂量的助凝剂,其作用可能不会十分明显。

第 6 单元

废水污染的综合影响

任何水体都能够同化一定程度的污染,而不会产生严重影响,因为水体具有稀释和自净两个因素。假如污染量增大,则受纳水体的性质会发生变化,其各种用途的适合性就可能随之削弱。理解污染的影响及可能采取的控制措施对于有效地管理水源是至关重要的。

在考虑废水污染问题时,除了产生溶解氧不足外,当然还有其他的影响。稀释程度不同,溶解固体、有机质含量、营养物(如氮和磷)、色度和混浊度都会随之大大提高。所有这些组分将导致水质的不良变化,特别是在提取下游水的情况下。在湖泊和流动缓慢的水域里,营养物的累积是一个严峻的问题,但是在江河中则不至于如此严重。然而应该牢记的是:许多从江河取水的供水项目中,原水处理前一般储存在不深的大水库中。这样,即使原水中营养物含量不高,也会导致藻类的大量繁殖生长,至使进行水处理时的难度比起原江河水要高得多。

在没有人为因素影响的情况下,所有的湖泊需要经过几千年完成其特性的自然变化。在荒野流域的湖泊主要从周围贫瘠的环境中承受进水,因此汇集的有机食物和无机营养物含量甚微。这种缺少营养的水域称为贫营养的,其特点是总溶解固体含量低,混浊度低和含有少量的生物种群。随着流域的老化(几乎和地质年代同步),营养物含量逐渐增加,因此生物繁殖力逐渐提高,导致了水质下降。随着营养物和生物繁殖力的上升,必然使水域营养物丰富或称为富营养的。营养物循环利用,在达到极端情况时,水域会被植被严重污染,由于腐烂的植物而引起低溶解氧,而且由于黑暗,很可能产生厌氧情况。所有湖泊发展必然结果是富营养的，但其发展速度，由于人类活动产生的人为富集而大大加快。氮和磷在富营养化过程中是最重要的营养物；同时，由于有些藻类能固定空气氮，所以一般认为磷是水中的限制营养物。磷的极限含量取决于许多因素，所谓极限，即超过这个极限将导致藻类的过度生长。污水出水中含有磷酸盐，部分是由于人粪尿，部分是由于人类使用的合成洗涤剂。

工业化地区常常发生的严重污染对河系会产生深远的影响，因此在河系中减少河流污染的工作必然是耗资巨大，不是一朝一夕所能完成的。理想的环境是条条河流无污染，游鱼成群，风景悦目宜人。在工业化国家里，从经济角度讲，防止所有的河流污染是行不通的，应该综观水资源的情况，把河流分门别类以适合各种专门的用途。

人们显然不希望河流受到污染，其原因有多种多样：
1. 给水受到污染——增加了水处理工厂的负担。
2. 限制了水上娱乐活动。
3. 影响鱼类生存。
4. 产生令人讨厌的外观和气味。
5. 沉淀固体的堆积妨碍了河道航行。

典型用水分类如下（按水质要求降低的顺序排列）：
1. 生活供水
2. 工业供水
3. 商业渔场
4. 灌溉
5. 娱乐和优美的环境
6. 运输
7. 废物处理

每一种用途对水质水量都有其特别的要求，有些用途是无法一概而论的。灌溉是消耗性用水，因为这种用途的水无法再回流江河。大量的冷却水由于蒸发而损失掉。虽然其他用途通常对水质会产生有害的影响，但一般不是消耗性的。作为生活供水提取的水以污水回流。水资源的保护取决于尽可能地实现水的综合利用。

第7单元

废水的三级处理

普通废水处理厂的任务是进行废水的一级处理和生物处理。然而，二级处理工厂的排水里仍然含有大量的各种污染物质。除了对生化需氧量产生影响外，悬浮固体会在河流里沉积下来，形成难看的淤泥堆。如果这种生化需氧量排入流速缓慢的河流中，则通过减少溶解氧仍然会破坏水生生物。无论一级处理还是二级处理都无法有效地清除磷和其它营养物或有害物质。

通过一种砾石过滤器的简单设备就可以有效地清除悬浮固体物质。该设备是一个装满砾石的箱子，安装在二次澄清池的边沿，这样所有的废水都必须流经滤床。砾石是如何截留絮状体的实际机理还不清楚。而只知道流过砾石过滤器的污水清洁了。

另一种复杂得多，且销路不错的精巧装置叫微滤器。微滤器是一只大圆筒，外面包着一层上面有小孔的不锈钢薄板。用泵把污水注入圆筒，清洁水就从小孔中滤出。当圆筒转动时，那些小孔通过喷淋得到清洗。

至今清除生化需氧量最常用的先进处理法是洁净塘，又称氧化塘。这实际上是地面上的一个坑，即一个大池塘，用来盛放排放前的工厂污水。这样的池塘是需氧的，因为阳光穿透对藻类的生长十分重要，从而池塘表面积要大。氧化塘里发生的反应情况见图7-1。如果废水流量小且氧化塘池面大的话，废水有时只需经过氧化塘一次处理步骤。

另一个清除生化需氧量的方法是活性炭吸附。这种方法还有一个优点：不仅清除有机物质，也清除了无机物质。活性炭的吸附机理包括化学和物理两方面，并利用细小的缝隙截留住胶粒和更小的微粒。活性炭柱是一根全封闭的管道，污水从底部注入，而清洁水从顶部流出。当炭里饱和了各种物质时，必需从炭柱中清除这些污物使其再生，或称为清洁。清洁过程常常是连续进行的，新炭从柱顶部不断加入。活性炭的清洁或再生通常是在无氧的条件下对炭进行加热。再生时，活性炭的效率会稍有下降，不断加入新炭以保证净水工艺的有效进行。

清除氮有两种方法。第一种方法是利用大部分氮即便在二级处理后还以氨的形式存在的特性，通过增加pH值，生成下列反应：

$$NH_4^+ + OH^- \longrightarrow NH_3\uparrow + H_2O$$

这样溶解于水里的大量氨气就从水里排入大气。但由此而产生的空气污染问题还没有办法解决。

第二种清洁氮的方法首先要对废水进行全面的处理，使其产生硝酸根离子。这样延长了二级处理的停留时间，致使像硝化杆菌和亚硝化单胞菌属这样的细菌把氨态氮转化成NO_3^-，这种转变过程称为硝化（作用）。其一系列反应式如下：

$$2NH_4^+ + 3O_2 \xrightarrow{亚硝化单胞菌} 2NO_2^- + 2H_2O + 4H^+$$

$$2NO_2^- + O_2 \xrightarrow{硝化杆菌} 2NO_3^-$$

这些反应速度缓慢，因此在曝气池里需要很长的停留时间，而且需要足量的溶解氧。这些反应的动力学常数很小，产量很低，因此，净产泥量不多，使冲洗始终是一种危险。

一旦氨转变成硝酸盐，由于多种兼性厌氧菌（如假单胞菌属）的作用而还原。这种称为反硝化作用的还原过程需要加碳，为此常常使用甲醇（CH_3OH）。

$$6NO_3^- + 2CH_3OH \longrightarrow 6NO_2^-\uparrow + 2CO_2\uparrow + 4H_2O$$

$$6NO_2^- + 3CH_3OH \longrightarrow 3N_2\uparrow + 3CO_2\uparrow + 3H_2O + 6OH^-$$

清除废水中的磷几乎总是用化学方法进行的。最常用的化学品是石灰[$Ca(OH)_2$]和硫酸铝（明矾）[$Al_2(SO_4)_3$]。钙离子在pH值高时，会和磷酸盐结合生成一种不溶于水的白色沉淀物，称为碱式磷酸钙，沉淀后被清除。另外还生成了不溶于水的碳酸钙，被清除出来后，置于炉内燃烧进行再循环。

$$CaCO_3 \longrightarrow CO_2\uparrow + CaO$$

生石灰（氧化钙）（CaO）加水消解，

$$CaO + H_2O \rightarrow Ca(OH)_2$$

这样生成的石灰，可以再利用。

从硫酸铝中产生的铝离子沉淀析出溶解性差的磷酸铝，

$$Al^{3+} + PO_4^{3-} \longrightarrow AlPO_4\downarrow$$

也形成氢氧化铝，

$$Al^{3+} + 3OH^- \longrightarrow Al(OH)_3\downarrow$$

该物质是粘滞性的絮体，有助于磷酸铝的析出，最常使用硫酸铝的地方是最终澄清池。

达到一定的除磷要求所需要的硫酸铝剂量取决于水中磷的含量，以及其它成分。所生成的污泥可以用化学关系式计算出来。

通过这种使用明矾（硫酸铝）沉淀磷的方法，（而且因为氢氧化铝的形成，这也是更有效的去除悬浮固体和生化需氧量的方法），我们达到了排污目标。

		原废水	一级处理	二级处理	三级处理
生化需氧量	毫克/升	250	175	15	10
悬浮固体	毫克/升	220	60	15	10
磷	毫克/升	8	7	6	0.5

一种代替高科技先进废水处理系统的方法是把二级处理的废水喷洒在地面上，让土壤微生物降解其中残留的有机物。这样的系统方法称为土壤处理法。多年来一直在欧洲使用，近年开始在北美洲使用。看来这样的系统是一种代替那些成本高的复杂系统的合理方法，特别是在较小的社区。

灌溉可能是最有前途的土壤处理法。一般作法是：废水流量为每秒一立方米时，需要土地1000至2000公顷，具体的用地量取决于作物和土壤。在二级处理出水中残留的营养物如氮和磷必然有利于作物的生长。

第8单元

工程人员在消除水污染中的作用

尽管以前一直声称控制水污染并不是高不可攀的技术问题，但是其涉及面广，且错综复杂，必须综合运用多门不同的学科，才能以最低成本获得最佳效果。消除水污染的系统方法涉及到许多学科的协作配合：(1) 工程及有关学科：卫生工程学（土木工程学）、化学工程及诸如机电工程、化学、物理学等其他工程领域；（2）生命科学：生物学（水生生物学）、微生物学、细菌学；（3）地球科学：地理学、水文学、海洋学；（4）社会和经济学科：社会学、法律、政治学科、公共关系学、经济学、管理学等等。

通常，学土木工程出身的卫生工程师由于时代的需要，首当其冲地承担起了控制水污染中采取各种工程措施的重任。这种局面要追溯到生活废水占主导地位的那些年代。生活废水的成分并不复杂，因此，制定的废水处理法都较规范，在处理程序中只包括数量有限的单元过程和单元操作。传统处理法使用大混凝土池对废水进行沉淀或曝气、经过滴滤池、加氯、筛滤，有时还经过一些其他工序。工程师主要关注的是有关结构和水力学的一些问题，当然，成为卫生工程师的先决条件是具有土木工程的学历或经历。

这种情况发生了变化，起初是渐渐变化，近来，随着工业化的到来日渐加快。由于各种各样新兴的工业过程，产生的废水品种繁多，需要更加复杂的处理过程。现代废水处理需要动用多种设备，进行多种单元过程和单元操作。显而易见，化学工程师在消除水污染的问题中已经起着举足轻重的作用了。化学工程师经过五十年的努力所形成的单元操作概念已成为科学地解决废水处理中所碰到的设计难题的关键。

事实上，今日城市废水也不同于过去的生活废水。实际上工业化地区所有的市政府都得处理混合的生活和工业废水。鉴于在这种处理中涉及到的经济和技术问题，工业废水在排入城市下水道之前进行单独处理（分流）是十分必要的。

随着当今一般家庭使用合成洗涤剂和其他一系列新产品的出现，即使是真正的生活废水，其性质也发生了变化。因此，欲用最佳方法处理生活废水，则需要改进过去沿用的处理方法。

总之，当务之急不仅要改进陈旧的水处理法，而且要创造新技术、新过程和新方法。今日之废水处理的形象不再是昔日的大混凝土池，而是一系列密切协调的单元操作。这些操作过程包括物理和化学两方面，必需根据每一种废水的具体情况加以协调。化学工程师在组合这些单元操作、使之成为行之有效的过程方面的才能，使他完全能胜任水处理设施的设计。

第9单元

持续发展的概念

满足人们的各种需求和愿望是发展的主要目标。但众多人们对衣食住行的需求尚未得到满足，而且在这些基本需求以外，人们尚有各种旨在改善生活质量的合理愿望。一个充满贫困和发展不平衡的社会是易于经常性地发生生态危机和其它危机的。持续发展要求满足所有人们的各种基本需求，并向他们提供机会以满足他们改善生活的愿望。

只有当各地消费标准注重长期持续性时，高于最低基本要求的生活标准才能得以维持。然而，我们许多人的生活，如在能量的使用方面，则超出了地球生态资源的限度。持续发展要求在生态学可能允许的范围以及人们合理的愿望内,提高促进消费标准的价值。

基本需求的满足在一定程度上取决于实现充分的增长潜力,持续发展明确地要求那些基本需求尚未得到满足的地区发展经济,而在其它地区持续发展则可与经济增长相一致,前提是其增长的内含能够符合持续性和不剥削他人利益的基本原则。但仅有经济增长是不够的。单一的经济增长将导致高水平的生产力与普遍的贫困同时存在,从而导致对环境的危害。因此,持续发展要求社会通过提高生产潜力和确保机会均等来满足人们的需求。

人口的剧增将增加对资源的压力并阻滞贫困地区生活标准的提高。虽然这并非仅仅是人口数量的问题,同时还是一个资源分配的问题,但只有当人口的增长与生态系统中不断变化的生产潜力相适应时,持续发展才能保持下去。

社会可以以多种方式(如过度地利用资源)来损害其满足人民未来基本需求的能力。技术的发展虽然能解决一些即时的问题,但也会导致一些更大的问题。考虑不周的发展可能会忽视许多人的利益。

农业的固定化、河道的改变、矿物的开采、热量及有毒气体向大气的排放、森林的商业化开发以及遗传控制都是人类在其发展过程中干预自然系统的例证。直至最近,人类对自然系统的这些干预还是小规模的,其产生的影响也是有限的。但今天,这些干预则规模较大,影响较深,因此更严重地威胁着地区性和全球性的生命保障系统。这种情况本来是没必要发生的。至少,持续发展不得危害保障地球生命的自然系统,即大气、水体、土壤和各种生物。

显而易见,经济的增长和发展包含着自然生态系统的变化。并不是各地每个生态系统都可避免受到外界干扰的。一般而言,像森林和鱼类这样的可更新资源,只要其被消耗的速率不超过其再生和自然生长的速率,不一定会消耗殆尽。但大部分可更新资源都是既复杂而又相互关联的生态系统中的一部分,在确定其最大可持续产量之前,必须考虑这些可更新资源的利用对整个生态系统的影响。

至于像矿物燃料和矿物这样的不可更新资源,对它们的使用将使其贮藏量减少而使后人难以为继。但这并不意味着不应该利用这些资源。一般而言,对这种资源的消耗速率必须考虑其临界性、各种降低其消耗速率的技术的有效性及可资利用的各种替代资源的可能性。因此,不能使土壤退化至无法进行正常恢复的地步。就矿物和矿物燃料而言,必须合理确定对它们的消耗速率,尤其是回收和利用的经济性,以确保其在获得可资利用的替代资源之前不至于消耗一空。

发展往往会简化生态系统并减少其物种的多样性。而物种一旦灭绝,则是不可更新的。植物和动物物种的损失将大大地限制后人的选择范围。因而,持续发展要求对植物和动物物种加以保护。

诸如水体和空气这样的所谓免费商品同样是资源。在各种生产过程中,仅有部分的原料和能量转变为有用的产品,而其余部分则作为废物而排出。持续发展要求降低对空气、水体和其它自然要素质量的不良影响,以维持生态系统的总体完整性。

实质上,持续发展是一个不断变化的过程,在这个过程中,资源的利用、投资方向、技术发展方向及制度的变化相互协调,有利于提高社会在目前和将来满足人们需求和愿望之潜力。

第 10 单元

环境影响评价

　　环境影响评价（EIA）的主要目的是对某一拟建工程项目对自然环境和城市环境将造成的任何不利（或有利）的影响进行预测。这样才有可能在实施该项目时采取措施以降低或消除其有害的影响。环境影响的预测或评价并非一件易事。此项工作的进行须有一支由不同学科组成的专家组，其中包括土木工程师和技术员、城市规划师以及生物学家或生态学家。对于大型且复杂的项目而言，尤其是涉及到敏感性环境问题时，专家组也可包括地质学家、考古学家、建筑师和社会科学家。

　　有些环境影响是可以直接而客观地加以评价的。它们不受主观或个人意见不同的影响。比如，因工程项目而引起的暴雨径流的增加量可以通过对现有的径流强度和径流量的计算和比较来进行预测，从而可预测径流量的增加对工地和河流下游特性的影响。这些影响包括洪涝、水土流失和水污染。

　　工程项目对大气质量的影响同样可借助于综合数学模型加以评价。通常，在土地开发项目中，汽车排放的一氧化碳对大气质量的影响尤其重要；汽车交通量的增加将直接造成这种影响。交通量的增加可利用基本交通工程原理将其作为人口密度和土地利用的函数来加以估算。根据此估算结果以及有关大气质量和主要气候条件的现状资料，便可对工程项目对其周围大气质量的影响进行预测了。

　　工程项目对植被和野生动物的影响是比较难以客观地加以评价的。虽然估算工程项目将要毁坏多少公顷或英亩的林地是比较容易的，但要对这种影响的价值或重要性取得一致的看法则要困难得多。当然，如果工程项目位于一个城市社区最后剩下的一片林地，或林地中有些树木是临绝物种的话，那么这种影响将比其它情形更为严重。

　　区分短期影响和长期影响是重要的。例如，项目施工中所造成的影响包括因重型机械而导致的周围噪声水平的暂时提高。但一当工程施工结束后，这些影响也就停止了；因而这些影响被认为是短期的。但工程项目完成后，其对诸如径流形式和当地含水层补给率的影响将不会停止；这些影响将是长期的。

　　几年来，人们业已提出了多种环境评价的方法。这些方法均以最客观地对工程项目进行综合性和系统性环境评价为基本目标。这些方法的复杂性从简单的列表法到较复杂的"矩阵"法各不相同。

　　列表法将工程项目的各种不同方案潜在的所有环境影响进行列表，用定性的方法来描述所预期的各种影响的大小。例如，用负号表示不利的影响。如用两个负号（——）表示小的影响或中等程度的影响，而用三个或四个负号（————）表示较严重的影响。有益或有利的影响则用正号（＋）来表示。若环境影响不适用于某一特殊的工程方案时，则用零（0）来表示。这样的一种表格可提供一种评价的直观看法。

　　所谓的"矩阵"法试图对各工程方案的相对影响进行定量化或"分级"，并为环境影响的比较和评价提供数值依据。各潜在影响的预期大小用等级（如 0 到 10）表示；等级数值越高则表示可能产生严重的不利影响，而等级数值越低则表示产生的影响不大或可以忽略。

零（0）表示对某一特殊的活动或环境组分不产生预期的影响。

矩阵法也利用数字权重因子来表示某一特殊影响的相对重要性。这些权重因子要取得专家评估组的一致认可，并根据其所在地和项目的特殊性来确定。例如，对某一特殊的地区而言，如果地下水是该地区的唯一饮用水水源，则可以认为工程项目对地下水水质的影响要比对大气质量的影响更为重要。因而可给地下水水质分配一个比大气质量高的权重，比如为 0.5，而大气质量的权重为 0.2。

权重因子可与相应的影响等级值相乘以直观地反映影响的大小。例如，虽然认为对地下水水质的影响等级值为 4，而对大气的影响等级值为 6。但通过对其进行权重（与权重因子相乘）后，我们则可以看到，对水质的影响（0.5×4＝2），总体上要比对大气质量的影响（0.2×6＝1.2）更为重要或严重。将所列出的所有经权重分析后的影响条目的大小加在一起，则可得到每个工程方案的综合分数或环境质量指标。总的来讲，指标数值最低的方案对环境造成的不利影响将是最小的。

第11单元

人类及其环境

人是一种动物。从解剖学和生理学的意义上讲，我们与哺乳类动物是一样的，而且我们和所有其它动物一样必须为生存而消耗食物和呼吸空气。然而，我们在技能和行为方面是与动物不同的。我们不仅拥有决定我们动物属性的基因遗传，而且拥有通过语言和符号传布知识和习俗的文化遗产。但和其它动物一样，我们也占据一个以空间和时间形式存在并形成我们环境的栖息地。尽管这是一个物理、化学和生物环境，但它同样是一个包含社会、政治、经济和技术各方面的文化环境。

环境的这种双重特性反映在人与环境相互关系研究的二分法之中：自然科学涉及自然环境；社会科学及应用科学涉及文化环境。研究人类与其环境相互作用的地理学反映了这种二分法。事实上，脱离开人类及人类与其环境之间的相互作用，便不能对环境的这两个组成部分加以充分地认识。但是，我们在考虑自然环境时绝对不能停留在表面上，而必须理解它。为此，本文主要对自然环境的物理、化学和生物组成、各组成部分之间的关系和各组成部分与人类之间的关系加以讨论。

我们应当怎样开始做这项艰巨的工作呢？我们可以像拆卸一部机器那样，先将环境分解成各个部分，看看它的组成是什么，它是如何工作的。此过程可以叫做环境的分析。这是科学的传统方法之一，由此可将不同的学科（或不同的学科分支）分解成各个不同的组成部分并对它们加以分别研究。因此，海洋学专门研究海洋，气象学专门研究大气，水文学专门研究水体，地质学专门研究岩石，生物学专门研究生物体，而物理学和化学则包罗了所有这些，但其涉及面要小一些、也更基础一些。

当我们试图将环境恢复原状时，这种方法将出现明显的问题：因为在从分析到综合的过程中，我们用不同的方式和不同的精确度对所选择的不同的环境组成部分作了观察，并提出了不同的术语，因此我们不再将它们看作是原来整体中的一部分了。由于我们忘了它们原来的组合方式，或者我们在分解环境之前未能弄清它们的组合方式，而使各个部分的重新组合变得更为困难。同样，有些部分因没有一个专门学科对其关心而可能被忽略掉了。因而问题的实质是缺乏任何真实的综合。翠鸟、集积中的雷云、汹涌的波涛和山崩之间有什么联系呢？虽然我们对它们中的每一个都知之甚多，但它们又是怎样组合成环境拼板玩具的呢？你或许会问这是否真的要紧。只要我们对它们有足够深的了解，有何必要将各个部分加以综合和重新组合呢？或许对这些问题最好作形象化的解答。

我们有限的自然环境不仅为人类及其动物需求提供了生存空间和资源，而且由于人类是一种文化型动物，因而它还必须为我们提供文化发展的基础。由于我们文化的复杂性、社会组织和技术能力的与日俱增，我们对环境的需求也不断地提高。此外，文化的发展使得我们对直接环境的依赖性越来越小，我们对直接环境的认识方法及与之相互作用的方式也发生了变化。我们对环境的利用、改造和损害或破坏业已达到了任何其它动物都无法比拟的程度。在20世纪，我们的需求已开始超过了环境的容量，我们明智地管理、保护和保存环境的能力已成了至高无上的东西。也正是由于对这种需要的认识，才促进了人们对各种保护政策的关心和支持。但我们必须首先理解环境，才能对环境进行管理。与其说是哲学思辨，不如说是这种迫切的需要，才促进了对人类自然环境的综合性研究。此外，它还强调将自然环境和文化环境隔离开来不仅是不现实的，而且也是危险的。要理解我们与自然环境之间的相互作用，则只有以我们对自然环境的认识并使我们的行为与之相协调为前提，而这两者都受到我们复杂的文化环境所制约。

第12单元

生物活性污泥法的设计

活性污泥或任何生物废水处理法的目的是花费最少的时间和资金，将有机物质尽可能彻底地从原废水中除去。原废水的性质及其流动特征确定了，便必须根据它们进行处理法的设计。仅在少数情况下，工业废水可排放到调节池以平衡有机物浓度和流量。

常规活性污泥的基本问题之一是微生物的优势种群易于变化。原废水中的有机物促进曝气池中某些菌种的生长。当除去有机物质，微生物进入内源期时，原有的用于稳定有机物的微生物群衰减以致死亡。第二批细菌利用原来的微生物死亡的产物并在曝气池的终端占据优势。当污泥回流到曝气池的首端时，原来的细菌群又必须重新生长起来。只有长的曝气时间，原来的细菌数量才能减少到某一水平，故需要较长的恢复期，来处理流量或浓度突然增加的废水。在以活性污泥处理不同的工业废水中，这是很重要的，并且也是活性污泥对冲击负荷反应缓慢的原因之一。

保持菌种均匀的唯一方法是保持有机物浓度的均匀。对于处理多变的废水来说，这是不可能的,但这种变化可保持在最小的限度。食料微生物比(F∶M)是细菌生长的关键。业已证明,高的食料微生物比使细菌迅速生长,而低食料微生物比使细菌生长不显著。在常规活性污泥法中,食料(F)和微生物(M)都在不断地变化,随着每一次循环,食料微生物比(F∶M)从最大值变为最小值。如果在完全混合的情况下,原废水由曝气池全部池水所稀释,该曝气池就成了一个巨大的调节池,减小食料(F)的波动范围。由于曝气池处于完全混合,食料(F)值变得最低,波动也最小,池中任何一点的微生物活动与任何其他点相同。微生物在整个正常生长期内的变化趋近一点,而不像在常规活性污泥法中那样是一条宽阔的生长带。因而,从微生物的观点看,完全混合系统的优点最多,缺点最少。

在任何废水处理问题中,有机物负荷都是固定的,因此只有通过调整微生物数量才能改变食料微生物比。通过调整食料微生物比,在细菌生长曲线的任何一点上进行处理都是可能的。现已清楚,就废水处理而论,在生长曲线上的某些段,并不能满意地进行工作。对于完全混合系统来说,其处理范围将处在生长下降阶段的某一点上。

最近的改革之一是让完全混合系统在生长下降阶段的较低端进行工作,此处污泥增加最小。剩余的污泥随出水排放,不致引起公害。出水中的活性与非活性固体之比必须与混合液中的相同。如果不能定期地除去悬浮固体(因为不能将这些悬浮固体随出水排放),那么完全氧化是否会大量用于处理生活污水,是值得怀疑的。

另一方面,含有可溶物质的工业废水形成惰性固体缓慢,其生物处理接近完全氧化。出水中剩余的固体与所处理的有机物质成正比,约有10%~13%的有机物质作为惰性固体存在于出水中。

在多数情况下,活性污泥必须有固体分离和排除装置。对于活性污泥法来说,仍须解决的主要问题之一乃是如何从液体中有效地除去和浓缩污泥。现行的方法则依靠重力分离,但浓缩污泥的能力有限。

如果污泥主要是活性的,就需要进一步稳定,才能最后进行处置。在正常情况下,厌氧消化用于污泥稳定,但近来在小系统中好氧消化也已达到相同的目的。决定采用何种方法,由经济因素决定,因为两种方法都会产生可以经过过滤除去其水分的稳定物质。如果污泥主要是非活性的,就不需要进一步稳定,污泥可以直接脱水。

第13单元

能源、经济和环境

伴随着工业化、城市化的不断发展及社会富裕程度的增强而导致的对能源需求量的日益增长,使得全球对初级能源的消耗量的分布变得极不均匀。例如,工业化市场经济中的人均能耗量为非洲撒哈拉沙漠周围地区的80倍以上。同时,占世界约四分之一的人口却消耗了世界初级能源的四分之三。

1980年,全球的能源总消耗量为10TW左右。如果人均能耗水平保持在目前的水准,则到 2025 年，全球人口达到 82 亿时，能耗量将约达到 14TW（其中发展中国家需消耗 4TW 以上，工业化国家需消耗 9TW 以上）——即总能耗量将比 1980 年增加 40%。但如果人均能耗量以目前工业化国家的能耗水平均匀分布的话，则到 2025 年达到上述同样数量的世界人口时，全球的能耗量将达到 55TW。

虽然上述能耗的"低"值或"高"值都很可能不能真实地反映将来能耗的实际情况，但它们至少粗略地估出了未来能耗量的变化范围。这其中可能会出现多种不同的情形，其中之一是假定发展中国家对能源利用率的提高。例如，如果低经济收入国家和中等经济收入国家的经济发展水平分别翻两番和翻一番的话，同时如果高经济收入的石油输出国、工业化国家及非工业化市场国家的能耗量保持在目前的水平的话，则中低经济收入国家和高经济收入国家的能耗量将大致相等。假定对初级能量的使用效率与目前相同，则中低经济收入国家需耗能 10.5TW，而三类高经济收入国家需耗能 9.3TW——全球总耗能为 20TW 左右。

这些情形的现实性如何呢？能源分析家业已对 2020 年至 2030 年的全球能源未来进行过许多的研究。虽然这些研究并未对未来能源的需求量作出预测，但它们对各种技术、经济和环境因素与能源的供给和需求量之间的可能的作用关系进行了探索。一般而言，较低的能耗需要提高能源的利用率，而较高的能耗则将加重自二次世界大战以来人们所经历过的环境污染问题。

未来的高能源需求在经济方面的含义是很令人不安的。世界银行最近的一项研究表明，在 1980～1995 年间，仅仅发展中国家年能耗增长 4.1% 就需要年均投资约 1300 亿美元（以 1982 年价计）。这些投资中约有一半要靠外汇，其余的则要靠发展中国家内部用于能源的开支。

未来的高能耗所带来的环境危机和不确定性同样是混乱，而且会导致其它问题。其中四个最明显的问题是：

（1）由于向大气排放多种气体，尤其是矿物燃料燃烧过程中产生的二氧化碳（CO_2），所产生的"温室效应"将极可能改变气候；

（2）由于矿物燃料燃烧所产生的大气污染物而导致城市-工业空气污染；

（3）由于上述同样的原因所引起的环境酸化问题；及

（4）核反应堆事故的危险性，核反应堆使用期结束后废弃物处置及设施的拆除造成的问题，与核能利用有关的核扩散的危险等。

除这些以外，发展中国家将出现的一个主要问题是燃料木材将变得越来越稀少。如果这种趋势继续下去，到 2000 年将有约 24 亿人口将生活在树木极其稀少的地区。

这些问题甚至将发生在能源利用量较低的地区。有研究表明，一种实用型燃料混合物——4 份煤、2 份燃气和 1.4 份油——将到 2020 年引起严重的全球气候变暖问题。目前尚无从矿物燃料燃烧过程中去除二氧化碳的技术。大量燃煤也将导致硫氧化物和氮氧化物排放量的增加，而这些氧化物中的大部分将在大气中转化为酸。目前，在一些国家，所有新设施甚至一些旧设施都要求使用这种硫氧化物和氮氧化物的去除技术，但这些技术将增加投资 15%～25%。如果有些国家不准备增加这方面的费用，那么这个办法也就行不通。这就将在很大程度上限制了未来在很大程度上依赖于矿物燃料的更高能量的使用。不久，全球初级能耗量增加一倍，也将不可避免地受到严重的经济、社会和环境的制约。

对于那些GDP增长不受限制而投资方向由建立较为初级的能源供应向开发和供应高效、节约燃料及废物利用设施的方向发展的国家，人们更愿意向低能耗的方向发展。这样，为满足社会所需的能量供应可大大减少初级能量的生产量。通过在经济各领域中使用目前所能利用的最为节能的技术和工艺，则年人均GDP增长速率可达到3%左右。这一增长速率至少与本文中所认为的实现合理发展的最低增长速率相等。但这一途径需要巨大的结构上的改变以使高效节能技术向市场渗透，但这似乎很难在今后的40年中被大多数政府所实施。

低能耗、高效率未来的关键点并不是它们是否能在建议的时间框架内得以充分的实现。而是要求在政治上和机构上作出根本性的变革，重新调整投资潜势，以走上低能耗及更高效率的道路。

委员会❶ 相信，21世纪的世界没有其它现实的选择。低能耗、高效率的思想并非是异想天开。提高能源利用效率业已表明了其成本效益结果。在许多工业化国家，产生一单位GDP所需的初级能源在过去的13年中已减少四分之一乃至三分之一，而其中大多数是因采取了提高能源利用率措施的结果。本世纪初，工业化国家通过合理的管理及采用提高能源利用率的措施而使其初级能源的消耗量得以基本稳定。它们也同样使发展中国家实现更高增长速率，同时大大降低投资、减少外债、缓解环境危害。但在21世纪的最初几十年中，它们不能最终缓解全球范围内对大量新能源的需求量。

第14单元

生态学——与其他科学的关系及与文明的联系

"生态学"一词起源于希腊语中的oikos（意为家庭）和logos（意为研究）。因此，环境家园的研究包括了其中所有的有机体及所有使得其适于居住的作用过程。那么，根据韦氏大词典中的定义之一，生态学顾名思义是"家居生活"的研究，它以整体性和有机体与其环境之间相互关系的形式为其重点研究内容。

"经济学"一词同样起源于希腊语中的词根oikos。由于nomics意为"管理"，故而经济学被翻译为"家庭管理"，因此生态学和经济学应当是两门关系极为密切的学科。遗憾的是，许多人却把生态学家和经济学家看作是观点对立的势不两立者。本文将考虑因生态学和经济学各自的观察面太窄而使它们间产生矛盾的问题，并努力设法在它们的差异之间架起桥梁。

在人类历史的早期，生态学就具有实用性。在原始社会中，人们为了生存而需要了解其环境，如自然力及其周围的动植物等。实际上，文明是伴随着火和其它用于改变环境的工具的使用而开始的。由于技术的进步，我们的日常生活需要对环境的依赖程度似乎越来

---

❶ 此处指世界环境和发展委员会。

越低了；我们忘却了我们还得继续依赖自然。而且，不管何种政治意识形态的经济体系都对人类所创造的、主要对个人有益的东西作出评价，而把那些对我们整个社会有益的自然界的物质和贡献看作是几乎没有价值的东西。在出现危机之前，我们通常把自然界的物质和贡献看作是理所当然的；我们总认为它们是取之不尽、用之不竭的或是可以通过技术的革新而加以取代的，而事实却与之相反。

极其令人费解的是，一些工业化国家以人类在短时期内与环境脱离的方式，通过利用正在迅速耗竭中的有限的天然矿物质而取得了成功。然而，文明仍然依赖于自然环境，不仅包括能源和物质，也包括那些诸如空气和水循环等的重要的生命支撑过程。自然规律是不以人们的意志为转移的，但其情形和定量关系却将随世界人口的变化而变化，惊人的能耗业已增加了我们改变环境的力量。因此，我们的生存依赖于知识和明智的行动，采取协调性的而非破坏性的技术来保护和提高环境的质量。

与其他学科一样，生态学自其有历史记载以来，也经历了断断续续而逐渐发展的过程。早在希波克拉底、亚历士多德和其它古希腊哲学家的作品中就清楚地涉及到了生态学问题。但当时的希腊语中还没有生态学一词。"ecology"一词产生的历史并不长，它是由德国生物学家爱伦斯特·海克尔在1869年首次提出的。在此之前，18和19世纪生物学复兴时期的许多伟人都对这个课题作过贡献，即便当时并没有使用"生态学"一词。例如，在18世纪初期，安东·范·列文虎克既是当时最著名的杰出显微镜专家，也是食物链和种群调节机制研究的先驱者。英国植物学家理查德·布莱德利的作品则表明他对生物的生产力有着相当的理解。而所有这三个学科都是现代生态学的重要内容。

生态学作为一种公认而独特的科学领域，可追溯到约1900年。但仅在过去的十年中，生态学一词才成为普通词汇的一部分。起初，这一领域被极为明确地划分为植物生态学和动物生态学，但F.E.克莱门兹和V.E.谢尔福德的生物群落概念、雷门德·里德曼和C.E.哈勤森的食物链和物质循环的概念以及E.A.伯杰和琼西·乔戴对湖泊整体的研究等则对普通生态学整体领域基本理论的建立起了帮助作用。

爆发于1968年至1970年两年间的那场环境意识运动是世界性环境意识运动最典型的例子。当时，大众媒介中有大量的篇幅提及环境问题，似乎一时间人人都关心起污染、自然界、人口增长和食物及能源消耗的问题来了。公众对环境问题关注程度的提高，对生态科学产生了深刻的影响。70年代以前，生态学在很大程度上被看作是生物学的一个分支。生态学家被安排在生物系工作，所开课程也只能见诸于生物学课程表。虽然生态学仍将以生物学作为其坚实的基础，但它实际上已作为一种新型的综合性学科而从生物学中脱胎而出，起到联结物理和生物学过程的作用，并在自然科学和社会科学之间架起了一座桥梁。

第15单元

环境伦理学

越来越多的公民正不仅从经济的角度，而且从环境质量的角度来考虑问题。律师、经济学家和政治家们正感到越来越难以回答这样一些问题："增长是否真有必要？"、"国民生产总值是否总该不断上升？"或"我们是否应该仅从金钱的角度来考虑公共项目的收益与成本？"。在几年前，这些问题会被认为是愚蠢的问题而被不屑一顾。但这些问题并不愚蠢，而应当给予明确的答复。

实际上，生态学和经济学是一对矛盾。人类不可能无限制地增加人口数量及其产出量（及对资源的利用），而不导至最终的自我毁灭。在目前的经济系统中，尚没有一种减缓有害于人类生存的各种过程的发展速度的反馈环节。

生态学家和经济学家之间的矛盾可归结为这样的顺口溜：

生态学不讲经济，

但是另一种逻辑，

经济学不讲生态。

虽然技术经济学家们认为环境伦理学已成为我们生活中永恒的一部分，但它尚处于其发展的初期，是一种新型而大胆的概念，其成熟和发展需要时间。其法律原理、经济计算方法及工程决策方法正处于迅速发展时期，其中有些尚不成熟。

伦理学一词起源于希腊语中的"ethos"，意指由一个人的行为所决定的个人特征。这种特征随着进化过程而不断得到发展，并受到适应环境之需求的影响。简言之，"伦理学"决定着我们的行为方式，这是我们受环境直接作用的结果。

当人们谈及"环境危机"时，他们的真正含义是指我们的思维方式和行为方式（我们的伦理）与环境不相适应。曾几何时，人类与环境是协调相处的，但不知何故，或是出于偶然或是由于被某种未知的力量闹了一个极大的恶作剧，使得人类这一物种的生活方式发生了改变，以至于与环境不再适应了。因而，在多年的发展过程中，使得我们与我们的环境变得不再适应的原因并不是"环境危机"而是认识上的危机。

根据生态学的观点，这种不适应性导致了两种结果：

1. 生物的绝种。
2. 生物进化成一种与环境再次相适应的形式和特征。

环境伦理学作为一种力量，它的诞生在一定程度上是出于我们对自身生存的关心的结果，同时也是我们对人类仅是生命形式的一种及我们应与我们的同伴共享地球的认识的结果。这不是一个宗教问题，因为伦理学不仅是建立在信念的基础之上的，也是建立在严格的事实和充分分析的基础之上的。

梭罗是最早认识到环境退化并提出关心自然的人之一。对此，他令人信服地指出关心就是让步的观点。这种观点在道义上是值得赞赏的，但在现实中却是没有什么作用的。在过去的十年中，我们所经历的正是梭罗的观点与能动主义相结合的过程。这是我们所关心的问题的一个方面，更重要的是，为提高对环境问题的关心程度，我们必须付诸行动。

自然主义者兼作家奥尔多·利奥波特曾为了对环境伦理学做出定义而最早作了卓有成效的努力。他提出：

只有那些以保护生命群体的完整性、稳定性及完美性为目的的决策才是正确的，否则便是错误的。

利奥波特采用环境价值而不是经济价值的主张是令人信服的，他的作品对环境意识的增长曾有过重要的影响。

环境伦理学是一门全新的学科，没有一种学说是镶铸于一成不变的法令和教条之中的。恰恰相反，与所有生命体一样，环境伦理学也将随着新的数据的获得而发生变化，以使我们人类能更加合理地认识自然并与之相处。

有些评论家错误地把伦理学的这种成熟看作是暂时的现象。这个问题如此重要，把伦理学仅仅当作一时的风尚也是荒谬可笑的。但这里的难题是：除非人们对问题的实质及解决问题的现实方法有普遍的认识，否则人们关心的程度将会迅速消失。公众必须有作为生存的动力的信心，环境科学家和工程师们必须通过正确分析和理解环境问题并提出和开发与我们的生态系统相协调的建设性设施，以使公众产生这样的信心。某些"环保主义者"、政治家以及一些善意的人们的危言耸听和赶浪头的做法会轻而易举地破坏公众对这个问题的关注，而这种公众的关注是解决我们共同面临的问题所必需的。

对公众进行环境问题及其解决途径的教育是极为重要的。人们必须具有环境污染控制的科学、技术、经济和立法等方面的鉴别能力和文化知识。

但这还不够，我们的生活必须符合环境伦理，必须认识到自然的力量，意识到在一个奇妙而仍然神秘的系统中，我们不过是沧海一粟。

第16单元

环境保护局必须面向未来

环境保护局科学咨询部担负着描绘未来环境景观蓝图的重任，按其观点在未来30年里，海洋保护、非癌症性人类健康影响、生态系统的持续性、"非常规环境压力因素"、及全球大气污染负荷将是环境问题的重要关注点。

在一篇咨询委员会认可的报告中，科学咨询部的环境前景委员会建议，环境保护局应将长远的、预见性的思想溶入日常工作中，并且着重了解那些促进改变环境的社会活动。报告指出，这个建议尚未成为该局的常规工作。

委员会主席，德州大学土木工程系的雷蒙德·洛伊说："环境保护局最根本的职责是要重视如何防止未来出现的环境问题，就像重视控制目前的环境问题一样。从某种意义上说，我们正寻求一种'代际公平'的形式，决不把我们现在可能回避的问题遗留给下一代。"

洛伊说，面向未来是环境保护局应做的，也是当初成立该局的目的。

在这篇报告之前，咨询部另外还有两篇着眼于未来的政策报告：一篇题为"未来的危机——90年代的研究战略",发表于1988年。另一篇为"减少危机——确立环境保护的优先地位和政策",发表于1990年,在环境保护局的请求下,咨询部于1993年7月正式开始行动。

未来的战略措施:

科学咨询部的报告突破了目前的范围:以其保护未来的远见,建议环境保护局采取下列步骤迎接未来环境问题的挑战:

* 如同控制当前环境问题一样,重视避免未来的环境问题。
* 建立一个"早期报警系统",发现未来将出现的环境危机,由环境保护局和其他组织机构提供出一、二个疑难问题以供在实验室的基础上作精密的分析。
* 鼓励联邦机构与民间组织更好地合作,以预测并采取相应的措施。
* 致力于环境领域内五个关键问题的基本研究:生态系统的持续性,非癌症性人类健康影响,全球大气污染负荷,非常规环境压力因素,及海洋保护。
* 根据国家的长远利益来认识全球环境质量,并采取将安全、对外关系、环境质量及经济增长相联系的政策。

在起草这篇报告时,委员会成员研究了未来学家的工作,并调查了科学咨询部常务委员会及环境保护局制定政策的人员,请他们确认对未来具有重要意义的问题。

委员会选择下列五项未来的关注点作为基本研究的领域,因为它们对人类健康和环境有着潜在的影响。

生态系统的持续性:由于毒性化学品的使用,土地占用日趋激烈的竞争及不断增长的人口压力,使得生态系统正面临着危险,环境保护局应该提出生态危机评价的标准及极限。

非癌症性人类健康影响:

科学研究表明,仿雌性激素类化合物诱发生殖问题和生育缺陷以及许多人和动物发育方面的非癌症问题。这些现象也许只是人类健康影响的微弱信号,但是环境保护局应该拓宽检测非癌症性疾病的途径,这些疾病是敏感的人群长期曝露于环境中而产生的。

全球大气污染负荷:

环境保护局不应仅致力于研究个别污染物的影响,而应探讨多种空气污染物的协同作用,这种协同作用可导致人类健康和生态方面无法预料的新问题。

非常规环境压力因素:

环境保护局应扩大其所关注的范围,考虑尚未充分认识的压力因素,开始监测新的压力因素(如:抑制抗体的细菌、植物和昆虫;新的水生病原体;及偶然或出于错误而引入的一些异种物)。进一步调查那些已熟知的压力因素的累积影响。

海洋保护:

由于不断增长的地球人口,海洋正面临着日益严重的压力,尽管目前所表现出的恶化迹象不明显,但是因为资源的范围和价值均面临危机,所以海洋所受的压力应被迅速地认识并受到及时的关注。

洛伊说,这份报告同时也建议在环境保护局内部设立一个关注未来问题的横向联系机构,这种机构设立在环境保护局较为合适。他估计一项未来的计划将会花费几百万美元,但有助于避免用于净化的更大的开支。环境保护局的对环境的关注将产生常被称为"环境伦理学"的东西,一种对我们地球的新的关注和认识。越来越多的公民考虑问题不光从经济的角度，而且从环境质量的角度来考虑。它同样将导致对公众进行环境问题及其解决方法的教育，使公众认识到有必要了解控制环境污染的科学、技术、经济和法律诸方面的知识。

Appendix III Key to Exercises

UNIT ONE
Reading Comprehension
I. 1. T 2. F 3. F 4. T 5. F
II. 1. b 2. e 3. d 4. c 5. a

Vocabulary
I. 1. has fallen into disuse 2. communal 3. solely
   4. rampant 5. prerequisite
II. 1. b 2. d 3. a 4. d 5. c

Writing (For reference)
water supply   sanitation provisions   sewage

UNIT TWO
Reading Comprehension
I. 1. F 2. F 3. T 4. F 5. T
II. 1. d 2. e 3. b 4. c 5. a

Vocabulary
I. 1. overlap 2. soluble 3. critical 4. routine 5. malformation
II. 1. d 2. b 3. b 4. a 5. c

Writing (For reference)
criteria,   drinking water,   raw water supplies

UNIT THREE
Reading Comprehension
I. 1. F 2. T 3. T 4. F 5. F
II. 1. e 2. d 3. a 4. c 5. b

Vocabulary
I. 1. resolution 2. depression 3. viable 4. inhabitant 5. contamination
II. 1. c 2. a 3. d 4. b 5. d

Writing

1. c   2. g   3. f   4. d   5. a   6. e   7. b

UNIT FOUR

Reading Comprehension

Ⅰ. 1. F   2. T   3. F   4. T   5. F
Ⅱ. 1. b   2. c   3. e   4. d   5. a

Vocabulary

Ⅰ. 1. strategy   2. spectrum   3. ambient   4. ranged from... to
    5. derive... from
Ⅱ. 1. b   2. d   3. c   4. c   5. a

Writing

1. the spectrum of various water quality management strategies.
2. the function of administrative interpretation of the law.
3. the reason why the water quality management professionals must often answer difficult questions.
4. an important element of successful water quality monitoring system design.
5. the difficulty of meeting the requirements directly stated in water quality management laws.
6. the first step in designing an effective water quality monitoring system.

UNIT FIVE

Reading Comprehension

Ⅰ. 1. T   2. F   3. T   4. F   5. T
Ⅱ. 1. d   2. a   3. e   4. c   5. b

Vocabulary

Ⅰ. 1. mutual   2. significance   3. dominant   4. repulsive
    5. in attempt to
Ⅱ. 1. c   2. d   3. b   4. a   5. d

Writing

1. c   2. a   3. d   4. f   5. b   6. e

UNIT SIX
Reading Comprehension
   I. 1. F   2. F   3. T   4. F   5. F
   II. 1. b   2. e   3. a   4. d   5. c

Vocabulary
   I. 1. would be impaired   2. prolific   3. deterioration   4. aesthetically
      5. gave rise to
   II. 1. b   2. d   3. a   4. b   5. c

Writing
1. It is important to understand the effects of pollution and the control measures in order to manage water resources efficiently.
2. The water in reservoirs is more difficult to treat than the original river water.
3. Eutrophication is accelerated by artificial enrichment due to human activities.
4. It is difficult and impossible to prevent all river pollution.
5. River pollution is undesirable for some reasons thus the use of water is classified accordingly.
6. Multipurpose use of water is an important way of the conservation of water resources.

UNIT SEVEN
Reading Comprehension
   I. 1. T   2. F   3. T   4. F   5. F
   II. 1. e   2. c   3. b   4. a   5. d

Vocabulary
   I. 1. expelling   2. saturated   3. beneficial   4. virgin   5. promising
   II. 1. c   2. d   3. a   4. c   5. b

Writing
   1. primary   2. secondary   3. tertiary treatment   4. suspended solids
   5. activated carbon adsorption   6. chemically   7. land treatment   8. irrigation

UNIT EIGHT
Reading Comprehension
   I. 1. T   2. F   3. T   4. T   5. F
   II. 1. d   2. c   3. b   4. e   5. a

Vocabulary

Ⅰ. 1. desirable   2. admirably   3. exceedingly   4. indispensable
   5. goes back to
Ⅱ. 1. b   2. c   3. b   4. d   5. a

Writing

1. broad   2. disciplines   3. domestic origin   4. concern   5. responsibility
6. domestic   7. industrial   8. chemical engineer

UNIT NINE

Reading Comprehension

Ⅰ. 1. T   2. T   3. F   4. F   5. F
Ⅱ. 1. e   2. b   3. c   4. d   5. a

Vocabulary

Ⅰ. 1. depleted   2. calibrating   3. degradation   4. orientation
   5. marginalized
Ⅱ. 2. a   2. b   3. c   4. d   5. d

Writing

Now societies are faced with such immediate problems as population explosion, resource overexploitation and environmental pollution during the courses of development. At least, sustainable development must not endanger the natural systems that support life on Earth: the atmosphere, the waters, the soils, and the living beings. Economic growth and development obviously involve changes in the physical ecosystem. People should take a scientific attitude in the tapping of renewable and non-renewable resources for the benefit of future generations, including the conservation of plant and animal species.

In its nature, sustainable development is a process of change in which things we are doing are all in harmony and enhance both current and future potential to meet human needs and aspirations.

UNIT TEN

Reading Comprehension

Ⅰ. 1. F   2. F   3. T   4. F   5. T
Ⅱ. 1. b   2. d   3. e   4. a   5. c

Vocabulary

Ⅰ. 1. evaluating   2. potable   3. in perspective   4. is implemented

5. describe

II. 1. b   2. d   3. a   4. c   5. a

Writing

The primary goal of the EIA procedure is to foretell the effects of a planned project on the natural and urban environment. The prediction of environmental impacts is not an easy task. It must be conducted by an interdisciplinary team, including experts from different academic domains.

Some environmental impacts can be evaluated directly and objectively; others can not. It is important to distinguish between short-term impacts and long-term impacts. Many procedures for conducting an environmental assessment have been developed over the years. They have in common the basic goal of providing an overall and systematic environmental evaluation of the project, with the greatest degree of objectivity.

Here are two popular methods, the checklist method and the matrix method. In the checklist method, all potential environmental impacts for the various project alternatives are listed, and the anticipated magnitude of each impact is described qualitatively. Negative impacts are indicated with minus signs (−) while positive ones with plus signs (+). In the matrix method, an attempt is made to quantify or "grade" the relative impacts of the project alternatives and to provide a numerical basis for comparison and evaluation. The magnitude of each potential impact may be rated on a scale of 0 to 10. Numerical weighting factors are also used in it to indicate the relative importance of a particular impact.

UNIT ELEVEN

Reading Comprehension

I. 1. T   2. F   3. F   4. F   5. T
II. 1. b   2. e   3. d   4. c   5. a

Vocabulary

I. 1. is transmitted   2. interactive   3. lie in   4. more than   5. outstrips
II. 1. b   2. b   3. d   4. a   5. c

Writing

1. inheritance   2. twofold   3. relationships   4. pieces   5. approach
6. integration   7. manage   8. conditioned

UNIT TWELVE

Reading Comprehension

I. 1. F   2. T   3. F   4. T   5. F

II. 1. d   2. e   3. b   4. a   5. c

Vocabulary
I. 1. levelled out   2. was dying off   3. to decline
   4. in direct proportion to   5. as far as ... is concerned
II. 1. b   2. a   3. d   4. d   5. c

Writing
The purpose of activated sludge is to remove the organic matter as completely as possible from the raw wastes with the least expenditure of time and funds. One of the basic problems with conventional activated sludge has been the variable predomination of the microorganisms. But now there has come into being some innovation of operating completing mixing systems at the lower end of the declining growth phase where sludge increase is minimal.

UNIT THIRTEEN
Reading Comprehension
I. 1. F   2. T   3. F   4. T   5. T
II. 1. c   2. a   3. b   4. c   5. d

Vocabulary
I. 1. c   2. d   3. e   4. a   5. b
II. 1. penetration   2. alleviate   3. proliferation   4. emission
    5. atmospheric
III. 1. b   2. c   3. a   4. d   5. a

Writing

The Abstract

The essay tells readers the relationship between energy, economy and environment.

With the development of industrialization and urbanization, the energy demand is growing rapidly.

In 1980, the world energy consumption reached about 10 TW. By 2025 that same global population would be expected to require about 55 TW.

The higher scenarios make worse the environmental pollution problems.

The "greenhouse effect" of gases emitted to the atmosphere will change the climate.

The atmospheric pollutants from the combustion of fussil fuels will cause urban-industrial air pollution and acidification of the environment.

Technologies to remove emissions of oxides of sulphur and nitrogen are now required in some countries, but they can increase investment costs by 15-25 percent.

The Commission believes that the ideas behind these lower scenarios are practical.

UNIT FOURTEEN

Reading Comprehension

Ⅰ. 1. F 2. T 3. T 4. F 5. T
Ⅱ. 1. c 2. d 3. a 4. e 5. b

Vocabulary

Ⅰ. 1. e 2. a 3. d 4. b 5. c
Ⅱ. 1. antithetical 2. uncouple 3. repealed 4. depleted 5. burst on
Ⅲ. 1. b 2. c 3. c 4. d 5. a

Writing

The Abstract

Both the word "ecology" and "economics" are derived from the Greek root "oikos" which means "household". Though different in meanings, they should be companion disciplines. Ecology was of practical interest in human history, but because of the technological achievements, we seem to depend less on the natural environment for our daily needs. The great paradox is that industrialized nations have succeeded by temporarily uncoupling humankind from nature through exploitation of finite, naturally produced possil fuels. Yet, civilization still depends on the natural environment, not only for energy and materials, but also for vital life-support processes such as air and water cycles. This unit describes mainly the origin of ecology and its development briefly.

UNIT FIFTEEN

Reading Comprehension

Ⅰ. 1. T 2. F 3. T 4. T 5. F
Ⅱ. 1. c 2. d 3. a 4. e 5. b

Vocabulary

Ⅰ. 1. d 2. e 3. a 4. b 5. c
Ⅱ. 1. bandwagon 2. standpoint 3. feedback 4. not withstanding 5. compatible
Ⅲ. 1. c 2. a 3. c 4. d 5. b

Writing

The Abstract

More and more citizens are considering questions not only from the standpoint of economics, but also from that of environmental quality, and many people are finding it more difficult to answer a question like "Is growth really necessary?". In the past, people thought that economy and ecology are on a collision course. But as a force, environmental ethic is partly a result of our own long-term survival, as well as our realization that humans are but one form of life, and that we should share our earth with our fellow travellers. This unit introduces briefly the birth of environmental ethic and its role in forming a bridge between ecology and economics.

UNIT SIXTEEN
Reading Comprehension
    I. 1. F   2. T   3. T   4. T   5. T
    II. 1. e   2. c   3. a   4. b   5. d

Vocabulary
    I. 1. b   2. a   3. d   4. e   5. c
    II. 1. initial   2. rigorous   3. susceptible   4. defects   5. exotic
    III. 1. b   2. a   3. b   4. d   5. c

Writing
The Abstract

    EPA must map the environmental landscape of the future. EPA will give much attention to avoiding future environmental problems.

    The essay raises the strategy for the future. It mentions to set up an "early warning system" to identify emerging future environmental risks. They will concentrate initial research on five key environmental areas: ecosystem sustainability, noncancer human health effects, total air pollution loading, nontraditional environmental stressors, and health of the oceans.

    The essay elaborates on the above-mentioned five key environmental areas.

图书在版编目（CIP）数据

建筑类专业英语. 给水排水与环境保护. 第3册 / 张文洁，濮宏魁主编. —北京：中国建筑工业出版社，1997（2023.6 重印）
高等学校试用教材
ISBN 978-7-112-03034-7

Ⅰ. 建… Ⅱ. ①张… ②濮… Ⅲ. ①建筑学-英语-高等学校-教材②给水工程-英语-高等学校-教材③排水工程-英语—高等学校—教材④环境保护-建筑工程-英语-高等学校-教材 Ⅳ. H31

中国版本图书馆CIP数据核字（2005）第106699号

本书按国家教委颁布的《大学英语专业阅读阶段教学基本要求》编写的专业英语教材。本册包括给水排水设备、水质监测、水污染及废水三级处理、人类及其环境、环境伦理学、生态学、环保面向未来等方面内容。全书安排16个单元，每单元除正课文外，还有两篇阅读材料，均配有必要的注释。正课文还配有词汇表和练习，书后附有总词汇表、参考译文和练习答案。语言难度大于一、二册，并配有科技英语写作的简要说明与写作练习。

本书可供本专业学生四年级上半学期使用，也可供有关专业人员自学英语参考。

高等学校试用教材
建 筑 类 专 业 英 语
给水排水与环境保护
第三册

张文洁 濮宏魁	主编
岑小平 吴儆武 任 瑞	编
蒋琴芳 蒋京东 蔡英俊	
沈耀良	主审

*

中国建筑工业出版社出版、发行（北京西郊百万庄）
各地新华书店、建筑书店经销
建工社（河北）印刷有限公司印刷

*

开本：787×1092毫米 1/16 印张：13 字数：316千字
1997年6月第一版 2023年6月第十三次印刷
定价：**18.00**元
ISBN 978-7-112-03034-7
(14977)

版权所有 翻印必究
如有印装质量问题，可寄本社退换
（邮政编码 100037）